To Philadelphia and back:
the life and music of
Joseph Parry

Dulais Rhys
and
Frank Bott

To Philadelphia and back

First published in 2010

Published with the financial support
of the Welsh Books Council

ISBN: 978-1-84527-302-6

Cover design: Sion Ilar/WBC

Published by Gwasg Carreg Gwalch,
12 Iard yr Orsaf, Llanrwst, Wales LL26 0EH
tel: 01492 624031
fax: 01492 641502
email: books@carreg-gwalch.com
internet: www.carreg-gwalch.com

Contents

List of Illustrations

Musical Examples

Preface

In the last quarter of the nineteenth century, there was no name better known in Wales and in the Welsh communities of the United States than that of Joseph Parry, Y Doctor Mawr – the great doctor. His music was sung in chapels and eisteddfodau throughout the country. He was in great demand as a conductor and adjudicator, and the nation was proud that a man of the people had risen to such eminence as to be awarded a doctorate in music from the University of Cambridge. Within a few years of Parry's death in 1903 his reputation had declined and by the middle of the twentieth century he was viewed with the same dismissive contempt as were other late Victorian figures. With the exception of *Myfanwy* and the hymn tune *Aberystwyth*, very little of his music was still performed, except perhaps in the smaller and more conservative eisteddfodau.

The story of Joseph Parry's life is a romantic and appealing one. It is not surprising that the writer Jack Jones made it the basis of his novel *Off to Philadelphia in the Morning*, published in 1947 and turned into a mini-series for television by BBC Wales in the early 1980s. This served to make the Joseph Parry story familiar to many to whom he would otherwise have been, at best, just a name. Unfortunately, this familiarity led to little if anything by way of more performances of his music.

Dulais Rhys first became interested in Joseph Parry as a result of hearing some of his work performed by the male voice choir in Carmarthen, in which his father sang. He later came to know and admire the music of *Blodwen* and *Emmanuel* through copies he found in the piano stool in his home. As a result of this interest, he was invited to prepare a performing score for a concert performance of *Blodwen*, which took place at the Menai Music Festival in 1978, a hundred years after the first performance of the opera. That performance was a success and it led to the release of a recording of the work.

The present book has its roots in the research carried out subsequently by Dulais Rhys, for which he was awarded a PhD by the University of Wales in 1986. This research was based on contemporary documents, largely in Welsh, from Wales and from Welsh communities in England and America. The work carried out for the PhD led to the publication in 1998 by the University of Wales Press of a book entitled *Joseph Parry: Bachgen Bach o Ferthyr* ('Joseph Parry: A Little Lad from Merthyr'). This book was initially to be simply translated into English by Frank Bott, but it was decided that significant changes were required to make it suitable for an English-speaking audience, and we have worked together to produce the present book.

Part One of this book takes the reader through Parry's life, his highs and lows, travels and tragedies. Part Two explores Parry the man and the musician.

The would-be biographer of Joseph Parry is faced with many difficulties. There is a shortage of primary sources relating to his life – we don't know how many letters he exchanged with members of his family but very few of them survive. Nor do we have many business letters written to him, although rather more business letters that he wrote to other people survive. His own attempt at autobiography is sketchy and was written late in his life, when his memory was unreliable. (A version of the autobiography, edited by Dulais Rhys, was published by the National Library of Wales in 2004.) The only full-length treatment of his life is *Cofiant Joseph Parry* ('A Memoir of Joseph Parry'), edited by E. Keri

Evans and published in 1921; this relied heavily on the autobiography and the resulting errors have been propagated in later works. Articles in the contemporary press sometimes confused him with other Parrys – there were at least three other Parrys writing music in the nineteenth century, including Sir Charles Hubert Hastings Parry, the composer of *Jerusalem* and *Blest Pair of Sirens*. Articles written about Joseph Parry after his death by those who knew him contain factual errors that may derive from confused memories, either on the part of the writer or on the part of Parry himself. Finally, although *Off to Philadelphia in the Morning* was intended only as a novel based on Parry's life, it has often been treated as a reliable biography and many of the author's inventions have become accepted as historical facts.

All these sources of error have had their effect magnified by the worldwide web. The web contains much that is valuable, but by its very nature there can be no guarantee of the accuracy of the information to be found on any individual page. A surprisingly large number of pages relate to Joseph Parry the composer, as well as to other Joseph Parrys. While some are accurate, others display a quite remarkable range of mis-statements, misunderstandings and plain mistakes.

There is, however, one important way in which the development of the worldwide web has made the production of this book significantly easier, as well as making it more useful to readers who are practising musicians. The IMSLP (International Music Score Library Project), also known as the Petrucci Music Library, is a publicly available website that holds the scores of several tens of thousands of works that are out of copyright. We have uploaded to this site the scores of most of the works by Parry referred to in this book. They are easily and freely available, and can be downloaded and printed. Since very little of Parry's music is in print, we hope this will encourage performances of his works. The address of the website is http://imslp.org/

A substantial reform of Welsh orthography was undertaken in 1928, following the report of a committee chaired by Sir John Morris-Jones. In most cases we have followed modern practice. One consequence of this is that automated searches may fail to find references to older editions of, say, 'Cytgan y Morwr', because they are indexed under the spelling used in the original document, that is, 'Cydgan y Morwr'. In the case of personal proper names, we have tried to use the same spellings as the owners of the names themselves – but they were not always consistent. And in the case of place-names, we have used English names where distinct English names exist (e.g. Cardigan and Fishguard), with the Welsh equivalent given in brackets on the first occurrence; for other place-names in Wales we have followed the practice of *A Gazetteer of Welsh Place-names*.

Finally, we would like to express our thanks to the many people on both sides of the Atlantic who have so generously given us their support and assistance. In particular, we would like to thank Rhidian Griffiths for his many helpful suggestions and corrections; Sis Hause and Fiona Siobhan Powell from Danville, Philadelphia, for contributing their local knowledge and making available photographs of nineteenth-century Danville; and Emeritus Professor David Wulstan, the *last* professor of music at Aberystwyth, for allowing us to use the drawing of Joseph Parry, the *first* professor of music at Aberystwyth, which is in his possession. John Gilbey gave us valuable assistance with some of the photographs, and the staff of the National Library of Wales and of Gwasg Carreg Gwalch, in particular our editor Jen Llywelyn, have helped us in many ways.

Dulais Rhys would also like to thank his research supervisor, John Hywel, formerly of the Music Department of the University College of North Wales, Bangor, without whose assistance, suggestions, criticisms and constant pushing the original research would never have been completed.

Just as Jane Parry had to tolerate the vicissitudes of life with Joseph, so our own wives, Leigh and Mary, have had to tolerate Joseph as an extra member of our families and we are most grateful for their support and forebearance!

Dulais Rhys
Frank Bott
March 2010

Part One

1

The Little Lad from Merthyr

Joseph Parry was born in 1841 in a house in Chapel Row in the Georgetown district of Merthyr Tudful, in what was then the county of Glamorganshire.

Until the middle of the eighteenth century, Merthyr Tudful, high up the valley of the River Taf, was a rural Welsh-speaking village. In 1750 its population was around 300. However, the discovery that iron could be extracted from iron ore using coke rather than the charcoal that had been used for centuries, suddenly made Merthyr, with its huge deposits of coal (from which coke is produced) and iron ore, an immensely attractive place to develop the new iron smelting industry. The first ironworks was opened there in 1759; three more had opened by 1784. The growth of the industry led to an explosion in the population: by the time of the first census, in 1801, the population was just short of 9,000; by 1851 it was almost 50,000. It was by far the largest town in Wales, way ahead of Swansea (Abertawe), Cardiff (Caerdydd) or Newport (Casnewydd).

This population growth was achieved very largely by immigration, predominantly from rural Wales, Cornwall and Ireland. Joseph Parry's parents were both part of the tide of immigrants from rural, Welsh-speaking Wales. His father, Daniel, was born in 1800, the son of John Parry, a farmer from the Moylgrove area of north Pembrokeshire, five miles south of Cardigan (Aberteifi). He moved to Merthyr in 1823.

We know rather more about Joseph's mother, Elizabeth

('Bet' or 'Beti') Richards. She was born in 1805 and baptized on 28 March 1805 in Capel Sul, an Independent[1] chapel in Cydweli in Carmarthenshire. She had been raised on a farm called 'Y Graig' near Mynyddygarreg, and moved to Merthyr in 1816, as a maid in the home of the Reverend Methuselah Jones, minister of Bethesda chapel. She was related to Henry Richard (1812–1888), Independent minister and Member of Parliament for Merthyr from 1868 till his death, and famous for his opposition to war.

Daniel and Elizabeth were married in the Merthyr parish church, the Church of St Tudful the Martyr, around 1825 – registration of marriages was not introduced until 1837, so the exact date is not known, nor was it possible to marry in a Nonconformist chapel. Various records suggest they had eight children, but only five are recorded in the 1851 census: Ann (born 1834), Henry (1838), Joseph (1841), Elizabeth (1844), and Jane (1847). It seems likely, therefore, that three children died in infancy. This would have been nothing unusual; infant mortality was high in Merthyr during the 1840s, with almost one in five children dying before reaching the age of twelve months, and a higher proportion dying before reaching the age of five.

Chapel Row, where Joseph was born in the evening of Friday 21 May 1841, was built in the early years of the nineteenth century, and named after the octagonal chapel that stood next to the first house of the row. The chapel was built toward the end of the eighteenth century by Richard Crawshay, the owner of the Cyfarthfa iron works, as a 'chapel-of-ease' for his workers, but by the middle of the nineteenth century the chapel was being used as a storehouse, a carpenter's workplace and as a rehearsal room for the Cyfarthfa Brass Band. There were at least five houses in Chapel Row, and number 4 is now preserved and open to the public as 'Joseph Parry's Cottage'. It is not certain, however, that this was the family home, because the 1841 Census states that the Parry family lived in 'the second house' and Parry's autobiography[2] describes his home as 'the second house'.

The 1851 census describes the eldest child, Ann, as a dressmaker and labels Henry, Joseph, Elizabeth (also known as 'Betsy') and Jane as 'scholars'. William Edmunds, in his book *Hanes Plwyf Merthyr*, states that there were thirty-two schools in the town in 1845, with between 6000 and 7000 children receiving formal education, based on the pioneering pattern of Lady Charlotte Guest in Dowlais. Joseph Parry was sent to the school associated with Cyfarthfa iron works.

It was usual for the works' masters in Wales and England to cater for the cultural needs of their workers, and in 1844 Robert Crawshay, Richard's son, set up a band for his workers. Cyfarthfa Band was one of Merthyr's musical highlights, proudly marching through the streets of the town in impressive uniforms. An article that appeared in Charles Dickens' journal *Household Words* shows the quality of the band and its effectiveness in nurturing an appreciation of instrumental music:

> Another set of harmonious blacksmiths awaken the echoes of the remotest Welsh mountains. The correspondent of a London paper, while visiting Merthyr, was exceedingly puzzled by hearing boys in the Cyfarthfa works whistling airs rarely heard except in the fashionable ball-room, opera-house, or drawing room. He afterwards discovered that the proprietor of the works, Mr Robert Crawshay, had established among his men a brass band which practises once a week throughout the year. They have the good fortune to be led by a man (one of the 'roll-turners')

who must have had somewhere a superior musical education. I ... was astonished at their proficiency. They number sixteen instruments. I heard them perform the Overture to *Zampa*, *The Caliph of Bagdad*, and *Fra Diavolo*, ... I have seldom heard a regimental band more perfect than this handful of workmen, located (far from any place where they might command the benefit of hearing other bands) in the mountains of Wales.[3]

According to his autobiography, this was one of Joseph Parry's first musical memories: 'I am following you as you play marching the streets of Merthyr, your music seems to satisfy my soul, more than food the body'.[4] Cyfarthfa Band's repertoire included Beethoven symphonies and it competed widely. For example, in May 1860, it won the first prize of £30 as well as a silver cup at the Crystal Palace in London, and it accompanied the 'Merthyr Tydvil Ball' – a grand ball for the rich of the area, held on the last day of every year at the Bush Inn in Merthyr.

The census for 1841, the year of Joseph Parry's birth, gives the population of Merthyr as 34,977. There were nineteen chapels, which were important centres for the native Welsh. Daniel and Bet Parry were staunch Independents, and the family attended Bethesda chapel on Bethesda Street hill half a mile from home. The chapel was built at the turn of the eighteenth century, then 'rebuilt', i.e. expanded, in 1829. The Reverend Methuselah Jones, Bet Parry's original employer, died in 1839. His successor was the Reverend Daniel Jones, who was young Joseph Parry's minister during his childhood.

As well as being staunch chapel-goers, the family were also enthusiastic musicians. Bet had a good alto voice, and was often called on to lead the congregational singing. Two of her oldest children were also musicians – Ann and Henry – and the two youngest girls – Jane and Betsy – were to develop excellent soprano and alto voices. There is evidence that the family sang as a group in Bethesda. The chapel had a thriving choir, which Joseph Parry joined as an eight-year-old; according to contemporary reports, he had an attractive alto voice and could maintain his part well. He was, however, no child prodigy – he could not yet read music, let alone compose.

The Bethesda choir conductor from 1845 was Robert James, known also as 'Jeduthyn'.[5] He was born in Aberdare (*Aberdâr*) but when he was two years old the family moved to Merthyr. It is claimed[6] that Robert James was Joseph Parry's first music teacher. There is no documentary evidence to support this, but he certainly was an early influence, both musical and moral, on Joseph – an influence that was strengthened when Robert married Joseph's sister Ann during the summer of 1852. A daughter, Lizzie Parry James, was born in 1854, but in January 1855 Ann died, just twenty years old. Robert James emigrated to Australia in 1857 and stayed there for five years – he was to return to Joseph Parry's life later on.

Another of Merthyr's committed musicians was Rosser Beynon. Like Robert James, he was born outside the area – in the Vale of Neath (*Cwm Nedd*) – but moved as a boy with his family to Merthyr. By the 1830s, Rosser Beynon had established music classes in Merthyr and Cardiff, with Robert James being one of his earliest students. But on Sundays, while Robert James attended Bethesda chapel, Rosser Beynon was one of Soar chapel's most faithful members: he eventually became *codwr canu*.[7] Beynon started a mixed choir in Merthyr, one of the first in the area, in around 1837, and Joseph joined it, as well as attending Beynon's singing classes.

Merthyr's population increased by around 25 per cent in the first ten years of Joseph's life. By this time the town was gradually becoming more anglicised as immigrants from England, Scotland and Ireland outnumbered those from rural Wales. Life was difficult and work was hard, so leisure and spiritual activity – especially the choir, eisteddfod and chapel – were vital. In April 1852, the Temperance Hall was built on the town's Market Square. It included halls and rooms for concerts, eisteddfodau, rehearsals, meetings, courts etc, and it was there that Rosser Beynon set up choir rehearsals every Sunday afternoon, with Joseph Parry as one of his youngest, most enthusiastic and faithful recruits. The choir won the first prize of three guineas for performing the choruses 'Worthy is the Lamb' and 'Amen' from *Messiah* at the Merthyr Cymmrodorion Temperance Eisteddfod of 1 June 1852, held at the Temperance Hall. On 4 August, the choir held a concert in the new Baptist chapel in Aberdare, with the programme demonstrating the variety of its repertoire – works that the young Joseph Parry will have benefited musically from singing. Selections were performed from Mendelssohn's *St Paul*, one of Handel's *Te Deums*, along with *Israel in Egypt* and *Messiah*, Mozart's *Requiem*, Haydn's *Creation*, as well as pieces by Cherubini, Byrd and several Welsh composers, for example, Robert James' winning anthem at the 1852 Merthyr Eisteddfod 'Clywch Tebygaf Clywaf Lais' (Listen, I Seem to Hear a Voice).

According to his autobiography, Joseph Parry worked as a pit-boy at Pwll Robbins[8] from the age of nine, earning half-a-crown[9] for working fifty-six or more hours a week. As we have already seen, however, the 1851 census records him still as 'scholar'. By 1852, at twelve years old, he was working in Cyfarthfa iron works, where his father, Daniel, worked as a refiner.

The young boy's life was full, especially on Sundays: to Sunday School at Bethesda at 9 am, then in the afternoon, to the Temperance Hall to rehearse with Rosser Beynon's choir, a service at Bethesda, singing practice, home for supper, a change of clothes then off to Cyfarthfa at midnight to begin his shift. In his autobiography Parry highlights two musical experiences that were vivid memories throughout his life.

The first was Merthyr's Cymmrodorion Eisteddfod at the Temperance Hall on Christmas Day 1853. The music adjudicator was Evan Davies, Swansea, who reappears later in the life of the young Joseph Parry. The test piece was J. Ambrose Lloyd's anthem 'Teyrnasoedd y Ddaear' (The Kingdoms of the Earth), which had been composed the previous year and had spread like wildfire through musical Wales. Nine choirs competed, with Joseph Parry singing in Bethesda chapel choir. The adjudicator could not decide between seven of the choirs, so he divided the prize of seven guineas equally between them.

The second was when Joseph sang alto in a performance of Mozart's Twelfth Mass, again at the Temperance Hall, on 5 June 1854, most probably under the baton of Rosser Beynon. It was a popular and successful occasion, bringing together choirs from Merthyr, Newbridge and Swansea, and accompanied by an orchestra – instrumental accompaniment was rare in those days.

The year 1854 saw a major upheaval in Joseph's life: his father Daniel Parry had decided to emigrate. In spite of the benefits of the industrial revolution, the common man worked long hours for little pay. In Merthyr, Cyfarthfa competed with three other iron works, and, although the Crawshay family was generous in its social provision (as the setting up of the Cyfarthfa Band and the provision of elementary education for its employees' children demonstrate) it ruled the workers with a heavy hand.

The newspapers of the day were full of reports about emigration – the following is typical:

> and this year, there are reasons for believing the number of emigrants will be fully as great, if not greater than usual. Activated by the various inducements of fanaticism, and of the noble desire of bettering their social conditions, one or more ship loads have left already.[10]

Attractive advertisements provided information about ships and travel prices to the New World. Crossing the Atlantic by steam ship from Liverpool to New York or Philadelphia was eight guineas, while a sailing ship – which was slower – cost between four and five pounds.

Between 1815 and 1859, 4,917,598 people emigrated from the nations of Britain, with the largest number – 306,500 – leaving in 1854. During the decade 1851–1860, 6,319 (out of a population of under a million) left Wales for America, with the majority emigrating for economic reasons, but another contributing factor was cholera.

Asiatic cholera had reached England for the first time in October 1831.[11] The following year saw a major epidemic of the disease across England, Scotland and Wales. The rapid increase in the population of Merthyr had not been matched by corresponding increases in the quantity of accommodation or the provision of clean water supplies or an effective sewerage system. It was not surprising, therefore, that Merthyr was particularly hard hit, with over 600 cases and some 160 deaths between 1 September and 19 November 1832. Cholera returned in 1849. Again Merthyr was badly hit, with 1,682 deaths out of a total of 4,564 deaths in Wales.

Toward the middle of January 1853, Daniel Parry sailed from Cardiff, probably to Philadelphia. He then went onward to Danville, a small town on the banks of the Susquehanna River in the middle of Pennsylvania's open hills. He soon gained similar employment to the post he left in Merthyr, as a 'roller' in the Rough and Ready Rolling Mills in Danville. After a year of settling and saving, he called on the rest of his family to join him. In July 1854, Bet Parry and her children Henry, Joseph, Betsy and Jane left on board the *Jane Anderson* for their journey from Cardiff to Philadelphia. Ann, who was already married to Robert James, stayed in Merthyr. By this time Joseph was thirteen years old. Bet and her children left Merthyr just in time to avoid the next cholera epidemic, which reached Merthyr at the beginning of September 1854 and resulted in 455 deaths there. This was not quite the last cholera epidemic in Britain, but improvements in the water supply and sewerage meant that subsequent epidemics were on a much smaller scale.

The sea voyage was terrible: six weeks and two days of storms and inclement weather. One seaman was washed overboard, and four passengers died. Bet Parry and her family reached Philadelphia safely toward the middle of September – many weeks late – but ready to start their new life in America.

Notes Chapter 1

[1] The 'Independents' ('Annibynnwyr' in Welsh) are a Welsh Nonconformist denomination that corresponds to the Congregationalists in English-speaking areas.

[2] Joseph Parry, *The Little Hero*, p. 8. All page number references to Parry's autobiography are to the version edited by Dulais Rhys and published by the National Library of Wales in 2004.

[3] Hogarth and Wills. 'Music in Humble Life', Household Words, 11 May 1850, pp. 161–164, as quoted in Herbert, 2000.

[4] Joseph Parry, p. 8.

[5] Following a practice introduced by Iolo Morgannwg, who was responsible for the revival of the eisteddfod in nineteenth-century Wales, members of the Gorsedd of Bards took pseudonyms when they were inducted. 'Jeduthyn' is an example of such a name. These names should not be confused with the pseudonyms used by competitors at the eisteddfod.

[6] David Morgans, *Music and Musicians of Merthyr and District*, p. 73.

[7] The role of the *codwr canu* was to lead the singing, a very important role at a time when few chapels could afford an organ. In the medieval church this was the role of the precentor but the modern ecclesiastical associations of the word are somewhat different.

[8] Parry's autobiography has 'Roblins' but this would seem to be an error.

[9] 12½p in modern currency, the equivalent of £10.37 in spending power in 2007. This and subsequent equivalences have been obtained from the web site http://www.measuringworth.com/

[10] *Cardiff & Merthyr Guardian*, 12 April 1851.

[11] See the article 'Cholera in Wales' by G Penrhyn Jones (*National Library of Wales Journal* Vol X/3, Summer 1958).

2

Growing up in America

When Bet Parry and her children arrived in Danville, in 1854, it was a much smaller town than Merthyr Tudful, with a population of only around 5,000. However, there was a substantial Welsh community and, just as in Wales, the chapel was at its heart. It did not take long for the family to find its place and the Congregational Chapel on Chamber Street, in the north of the town, built in 1852, became their new spiritual home. The family lived initially close to the chapel, on the western side of South West Upper Mulberry Street in northern Danville, in a redbrick house which was rented from a Mr Richards. Daniel Parry later bought two lots in Elm Street (now lower Railroad Street) on which he built houses, into one of which the family moved. The tax rolls for 1860 show him as paying tax on both properties.

Joseph sang in the chapel choir, and regularly attended the three Sunday services, the Debating Society every Saturday evening, the Young Men's meetings and Sunday School. Like other immigrant communities, the Welsh in Danville sought to build a society and a way of living that reflected the one they had left behind in the 'old country'; this meant not just the chapel but the eisteddfod, which was to be so important to Joseph's career.

Joseph and his brother Henry joined their father working at the Rough and Ready[1] Rolling Mills soon after they arrived. The mill had been established in 1847 on the site of the old Glendower iron works at the corner of Railroad and East Market Street in Danville; the name of the old iron works suggests a Welsh connection. The rolling mill was not as big as Cyfarthfa, but it was one of Danville's principal employers. Joseph was initially employed as a 'puddler's boy' and his father was a refiner. Joseph worked full-time at the rolling mill until Christmas 1865, eventually becoming head roller. Rolling mills were dangerous places and he was twice fortunate in avoiding death or serious injury in accidents at the mill. The first was when a nearby boiler exploded, killing one of his fellow workers, and the second when a wheel broke off its axle and caused much damage nearby. The diary of his good friend Thomas Roderick records that 'Jo Parry burned his arm last night at the mill' but the tone of the entry does not suggest a serious injury.

There were substantial Welsh communities in many parts of the United States, as far west as Milwaukee, but they were particularly strong in Pennsylvania, because of the prevalence there of the traditional Welsh industries – coal mining especially, but also iron, steel, and slate. Like other immigrant groups, the first generation tended to congregate in communities where they could maintain their language and cultural traditions; inevitably, however, the need to speak English in daily life would lead to a decline in the use of the language and this, in turn, would mean that many traditions would slowly disappear. However, when the young Joseph Parry arrived in Pennsylvania, the language and the tradition of chapel, the *cymanfa ganu* (hymn singing festival) and the eisteddfod, were still strong, precisely because they were being refreshed by new immigrants such as the Parrys. Remarkably, although the Welsh language completely disappeared from Pennsylvania, the *cymanfa ganu* and the eisteddfod survive to this day and have served to encourage a new generation to learn Welsh.

One of Joseph's colleagues at the mill was John Abel

Jones, employed as a heater. He had emigrated from Merthyr to Danville, with his family, around 1830, when he was four years old. A keen amateur musician, he took the young Joseph Parry under his wing and found his student to be every bit as enthusiastic. Every Saturday Joseph Parry went to John Abel Jones' house – their homes were opposite each other – for an hour's lesson at 3 pm for a fee of 25 cents. According to Parry's autobiography, Jones was his first music teacher. Some of Joseph's fellow workers also attended, since Jones' home was open to anyone from the Rough and Ready Rolling Mills who wanted to learn about music. Jones also ran a choir, and Joseph soon became a faithful member. In his autobiography he notes that it was there that he learned to read staff notation, stating 'I am thus seventeen years of age before I can understand a single note of music (though I had sung in several oratorio and Mass performances at Merthyr).'[2] He also learned sight-singing. In fact, his musical enthusiasm was such that his teacher would complain: 'The little devil is at me all the time.' His student's reaction, according to his autobiography, was 'Now from this date onwards, I am music's willing servant.'[3]

Joseph Parry's workbook with John Abel Jones was *A Catechism of the Rudiments of Harmony and Thorough Bass* by James Alexander Hamilton. It seems that Joseph worked through the book diligently, because by 1860 he was transferred to John M. Price – another Welsh musician who had emigrated to Danville, from Rhymney in the old Monmouthshire, and also worked at the Rough and Ready Rolling Mills. Parry 'held' the metal for Price, that is, he was Price's 'puddler's boy', and, during their brief breaks, Parry, Jones and Price would meet at the rollers' cupboards to discuss music. His dedication to music tended to keep Parry apart from his co-workers and he became known as the 'lone wolf'.

John Price accepted Joseph on John Abel Jones' recommendation, teaching him every Saturday afternoon, and later at 9 am on Sundays as well. Joseph's new teacher's strength was harmony, but John Price was amazed at his student's apparent ability to hear in his head the effect of written chords. A decade later, Joseph wrote to 'Mynorydd' (William Davies), conductor of the London Welsh Choral Society, saying

> if I have succeeded in doing anything with music, it is because of these two men, my personal and Creator's diligence ... they were men of extraordinary talents, that did so much for Music, even though they were amateurs.[4]

Amateurs they may well have been, but from the standpoint of their ability to encourage, develop and support a budding young musician such as Joseph Parry, Jones and Price were worth their weight in gold for their diligence and vision.

Vocally, by now Joseph was a tenor and a member of the Pennsylvania Male Glee Party, which sang, according to his autobiography, the 'best English glees', but, more significantly, these English glees were to have an influence on his development as a composer. (A glee is a part song usually, but by no means always, for unaccompanied voices.)

In 1860, the Congregational Chapel advertised in the local newspaper that they were 'looking to buy a melodeon for some of our talented young men.' The melodeon was a type of four-octave pipe organ that was light enough to be portable. Parry remembered playing his first music on the new instrument – the first three chords of 'Queen of the Valley Thou Art Beautiful', a five-part glee by John Wall Callcott. To him, this simple organ was not merely an ordinary instrument, but: 'is to my soul as a *great pipe organ*, or a *full orchestra!*'[5] He began to carry the melodeon on his shoulder to chapel meetings, just in case any singing started up, and needed accompaniment.

Joseph's enthusiasm for music increased steadily, focusing especially on composition. By 1860, at the age of nineteen, and encouraged by John Price, he felt confident enough to submit work to two Christmas eisteddfodau.

Danville was the first success: he won first prize with a choral piece, 'A Temperance Vocal March', reflecting the teetotal ethos so prevalent among Welsh Americans at that time. Joseph's family were total abstainers in the Welsh Nonconformist tradition, and he stayed faithful to the cause throughout his life. Many of his compositions reflect this, and he attended many a temperance eisteddfod and meeting. No copy of 'A Temperance Vocal March' has survived, but we know that, despite awarding it first prize, the adjudicator had reservations about the style of the piece, which suggests there was something novel in young Parry's music.

His second eisteddfod success was at the Christmas eisteddfod in Fairhaven, Vermont, where he shared first prize in the competition for writing a hymn tune with a Mr Pritchard, an old hand in this field, according to Parry. The hymn tune survives, although it was never published, and is included here as Example 1.

Musical Example 1

*Parry's hymn tune 'Fairhaven', which won him first prize
at the Fairhaven Eisteddfod in 1860*

From this time onward, Parry was strongly committed to composing. From 1861 to 1866, he was to hone his musical skills at eisteddfodau in America and in Wales and his name began to become familiar to Welsh people on both sides of the Atlantic.

As a consequence of his success in the Danville eisteddfod, and with his teachers' encouragement, enough money was raised to enable Joseph to attend a one-term summer course in Geneseo, a small town on the western edge of the Fingerlakes region in up-state New York, some two hundred miles from Danville. It was not a small step for the twenty-year-old Welshman to leave home and be among strangers for eight weeks. The course, which followed similar successful courses in the previous year, was offered by the Normal Academy of Music[6] in the third term, commencing on 3 July 1861; according to the advertisements, it would offer 'a Thorough Musical

Education'. Joseph studied singing with the Academy's principal, Carlo Bassini, and received tuition in organ, harmony and composition from Professor T. J. Cook.

Cook was a versatile musician, who had composed many small-scale works such as piano pieces and hymn tunes, as well as editing singing books for school children. He was also the editor of *The New York Musical Pioneer and Chorister's Budget*, a magazine published in that city in the 1850s and 1860s. In 1862, Parry's anthem 'O, Give Thanks unto the Lord' appeared in volume VII, probably as a result of the impression his music had made on Cook – the piece was published within a year of the course at Geneseo, and this anthem was probably the first of his compositions to get into print.

Joseph returned to Danville and to his work at the rolling mills with his zeal for music augmented. 'Composition has a firmer hold upon me', he wrote.[7] His next musical success was to come in the Utica Eisteddfod at the end of 1861.

From the beginning of the nineteenth century, Wales sent more immigrants to Utica (in New York State) than any other nation, and the town's eisteddfod was a major event. It was held in the Mechanics Hall on 31 December and 1 January 1862. Parry submitted an anthem and a glee to the composing competition. He won, actually beating the man who had adjudicated his compositions the previous year at the Danville Eisteddfod.

The third important event of 1861 was Joseph falling in love with Jane Thomas. Both her father and mother were from Blaenafon in Monmouthshire but Jane and her brother, Gomer, were born in Pennsylvania. Jane was born on 27 March 1843. Her father owned a music store on Mill Street in Danville. Her brother was an organist; he and Joseph studied music together and he later became one of

Joseph's main music publishers in the United States. It seems that Gomer and Thomas Roderick, whose diary is quoted above, befriended Joseph when he first arrived, and they were all puddler's boys together. Gomer was later to marry Thomas's sister.

Joseph and Jane were married on his twenty-first birthday, 21 May 1862. The wedding service was held in Welsh, at the Parry chapel on Chamber Street, and at the reception, Joseph and his friends performed a glee that he had written specially for the occasion: 'Cupid's Darts'. Joseph was fond of composing for special occasions. As Arthur Foulke wrote: 'Every birth, marriage or death was for [Joseph Parry], a musical occasion, and he would seize every such opportunity to compose and sing'.[8]

After their marriage, Joseph and Jane lived at 421 Railroad Street, which they rented from Jane's father, Benjamin Thomas. Bet Parry seems not to have been entirely happy about the marriage. As a second generation immigrant, Jane's knowledge of Welsh would have been limited and she and her parents were members of the Mahoning Presbyterian Church, an English-language church, which was frequented by some of the more prominent local citizens. After they were married, Joseph became organist at Mahoning. Bet might have worried that Joseph was 'betraying' the good Welsh chapel for the sake of enhanced social status. Such an attitude persisted long in Welsh Nonconformist communities.

Bet Parry was unhappy at having a daughter-in-law whose Welsh was limited and who saw herself as part of the English-speaking community. Until the Hispanic immigration of the late twentieth century, all immigrant communities in the United States lost their language after a couple of generations. Joseph's mother was afraid that Joseph's children would lose their Welshness and their connections with Wales. Welsh had been the language of the Parry household in Merthyr and it was the language of the chapel around which their social life revolved. Joseph would have learned to read and write Welsh in the Sunday School. However, as a result of the large number of immigrants from England and Ireland, English was spoken widely in Merthyr. It would have been the main language of the Cyfarthfa ironworks and of the company school in which Joseph received his only formal education. English would have been even more in evidence in Danville, with Welsh being the language of only a minority, substantial though their numbers were. Joseph must have rapidly become fluent in spoken English, but his limited formal education in the language meant that, throughout his life, his command of written English left something to be desired. However, in the latter half of the nineteenth century Welsh was increasingly regarded as a language fit only for the home and the chapel, so that he wrote mostly in English and would very often expect to speak English even with other Welsh speakers.

Later in 1862, Robert James, Joseph's brother-in-law arrived in Danville. He had been a widower since the death of Ann in 1855, and had spent the previous five years in Australia. He returned to Wales for a six-month concert tour before emigrating to Danville. He and Joseph, along with John Abel Jones and John Price, decided to form a vocal quartet. The male vocal quartet had had something of a vogue among fashionable men in England in the late eighteenth and early nineteenth centuries, mixing madrigals with glees and catches. By the middle of the nineteenth century it was on the wane in England but was still growing in popularity in America. Indeed, to this day the older American universities still have their glee clubs – those at Harvard and Yale are particularly well known. What the quartet sang is not known, but it possibly included some of their own compositions – Joseph was certainly composing pieces for male voices at that time, including glees.

This was a happy period for Joseph, even though his adopted country was in turmoil due to the 1861–65 Civil War. Groups of men wandered the states press-ganging their peers to join the Yankee army. Joseph's brother, Henry, signed up in Minersville, Schuylkill County on 8 August 1862, and during 1863–64 Joseph was twice drafted. He managed to avoid joining up each time by paying others to go in his place, a common enough practice at the time. Indeed, it seems likely that his friends encouraged him and may have helped him find the money to pay others to go. Certainly there is no sign that his avoidance of the draft engendered any ill feeling; his friend Thomas Roderick, who served throughout the Civil War, wrote warmly and kindly about Joseph, and Joseph visited him when he was stationed close to Danville.

In 1862, Parry adjudicated in an eisteddfod for the first time – at Hyde Park, Pennsylvania, a Welsh area of the city of Scranton. In two years, he had risen from being an eisteddfod competitor to adjudicator. According to his autobiography[9] he couldn't sleep the previous night due to worrying over the responsibility of the following day's work.

Although the tradition of the eisteddfod can be traced back over a thousand years in Wales, the first eisteddfod that can be recognised as a *national* eisteddfod along the now familiar lines was held in Aberdare in 1861. The 1863 National Eisteddfod was to be held in Swansea and John Abel Jones and John Price encouraged Joseph to enter some of his compositions. The 1863 competition requirements appeared in newspapers in Wales and America in February that year. There were seven composing competitions, with honour and generous prizes to be won, and with adjudicators of renown: Brinley Richards,[10] John Thomas[11] ('Pencerdd Gwalia'), Owain Alaw,[12] J. Ambrose Lloyd[13] and Ieuan Gwyllt[14].

By August 1863, the competitors' pseudonyms had appeared in the newspapers. Parry's choices were particularly interesting:

1. *Motet* – 'Bachgen bach o Ferthyr erioed, erioed.' (A little boy from Merthyr always, always.)
2. *Two hymn tunes* – 'J. P. Bach' – J. P. were his initials, after all, and there is a punning element here since 'bach' is the Welsh for small.
3. *Three glees* – 'Hoffwr Amrywiaeth' (A lover of variation).
4. *Duet* – 'Bassini' (his singing teacher's name on the music course at Geneseo).

Parry won first prize with his motet for five voices, setting Psalm 86, 'Gostwng, O Arglwydd, dy Glust' (*O Lord, Incline thine Ear*), winning £8 and a medal worth £2. The piece was described by two of the adjudicators – J. Ambrose Lloyd and Owain Alaw – as 'truly excellent' and head and shoulders above the rest. 'Gostwng, O Arglwydd, dy Glust' is probably the first Welsh motet, and Parry's only attempt at that form. Psalm 86 was set for a five-part choir and accompaniment, a big step forward from the trio and chorus 'O Give Thanks unto the Lord' of the previous year. One of the competition's requirements was that the motet followed the form of Mozart's 'Splendente Te, Deus', so 'Gostwng, O Arglwydd, dy Glust' is long and complicated. Stylistically, it is derivative, as might be expected of a piece written so early in the composer's career and constrained to follow the Mozartian model.

According to his autobiography,[15] Parry won the first

prize of five guineas for the hymn tunes, but it seems that the first prize was shared: Brinley Richards stating in his adjudication that of the 137 tunes submitted, ' ... two were better than the rest ... one of which was Mr David Lewis, Llanrhystud, while there was no reply to the other, his pseudonym being 'J. P. Bach'.' Without knowing the identity of 'J. P. Bach', Brinley Richards was reluctant to award the prize to an anonymous composer, and in a letter to Parry, dated 13 July 1871, remembered that one tune was 'so far above the usual standard for such pieces, that I doubted its authenticity – I thought it had been stolen!' His friend and fellow musician, William Sterndale Bennett, concurred, and suggested that Richards search volumes of Bach chorales in order to check for plagiarism. Parry's prize was withheld until he convinced Richards of his authorship by sending him the first three hymn tunes from a collection of a dozen composed the previous year, 1862, thus conclusively demonstrating his ability.

There were no such difficulties with the three glees with Welsh words. Joseph Parry won the first prize of five guineas, beating experienced composers such as 'Gwilym Gwent'[16] and John Thomas (Blaenannerch). 'Man as a Flower',[17] 'Rhowch i mi fy Nghleddyf' *(Give me my Sword)* and 'Ffarwel i ti, Gymru Fad' *(Farewell to thee, Fair Wales)*, according to Ieuan Gwyllt's adjudication, showed that here was a composer who had 'talent, taste and ability, that we do not come across every day.' Parry's glees beat Gwilym Gwent's 'Y Clychau' *(The Bells)*, and 'Yr Haf' *(Summer)* and 'Nant y Mynydd' *(The Mountain Stream)* by John Thomas, even though these last two glees were to become as popular as eisteddfod test pieces as Parry's winning 'Ffarwel i ti, Gymru Fad'.

In the duet competition, Joseph Parry shared the first prize with Gwilym Gwent but Parry's successful duet is not named, and no duets of his from this period have survived. In an anonymous article 'Y Buddugwr Anhysbys yn Eisteddfod Abertawe' *(The Anonymous Winner in the Swansea Eisteddfod)* in *Y Cerddor Cymreig*,[18] Parry is described as having won 'the highest degree of respect among his fellow Welsh Americans', and that his compositions – under their various pseudonyms – were 'all the work of one composer; and others doubted that they were the work of anyone who currently competes in Wales'.

Back in Danville, Joseph Parry was by now the organist and choir-master at Mahoning Presbyterian Church, 218 Ferry Street. Indeed, in his autobiography[19] he claims to have held that position for twelve years, probably until he commenced his concert tour of 1866. On the face of it, this seems improbable, since it would mean that he became organist in 1854, when he was only thirteen, when, by his own confession, he did not learn to read music until he was seventeen. In any case, he states elsewhere in his autobiography that the melodeon, which he began to play in 1860, was his first musical instrument. However, there is no doubt that he was organist at the Mahoning Church during the mid-1860s, and it seems likely that he was organist at the Welsh Congregational Church before this.

Jack Jones in *Off to Philadelphia in the Morning* seems to have been responsible for the myth that Parry was the organist at the Welsh Congregational Church, then the English Congregational Church in New York City during this period. This would have been physically impossible given his commitments in Danville, and the fact that the 140-mile journey from Danville to New York City could not be completed in less than seven hours. He probably played the organ in those churches once or twice on occasional visits and, as his fame grew, the length and significance of those visits was exaggerated.

The successes in Swansea gave Joseph a taste of national fame but he still competed, with success, in lesser eisteddfodau in the United States, for example, his glee 'Heddwch' *(Peace)* won at the eisteddfod held in Pittsburgh, Pennsylvania. In August 1864, he was again successful at the Welsh National Eisteddfod, in Llandudno. According to his autobiography,[20] he won a total of £24 and a medal, which were the prizes for the four competitions he'd entered – glee, canon, anthem and part-song.

Nineteen glees for mixed voices had been submitted, with Brinley Richards as the adjudicator, Joseph Parry won the £3 first prize for his glee 'Y Chwaon Iach' *(Wholesome Breezes)*. There seems to have been some confusion over his pseudonym but it is most likely that it was 'Ap ei Wlad' *(His Country's Son)*. 'Sir George Smart' – David Lewis, Llanrhystud – received the £2 second prize, with the third prize of £1 going to 'Mynyddwr' – Gwilym Gwent.

The third competition section was composing an anthem – a verse and chorus on the composer's choice of words. This was Joseph Parry's best result, since he won both first and second prizes, out of eighteen entrants, adjudicated by 'Pencerdd Gwalia' (John Thomas) and 'Tanymarian'.[21] Joseph Parry's first prize was £10 and a medal for his 'Clyw, O Dduw fy Llefain' *(Hear, O Lord, my Cry)*, under the pseudonym of 'Sebastian'; the second prize was £5 for 'Achub fi, O Dduw!' *(Save me, O God!)*, under the pseudonym 'Alltud o Wlad y Gân' *(An Exile from the Land of Song)*.

Lastly, Joseph Parry – with the cheeky pseudonym 'Brinley' – won the first prize for composing a part-song, title unknown. There were six entries, with 'Bardd Alaw' (John Thomas, Blaenannerch) coming second. Thomas, along with David Lewis, was also successful in the competition for composing a hymn tune. Joseph Parry's name is not in the list of winners for this section: either he did not compete or was unsuccessful.

A year earlier, the National Eisteddfod had no idea who this stranger was who won the composing prizes at Swansea, but things were different in Llandudno in 1864, with 'Mr Joseph Parry of America, formerly of Merthyr Tudful' announced from the stage as the victorious musician. He was not present, but was represented by Mr W. J. Jones, owner and editor of the Welsh American newspaper *Y Drych*.[22]

It is an indication of the esteem that Parry had won with his entries for the Swansea Eisteddfod of 1863 that the test piece for the mixed voice choir (twenty to forty voices) competition at the Llandudno Eisteddfod in the following year was his winning motet 'Gostwng, O Arglwydd Dy Glust'. And in the Rhyl Cymmrodorion Eisteddfod at Christmas 1863, the motet's closing chorus was again set as the test piece.

While all this was going on in Wales, Joseph was still in Danville, and composing, as ever, in his spare time. By now he was 'chief roller' at the mills, working the 6 pm to 1 am shift nightly.

For Joseph and Jane 1864 and 1865 were happy years. Their first child, christened Joseph Haydn Parry, was born on 27 May 1864 and their second, called 'Mendy' after his middle name, Mendelssohn, in July 1865. Mendy's full name is usually quoted as 'D. Mendelssohn Parry'; according to *Off to Philadelphia in the Morning*, the D stood for 'David', after one of Jane's brothers. However, the Danville census returns show Jane as having only one brother, Gomer. According to Eleanor Deutsch, who did much to keep the name of the Parry family alive in Danville, the D stood for Daniel, after Joseph's father. Although registration of births had become compulsory in Wales and

England in 1837, there was no such registration system in America even by 1865 and so it must remain a matter of conjecture, but Daniel seems the most likely.

Two months after the new arrival, the 1865 Eisteddfod was held in Aberystwyth. This time Joseph decided to go to Aberystwyth to pick up his prizes in person, a reflection of the 24-year-old composer's confidence in his musical ability. Five Welsh Americans went to Wales for the Eisteddfod: the vocal quartet from Danville, and the singer, teacher and composer, J. R. Thomas, born in Newport (*Casnewydd*, Gwent) and well-known on both sides of the Atlantic. But before they left, they were contacted in New York City by another Welshman, John Griffith. As a lifelong and much-respected journalist, he was almost universally known by the Welsh word for journalist, 'Gohebydd'; he had made his reputation by sending high quality articles from overseas to Thomas Gee's newspaper *Baner ac Amserau Cymru*[24] in Denbigh (*Dinbych*).

Gohebydd was sent to the United States for a year, arriving in June 1865. At the beginning of August, he read in the New York Times that Mr J. R. Thomas, 'the well-known composer and baritone', was about to leave for Europe. Gohebydd made inquiries at *Y Drych*'s Utica office and discovered that Thomas was one of a group of musical Welsh Americans leaving for the Old Country. They were staying at the Cambrian Hotel in Manhattan, and Gohebydd and Eleazar Jones from Utica went to meet them. Gohebydd's first reaction was disbelief that so young a man as Joseph Parry had won so many prizes at the National Eisteddfod. And as he interviewed the group, his attention focused on Parry, and upon hearing about the personal and musical events of his life thus far, decided that here was a good story that was sure to win the attention and sympathy of *Y Faner*'s readers back in Wales.

There was instant friendship between Joseph Parry and John Griffith, a relationship that was to flourish and strengthen with time; indeed, Gohebydd was eventually to prove an important force in advancing Joseph's career. In his autobiography, Joseph calls him 'the King of all my innumerable, invaluable and *never* to be *forgotten friends* in New York City'.[24] In an article in *Y Faner*, Gohebydd described Joseph's successes in Swansea and Llandudno, and asked:

> Is there a way to give this young man, Joseph Parry, a start so to set him up in a situation that would be more in tune with the musicianship in his soul, so that he may truly serve his nation, his time, and the world, rather than spend his energy and days in front of Danville's furnaces, smelting iron? ... Here's a lump of genius! There's no two ways about it.[25]

He suggested that, after the National Eisteddfod in Aberystwyth, Parry be sent for a term of basic general education with Dr. Evan Davies in Swansea, or someone who could offer similar tuition, then to the Royal Academy of Music in London to complete his music education. And he added that he would be handing Joseph's cause over to the Reverend John Griffiths, Rector of Neath (*Castell-nedd*), and chairman of the National Eisteddfod Council. The timing of Gohebydd's article was crucial, because the Eisteddfod was to be held in Aberystwyth in a few weeks, and Parry was already on his way there.

He and his party left New York on 18 August aboard the steamship *City of Washington*, reaching Liverpool toward the end of the month. By 12 September they had reached Aberystwyth, but to Joseph's great dismay his compositions had not reached the adjudicator. John Abel Jones had travelled especially to New York to mail them, and Joseph Parry himself thought they had been stolen, asking in his autobiography, 'Where are they? Who has them? And what the motives? These questions will never be answered.' Perhaps his feeling of paranoia was justified: here was a talented, young – but exiled – composer, winning prizes in the National Eisteddfod of *Wales*. Was this too much for some unscrupulous over-competitive musicians? In a letter dated 18 February 1865 to David Lewis, John Thomas, Blaenannerch, asks:

> What shall we do with this creature that comes over from America to sweep up our music prizes, Dafydd? Surely we must set to it at once, and show him that the best thing for him would be to be at home rather than come over here prize-gathering.[27]

There was clearly a natural element of jealousy at the success enjoyed by this stranger from far away, but there is no evidence to justify suspicions of foul play, and the disappearance of the compositions remains a mystery.

In spite of this disappointment, the 1865 Aberystwyth National Eisteddfod was a success for Parry, albeit for other reasons: he had the opportunity to meet other famous Welsh composers of the day; he heard his composition as a test piece; he was accepted into *Gorsedd y Beirdd* (the assembly of bards); and he had the opportunity to have a piece published. The well-known Welsh musicians at Aberystwyth included J. Ambrose Lloyd, Brinley Richards, Ieuan Gwyllt, 'Tanymarian', John Thomas ('Pencerdd Gwalia'), 'Alaw Ddu',[28] 'Gwilym Gwent', John Thomas[29] and Emlyn Evans.[30] Parry was only twenty-four years old, an exile, but he was warmly accepted into this élite circle. He also had the opportunity to sit at the adjudicators' table to hear his 'Gostwng, O Arglwydd Dy Glust' performed as the mixed choir test piece. And, to crown it all, along with J R Thomas, one of his travelling companions from America, he was presented to the audience, from the Eisteddfod stage, by John Griffiths, Rector of Neath and chair of the Eisteddfod Council; the audience gave them an enthusiastic welcome.

More honours were to follow. The Eisteddfod Gorsedd met at Aberystwyth castle on the Friday morning, with John Thomas ('Pencerdd Gwalia') in charge of the ceremony. Parry and J. R. Thomas were both accepted into the bardic 'Guild of Musicians' – the composer as 'Pencerdd America' (Leading Musician of America) and the singer as 'Alawn Gwent'.

The last of Parry's successes at the Eisteddfod – and the least expected – was that one of the missing compositions was accepted for publication by Hughes & Son, Wrexham (*Wrecsam*). This showed the company's generous faith and belief, firstly because of the commercial risk in publishing the music of a young composer from overseas and secondly the risk of agreeing to publish even though the manuscript was lost. Parry copied the music for his four-part glee 'Ar Don o Flaen Gwyntoedd' (*On the Sea in the Face of the Winds*) from memory – he had a tremendous musical memory – and sold it to Hughes in return for 500 copies, 'feeling *delighted* with the *great bargain*' according to his autobiography.[31] Parry did quite well out of this deal. In Wales, Hughes a'i Fab were selling copies in staff notation at four pence each. Parry's 500 copies would have raised over £8 if sold at this price, a fairly generous fee. In practice, Parry would be selling them in the United States, where he would have a monopoly of the market and could probably sell them at a higher price. In the long term, Hughes must also have made a considerable profit out of the gamble because the glee was reprinted many times and a revised version was produced that included a translation of the Welsh words and corrected a number of errors. This was the first of his pieces to be published on its own, although many had been printed in magazines, for example 'Gostwng, O Arglwydd Dy Glust' in an edition of *Y Gyfres Gerddorol Gymreig*. Publishing 'Ar Don o Flaen Gwyntoedd' was a major coup for Parry, and by 1868 it was a test piece in the Ruthin *(Rhuthun)* National Eisteddfod.

So the 1865 Aberystwyth National Eisteddfod was a mixture of success and disappointment for Parry, and at the end of the week, his group left for south-east Wales for three concerts in the Merthyr area. Joseph visited the family home and nearby relations; he says in his autobiography[32] that he was deeply affected by the visit, which evoked the emotions that he had tried to express in his song 'O Give me back my Childhood Dreams', composed earlier that year. On 18 September, he visited the Gwent and Morgannwg Temperance Cymanfa in Cardiff, addressing the audience as well as performing an arrangement – or 'harmonization' as it was described in the programme – of the traditional tune 'Gwŷr Harlech' *(Men of Harlech)*.

On 23 September, the quartet gave a successful concert in the Temperance Hall in Merthyr, with the hall full to capacity to hear songs, part-songs and glees by Parry, with the Cyfarthfa Brass Band also contributing items. The following evening, Joseph Parry was accompanying on the harmonium as well as singing with the quartet at a similar concert held at the British School in Hirwaun.

The quartet left for America at the end of September, sailing on the *City of New York* from Liverpool to New York, Parry's third trans-Atlantic voyage. The *City of New York* was a new ship that had been launched earlier in 1865; like the *City of Washington*, she was a hybrid – a steamship that also carried sail but she was a faster ship, making the crossing from Cork in an average of ten days, rather than the twelve required by the *City of Washington*. However, a lengthy spell of severe storms made the crossing very unpleasant and the ship had to be repaired after docking. During the journey, there was plenty to think over. Following Gohebydd's reports in *Y Faner*, and with an offer of support from the Rector of Neath, the Eisteddfod Council decided to pay for two years of tuition for Joseph Parry, a year of general education with Dr Evan Davies in Swansea, followed by a year's musical education at the Royal Academy of Music in London.

The Academy was the natural choice – London was the leading musical centre in England and it is unlikely that the Council would have thought of anything further afield – but sending Joseph first to Dr. Evan Davies was unexpected. Evan Davies was an enthusiastic musician, a singer, an eisteddfod adjudicator, the conductor of Swansea Choral Society, and Principal of 'Swansea Normal', the local teacher training college. The Eisteddfod Council felt that Joseph's general education was rather basic, and that a year with Evan Davies would fill the gaps. As far as his musical education in London was concerned, John Thomas ('Pencerdd Gwalia') presented his case to the Academy officials, and Brinley Richards wrote to the Principal, William Sterndale Bennett, describing Parry's musical talent and supporting Joseph's application to study there. New doors were opening for Joseph, but before coming to a decision, he had to discuss the matter with his wife Jane. He was a family man, and there was one other consideration – money. How to pay for moving his family from one side of the Atlantic to the other? Back in Danville the options had to be weighed carefully.

There, Joseph Parry returned to his post as 'head roller', where he was to remain until the end of 1865, considering his future. During his work, his mind was elsewhere, as his autobiography shows:

> How *musical* are some noises of this mill to me, the humming of your huge fans, the rhythm of your engines and machines, the very *flashes* of your rolls are picturesque to my eyes ... all [my compositions] have their origin in your companionship.[33]

The work was physically demanding, with only his little spare time giving Parry the chance to pursue his musical education. He continued to compose prolifically, and despite the disappointment of losing the compositions for the Aberystwyth National Eisteddfod, he continued to win prizes in American eisteddfodau: for example 'Yr Eneth Ddall' *(The Blind Girl)* was the winning song at Pottsville Eisteddfod, Pennsylvania, on 4 July 1865. He also served as an adjudicator, and on Christmas Day that year he adjudicated at the Youngstown Ohio Unitary Eisteddfod at the Arms and Murray Hall, an occasion that was to be a turning point in his musical career.

The first of two meetings was held at 10 am, and following a speech by the chairman D. J. Nicholas (Ivor Ebwy), Joseph Parry sang an 'Eisteddfod Tune', accompanying himself at the harmonium. Parry's song 'O give me back my childhood dreams' was the solo set piece. Gohebydd was also present at the Youngstown Eisteddfod, and following his suggestion, a special meeting was held on 26 December – the day after the eisteddfod – to discuss Joseph's situation. This meeting was held at 10 am at the Welsh Congregational Church on Elm Street, Youngstown, with Gohebydd once more presenting the case for supporting Joseph. It was agreed that a 'Parry Fund Committee' be established, with David John as treasurer and Joseph Aubrey as secretary. With perhaps an oblique reference to the slowness of the Welsh National Eisteddfod Council, the Committee decided 'to work while others talk',[34] and Gohebydd and John Jehu agreed to write letters to Welsh Americans. Three months had elapsed since Joseph Parry had been promised aid by the Eisteddfod Council but he was still at work in Danville.

A General Committee was formed to administer the Parry Fund. As an example to the rest of Welsh America, the Youngstown Eisteddfod Committee gave a donation of $50, followed shortly after by a similar sum from eight other well-known Welsh Americans. Parry's own contribution would be via a concert tour of Welsh-American communities, from the east to the mid-west. He started more or less immediately after the Youngstown Eisteddfod, forming a choir of approximately twenty local singers, including Joseph Aubrey, the Parry Fund secretary, and criss-crossing the countryside on a sled from concert to concert. This experience possibly inspired Parry to compose his light-hearted and descriptive 'Sleighing Glee' (Example 2) in Danville in 1873, prompting one anonymous journalist to comment:

> Next to the surprise that a musician of Mr Parry's stature has composed such a non-sense is the worry that any poet [Cynonfardd] in the world could ever write 'Jing jingle jing, now let us sing, peth jolly yw sleigh ride y gaeaf'. [35]

The journalist has missed the point. The glee is just a piece of fun, as shown by mixing the Welsh and English words, and is to be sung with *hwyl*; it shows the light-hearted side of Parry as a composer.

Joseph Parry on his appointment to the Chair of Music in Aberystwyth in 1874
[From the John Thomas Collection, by permission of Llyfrgell Genedlaethol Cymru/
the National Library of Wales]

Drawing of Joseph Parry's birthplace in Merthyr Tudful, taken from
Cofiant Joseph Parry *(published 1921)*

Mill Street, Danville, Pennsylvania, around 1860

The Rough and Ready Rolling Mills in Danville, where Joseph Parry worked as a puddler's boy from 1854 to 1865

Mahoning Presbyterian Church, Danville, in the 1860s

Joseph Parry's house, Glanbrenig, St David's Road, Aberystwyth, as it is today; the plaque (right) is on the gatepost

'Gohebydd' (John Griffith), who championed Joseph Parry as a young man, and was largely responsible for his appointment to the Chair of Music in Aberystwyth.
[From the John Thomas Collection, by permission of Llyfrgell Genedlaethol Cymru/ the National Library of Wales]

Plaque commemorating the first performance of Parry's hymn tune Aberystwyth. *The former Congregational church is now the surgery of a GP practice in Portland Road in the town.*

The front (above) and back (below) of the medal presented to Joseph Parry for the best motet at the Swansea Eisteddfod in 1863. [By permission of the Cyfarthfa Castle Museum and Art Gallery, Merthyr Tudful]

Joseph Parry's mixed Welsh choir in Danville, around 1873. Parry is in the centre (no. 53).

'Dewi Môn' (Rev. David Rowlands, 1836–1907). He wrote the English words for Blodwen and continued to collaborate with Joseph Parry to the end of his life.
[From the John Thomas Collection, by permission of Llyfrgell Genedlaethol Cymru/ the National Library of Wales]

The only known photograph of Joseph Parry and his family, probably taken around 1886. Back: Haydn, Mendy, Willie; Dilys is on Joseph's lap, holding Jane's hand; front left: Edna

Jane Parry, taken some time after Joseph's death (c. 1915). Round her neck she is wearing the medallion that can be seen in the photograph of Joseph on page 49

Joseph Parry's birthplace in Merthyr Tudful, as it is today

BLODWEN;

(White-Flower.)

A

WELSH OPERA, IN THREE ACTS.

THE MUSIC BY

DR. JOSEPH PARRY,

Professor of Music at the University College of Wales.

THE WELSH WORDS BY

The late MYNYDDOG.

THE ENGLISH WORDS BY

PROFESSOR ROWLANDS,

Brecon College.

J. PARRY AND SON, ABERYSTWITH.

PRINTED BY F. PITMAN, 20, PATERNOSTER ROW, LONDON.

Title page of the score of Blodwen. *Note the spelling of Aberystwyth.*

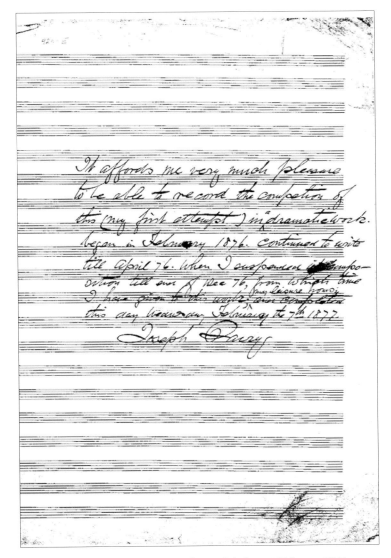

Parry's note recording the completion of Blodwen, *7 February 1877*
[By permission of Llyfrgell Genedlaethol Cymru/the National Library of Wales]

*The Calvinistic Methodist (Presbyterian) ministers of Glamorgan (around 1880),
including Parry's friend and supporter, the Rev. Thomas Levi*
[From the John Thomas Collection, by permission of Llyfrgell Genedlaethol Cymru/
the National Library of Wales]

Edith Wynne ('Eos Cymru' – the Welsh Nightingale) (1842–1897),
who sang with Joseph Parry and adjudicated alongside him
[From the John Thomas Collection, by permission of Llyfrgell Gernedlaethol Cymru/
the National Library of Wales]

Joseph Parry at the organ in his later years

The memorial to Joseph Parry and his son Mendelssohn (Mendy),
in the graveyard of St. Augustine's Church, Penarth

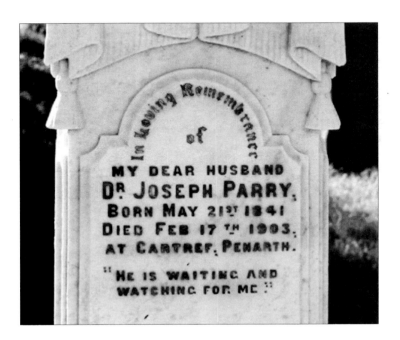

Drawing of Joseph Parry by E. J. Edwards of Penrhyndeudraeth. The drawing won first prize in an eisteddfod in Pwllheli in 1909. It is now in the possession of Emeritus Professor David Wulstan, the last professor of music at Aberystwyth, by whose kind permission it is reproduced here.

Musical Example 2

The first part of Parry's 'Sleighing Glee'

In his autobiography, Joseph thanks the Youngstown Eisteddfod Committee and his 'CambroAmericans' [*sic*] for their support and faith. He gave up his job at the mills in Danville and by the end of 1865 was a professional musician, even though, according to his autobiography, he was 'much afraid of my non-success'.[36]

On New Year's Eve 1866 the town of Newburgh, Ohio was the scene of a successful Parry Fund concert under Joseph's leadership. There he completed his cantata 'Y Mab Afradlon' (*The Prodigal Son*). The work had been in progress for some time, with Parry working on it on trains, ships and at various homes. The words, by 'Eos Bradwen',[37] had won first prize at the 1865 Aberystwyth National Eisteddfod in a competition to write a cantata libretto based on a Biblical subject. Setting those words to music was one of the composition competitions for the 1866 National Eisteddfod, held in Chester on 4–7 September. The adjudicators were Brinley Richards, John Thomas (Pencerdd Gwalia) and Edward Stephen (Tanymarian). The town mayor read the adjudication from the stage. Joseph Parry – pseudonym 'Crwydryn' *(Wanderer)* – won the £20 and silver medal first prize, with his cantata being described as 'by far the very best composition which has been sent in for competition to any Eisteddfod in our recollections.' 'Y Mab Afradlon' contains many of the features that were to characterise Parry's more mature style and makes effective use of the hymn tune 'Talybont'.

'Y Mab Afradlon' was – as far as is known – Parry's final attempt at competing in the National Eisteddfod of Wales. He continued to compete occasionally in America but he is not recorded as winning any more prizes in Wales. This had been a comparatively short period of competing – from 1863 to 1866 – and Parry does not offer any explanation for retiring from the competition circuit. Or he did compete after 1866, without success, and keep it quiet? The most likely explanation is that, while the prize money certainly helped his finances, he felt that the status that he had by then achieved as a composer put him above such competitions. His name had begun to become well known in Wales and America, and perhaps he did not now feel the need to prove himself as a composer. But although 'Y Mab Afradlon' was a success in the Chester Eisteddfod, it was not in great demand for performance; Parry's smaller scale works, such as the songs, anthems and glees, appealed to the public much more.

Also in 1866 Daniel Parry, Joseph's father, died, aged sixty-seven, and was buried in the Christ Episcopal cemetery north of Danville, but Joseph does not mention this in his autobiography. The grave, with its splendid slate headstone, was restored in the mid 2000s.

Joseph's concert tour was going from strength to strength, visiting Welsh communities across New York State, Ohio and Pennsylvania, and even going as far afield as Chicago and Milwaukee.

In June 1867, the Danville Choral Society arranged two concerts in aid of the Parry Fund, one in Mahoning Church and one in Thomson's Hall. The programme included a variety of solos, duets, trios, quartets, with Joseph himself singing while accompanying himself at the organ (probably a harmonium); among the pieces performed were 'Friend of my Youth', 'Y Trên' *(The Train)*, 'Y Gwallgofddyn' *(The Madman)*, 'Y Plentyn yn Marw' *(The Dying Child)* and 'Gwraig y Meddwyn' *(The Drunkard's Wife)*, the last of these sung by Joseph's sister, Jane, by now Mrs Jane Evans.

In August 1867, Parry was in Hyde Park, Pennsylvania, where he conducted, sang and played the organ at a farewell concert for the Reverend Thomas Levi, who was visiting from Wales. The farewell concert was held in a Calvinistic Methodist chapel on 9 August. The concert was a rousing success, as was Parry's own contribution. But in the longer term the concert was important because it saw the start of the friendship between Parry and Levi, which was to be so helpful to Parry over the next few years.

The concert tour continued to be a resounding success and, if anything, the demands on Joseph increased. On 14 and 16 December 1867, for example, he held concerts at Fairhaven and Middle Granville, in the Slate Valley district on the border between New York State and Vermont – an area where slate mining had led to the development of very substantial Welsh communities – and then the next day he had a concert in Jamesville, near Syracuse. The distance from Fairhaven to Jamesville as the crow flies is around 130 miles; by train it was more like 170 miles and in the 1860s the train journey would have been awkward and slow, with several changes. What is more, by December, upper New York State is very cold and prone to heavy blizzards, which cannot have made travelling a pleasant experience.

On Christmas Day 1867, Joseph returned to Youngstown Eisteddfod, where his concert tour had been born two years earlier. Two of his compositions were test pieces: the first movement of the motet 'Gostwng, O Arglwydd, Dy Glust' and the glee 'Ar Don o Flaen Gwyntoedd'. He was also the principal performer in a concert held in the evening at the Excelsior Hall.

By the spring of 1868, the Parry Fund had reached $3,500, and by the summer had doubled to $7,000, enough to fund three years of study for him at the Royal Academy in London. During his concert tour, he had been asking people for their opinions on what kind of an education he should pursue on the other side of the Atlantic, and by January 1868 the Parry Fund Committee had decided that there was no need for him to study with Dr. Evan Davies in Swansea after all, since he had received 'a preparatory education in Danville'.[38] But the Parry Fund was not large enough to support the composer's wife and young family in London, so that Joseph left New York on 19 August 1868, for his fourth trans-Atlantic crossing, on his own. He says in his autobiography[39] that he sailed on the *City of Brussels* but his memory must have been at fault – he was writing some thirty-four years after the event – because the *City of Brussels* did not make her maiden voyage until October 1869.

Parry would have embarked on the voyage with very mixed feelings. He must certainly have felt sadness at leaving his wife and two young sons behind, as well as trepidation at the prospect of the loneliness awaiting him in a city where he knew almost no-one, but he must also have been anticipating eagerly the opportunity of studying full-time at the leading institution for musical education in the English-speaking world.

Notes Chapter 2

[1] US President Zachary Taylor was known as 'Old Rough and Ready' and the mills were named after him.

[2] Joseph Parry, p. 12.

[3] Joseph Parry, p. 12.

[4] Letter dated 10 March 1869 to 'Mynorydd' (William Davies), conductor of the London Welsh Choral Society.

[5] Joseph Parry, p. 14.

[6] The Normal Academy of Music in Geneseo was founded in 1860 by William B. Bradbury and certainly continued to operate until 1864.

[7] Joseph Parry, p. 9.

[8] *My Danville*, p. 98.

[9] Joseph Parry, p. 18.

[10] Henry Brinley Richards (1817–1885), pianist and composer, was born in Carmarthen and educated at the Royal Academy of Music, where he subsequently taught. He is remembered today for his collection of Welsh traditional songs, *The Songs of Wales* (1873), and perhaps for his song *God Bless the Prince of Wales*.

[11] John Thomas ('Pencerdd Gwalia') (1826–1913), harpist and composer, was born in Bridgend and, like Richards, was educated at the Royal Academy of Music. As a harpist, he was well known throughout Europe and in 1871 was appointed Harpist to Queen Victoria. He founded the London Welsh Choral Union. Although not remembered today, he was a much more serious composer than Richards, with a number of large scale instrumental works to his credit.

[12] 'Owain Alaw': John Owen (1821–1883), organist and music publisher.

[13] J Ambrose Lloyd (1815–1874), from Mold, was a prolific composer of hymn tunes and anthems, of which the best known is 'Teyrnasoedd y Ddaear' *(The Kingdoms of the Earth)*.

[14] 'Ieuan Gwyllt': Rev John Roberts (1822–1877) was successful in many fields, as teacher, editor, Welsh Calvinistic Methodist minister, journalist, lecturer, poet, composer and conductor. In 1859 he published *Llyfr Tonau Cynulleidfaol* ('The Book of Congregational Tunes'), a collection of hymn tunes from various sources that set a new standard for congregational singing.

[15] Joseph Parry, p. 18.

[16] 'Gwilym Gwent': William Aubrey Williams (1834–1891). Born in Tredegar, he was a blacksmith by trade who became a prolific and successful composer. He emigrated to Plymouth, Pennsylvania, in 1872, where he remained until his death.

[17] This is how Parry refers in his autobiography to the first of the glees. Presumably the words were in Welsh but we have no record of them.

[18] 1 January 1864.

[19] Joseph Parry, p. 28.

[20] Joseph Parry, p. 18.

[21] 'Tanymarian': Edward Stephen (Jones) (1822–1885). Born in Maentwrog, Merionethshire as Edward Jones but changed his name to Edward Stephen. He was a Congregationalist minister, composer (remembered now chiefly for some fine hymn tunes), singer, lecturer, journalist, conductor and adjudicator.

[22] *Y Drych (lit. The Mirror).* For information about this and other newspapers and periodicals referred to, see the Bibliography.

[23] Details of the Welsh newspapers and magazines referred to will be found in the Bibliography.

[24] Joseph Parry, p. 20, Parry's emphasis.

[25] *Y Faner,* 6 September 1865.

[26] Joseph Parry, p. 20.

[27] NLW MS 8271C no 10.

[28] 'Alaw Ddu': William Thomas Rees (1838–1904). Born in Pontrhydyfen, Glamorgan, in 1851 he moved to Aberdare to work as a miner. He subsequently moved to Llanelli (then spelt Llanelly), where he founded the Llanelly Philharmonic Society. He composed songs, hymn tunes, cantatas and four Requiems.

[29] John Thomas (1839–1921). Born in Blaenannerch, Ceredigion (and not to be confused with John Thomas, Pencerdd Gwalia). Poet and composer of songs, anthems and hymn tunes, a few of which are still sung. In 1871 he married Anne, daughter of the family who kept the Post Office in Llanwrtyd, and moved to Llanwrtyd; he is therefore sometimes referred to as John Thomas of Llanwrtyd.

[30] David Emlyn Evans (1843–1913). Born in Newcastle Emlyn, Carmarthenshire. As well as the usual songs, anthems and hymn tunes, he wrote an operetta *Y Tylwyth Teg (The Fairies)* based on Welsh folk tunes, a cantata and an oratorio.

[31] Joseph Parry, p. 22.

[32] Joseph Parry, p. 20.

[33] Joseph Parry, pp. 23–24, Parry's emphasis.

[34] *Y Drych,* 25 January 1866.

[35] *Y Gerddorfa,* 1 March 1873.

[36] Joseph Parry, p. 24.

[37] 'Eos Bradwen': John Jones (1831–1899), poet and musician, born near Tal-y-llyn. From 1863 to 1878 he was leader of the choir at S. Asaph cathedral, where he worked for fifteen years. He won many prizes for poems at various eisteddfodau.

[38] *Y Drych,* 13 February 1868.

[39] Joseph Parry, p. 28.

3

The Royal Academy

When Joseph arrived in Liverpool, around 10 September 1868, he went first to Merthyr Tudful, where, according to his autobiography, the following words came to his mind:

> O! give me back my childhood dreams,
> O! give them back to me;
> When all things wore the hue of love,
> The heart from grief was free.

These are the opening words of the song composed in Danville *c.* 1865, on lines he apparently wrote himself. The song was later translated into Welsh by the poet Mynyddog[1] as 'Breuddwydion Ieuenctid'.

Joseph went on to visit his mother's family home in Mynyddygarreg before travelling to Morriston *(Treforys)* to visit the Reverend Thomas Levi. The minister had organised a concert in Swansea on 17 September; despite the fact that it had been arranged in some haste, the Music Hall was full to capacity to hear him as principal soloist and accompanist. There were items by local performers such as a brass band, soloists – including Silas Evans, one of Swansea's leading musicians, and the Glantawe choir under the baton of John Watkins, Morriston. Joseph sang his own songs, accompanying himself at the harmonium. His programme included 'The Home of My Childhood', composed on Parry's own words during his recent sea voyage, 'Yr Eneth Ddall', 'Y Trên', 'Dangos dy fod yn

Gymro' (*Show you're a Welshman*), 'Gwraig y Meddwyn', 'Y Ty ar Dân' (*The House on Fire*), and 'Jefferson Davis' – a song mocking the Confederate leader during the American Civil War. The choir sang Parry's arrangement of 'Gwŷr Harlech' as well as the glee 'Ar Don o Flaen Gwyntoedd', with the composer accompanying both items. Reviewing the concert, *Y Faner* described Parry as:

> a young, exiled and brilliant Welshman ... no Welsh person had received such a warm and heartfelt welcome on his first appearance in the country of his birth. It's obvious to the weakest eye that Mr Parry is a mass of musical genius.[2]

The following day, Parry left Swansea for London, registering at the Royal Academy of Music on 19 September 1868, and lodging at 27 Thavies Inn, London (EC4 today), close to Holborn Circus. At that time, the Academy occupied 4–5 Tenterden Street near Hanover Square, just south of Oxford Street and west of Oxford Circus, around a mile and a half from Parry's lodgings.

The Principal of the Royal Academy was William Sterndale Bennett, who had come into indirect contact with Joseph over a decade previously when his friend Brinley Richards had consulted him about the originality of some of the eisteddfod entries. It was Richards who brought Parry to the attention of the Academy when he was seeking admission and this was doubtless a factor in Sterndale Bennett's decision to teach Joseph himself. Joseph was fortunate to have this opportunity. Sterndale Bennett, was undoubtedly the best of the English composers of the first three-quarters of the nineteenth century. A fine pianist, he wrote five piano concertos, and was a friend of Mendelssohn. It was this friendship that that led Sterndale

Bennett to his admiration of J. S. Bach and to his founding of the Bach Society in 1849, to bring the works of the composer to London audiences.

Parry's education was not, however, to be limited to composition; after all, he was familiar to his audiences as a singer and organist as well as a composer. He received singing lessons from Manuel Patricio Rodríguez García (1805–1906), the son of the famous Spanish tenor Manuel del Popolo Vicente García: he taught at the Paris Conservatoire from 1830 to 1848 and at the Academy from 1848 to 1895, and was perhaps the most famous singing teacher in Europe at the time, numbering Jenny Lind among his pupils.

Parry was taught the organ by Charles Steggall (1826–1905). Steggall himself had been a student of Sterndale Bennett's at the Academy from 1847 to 1851 and was the secretary of the Bach Society throughout its life. He was an organist and composer, who is now remembered chiefly for a few hymn tunes, in particular *Christchurch* ('Jerusalem on high my song and city is'), and for a number of organ pieces.

At twenty-seven years of age, Joseph was older than his fellow students, but this personal and musical maturity worked in his favour. He was eager to take advantage of the opportunities for musical education that were so much wider than those that had been available to him so far. He was to work conscientiously and diligently throughout his three years in London. This was his nature but he was fully aware of the huge efforts that had been made, on both sides of the Atlantic, to support him. He was also aware that the eyes of the press, both in Wales and in America, were upon him and that his academic career at the Academy was constantly being reported, making his working conditions very different from those of his peers. Finally, he was bound by ties of personal friendship to some of his most important supporters, in particular Gohebydd and Levi, and he would not have wished to let them down in any way. All these pressures might easily have proved too much for a younger and less experienced man.

London was a new and strange place for him, but Joseph continued to cling to his Welshness and his Nonconformist ways. He attended the Welsh Independent chapel in Fetter Lane, close to his first London lodgings in Thavies Inn. He was a faithful member there for the whole of his three years in London, eventually becoming *arweinydd y gân* (leader of the congregational singing) and organist; Fetter Lane was said to have the best chapel singing in London.

Joseph kept in close contact with Wales, taking every opportunity to return to the country to perform, conduct a *cymanu ganu* or adjudicate in an eisteddfod. He held concerts all over Wales, with every occasion more or less following the same pattern as the Swansea concert. As well as being a platform for his music, every event promoted Parry the musician. Danville songs – from *c.* 1861–68 – were the main content of the Swansea concert, but from then on, his concerts in Wales would be an opportunity to perform new music, mostly solos, composed in London. One of these, 'Hoff Wlad fy Ngenedigaeth' *(Dear Land of my Birth)*, is an early example of the co-operation between Joseph Parry and the poet 'Hwfa Môn' – the Reverend Rowland Williams, minister of Fetter Lane chapel from 1867 to 1881.

At the end of the 1868 Autumn term, Joseph had a month's vacation. He used this to hold a concert tour. On Christmas Day, he acted as music adjudicator and concert soloist at the Merthyr Tudful Cymmrodorion Eisteddfod, where his winning glee at the 1867 Utica Eisteddfod, 'Rhosyn yr Haf', was one of the set pieces. (This glee was also the set piece at the Tabernacl Eisteddfod held in the

Drill Hall, Merthyr on the same day.) On 7 January he sang in a concert at Aberdare with Megan Watts,[3] a promising young singer who was beginning to make a name for herself. On 15 January he sang and accompanied the choirs at a concert in Porthmadog, arranged by Thomas Levi, to raise funds for the purchase of a new harmonium. On 16 January he gave a concert at Waunfawr, near Caernarfon, where every song was encored, and Parry was described by *Yr Herald Cymraeg*[4] as one who has 'greatness in his simple and unaffected style' along with an ability 'to throw into his singing 'that something special' that touches the heart of man'. After his concert in Caernarfon on 18 January the following prescient comment appearing in *Yr Herald Cymraeg*: 'It's obvious that the Pencerdd's stay and studies at the Royal Academy in London have resulted in a good impression; and from what we can judge, an illustrious career awaits our talented fellow countryman.'[5] Similar concerts took place in Bryn Menai, Swansea, Dowlais and Llanelli. The tour was a success in every way – Parry's compositions and his solo performances were well received and the financial outcome was gratifying.

A nineteenth-century musical phenomenon was the 'benefit concert', with the proceeds often going toward securing the education of an individual. Most of the concerts held during Joseph's first college vacation benefited him both educationally and personally, and many other tours were to follow. The hand of Thomas Levi was often visible in the arrangements, and at the beginning of 1869 Gohebydd returned to tour Wales with his lecture on 'This and that in America'. He took every opportunity to mention Joseph and his friendship with him. Such publicity often resulted in an invitation to Joseph to perform in the area.

Back in London, Joseph continued his academic career,

working diligently without venturing far away from the Academy, the chapel and his lodgings. Occasionally he had an opportunity to socialise more widely; on 24 February 1869, for example, he attended a grand dinner held by the London Welsh in the Freemasons' Hall in Holborn and attended by other Welsh musicians such as Brinley Richards, Megan Watts and Edith Wynne.[6] But such an occasion was exceptional and even though London was one of Europe's great musical centres, he seemed reluctant to take advantage of its opportunities. He mentions attending but few musical events, and even scarcer was his contact with activities that were not Welsh in some way. Although he had become a Freemason in Danville in 1867 and seems to have transferred his membership to the London Welsh Lodge, Freemasonry does not appear to have figured significantly in his life in London. For the three years that he was at the Academy, Parry's world during term time consisted of his academic work and the chapel, along with his family from June 1869 onwards. His vacations were largely spent performing as singer and organist in concerts in Wales.

The most important domestic event of 1869 was the arrival of the rest of the Parry family during mid June. Joseph himself paid for their passage out of his concert income. The family moved into accommodation at 193 Euston Road.

The Academy's academic year closed on 23 July with a concert and award ceremony at the Queen's Concert Rooms in Hanover Square. Of the seventy-five students, twelve received a special award, with Parry among them – no mean achievement considering that the other eleven had been students there for three or four years. The prizes were distributed by Mrs Gladstone, the wife of the Prime Minister and one of the Academy's benefactors, and she and Joseph expressed their shared pride in their Welshness.

Parry had already been to Wales to hold concerts before the end of term. On 14 July, for example, he had been at the Fourth Eryri Temperance Union Musical Festival held in Caernarfon castle. The Union included thirteen local choirs, and during the afternoon session, Parry's glee 'Ar Don o Flaen Gwyntoedd' was sung with great passion. The following evening he was in Blaenau Ffestiniog for a benefit concert in aid of Tanygrisiau British School – an event that prompted this comment: 'The Pencerdd is a fine lad, an honour to his country, and his name has a charm for every Welshman who appreciates real music.'[7] Parry himself was in Tanygrisiau the following evening going through his usual programme, but which also included the first performance of a new glee 'Gweddi Gwraig y Meddwyn' (*The Drunkard's Wife's Prayer*), on words by Thomas Levi. Levi was gradually associating himself with Parry's public appearances and becoming, in effect his (possibly unpaid) agent. At the beginning of August, an appeal was made via the newspapers for those areas wishing to secure an appearance by Joseph Parry to confirm that as soon as possible, with all correspondence after 9 August to be directed through Thomas Levi in Morriston.

Joseph's first concert of the summer vacation was another visit to Llanelli on 6 August, followed by concerts in Treuddyn near Mold (19 August), Waunfawr (21 August) – where the proceeds came to £18 – Caernarfon (23 August), Pen-y-groes (26 August), Amlwch (27 August), Llanberis (30 August) and Llanwrtyd (2 September). On 4 September he was in Cwmaman, prompting the comment by an anonymous journalist in *Y Faner* that one of the musical reasons why he was 'world-popular' was: 'New songs from his own pen, rather than grinding out the age-old 'golden oldies' e.g. the 'A.B.C. duet' (by John Parry).'[8] Part of Joseph Parry's appeal was certainly that he was a young musician who was prepared to present his audience with new songs, performed with attractive enthusiasm – thanks to his vocal training at the Academy as well as his outgoing personality. The rest of September and the end of his summer vacation saw concerts in Rhosymedre, Rhymni, Ebbw Vale (*Glyn Ebwy*), Dolgellau, Rhiwabon and Dowlais, and at the end of the tour *Y Cerddor Cymreig*'s comment was that Parry succeeded at every event 'to cause not only musicians, but the general public, to think even more highly of him than previously. His compositions were so new'.[9]

During this period, Parry was in regular contact with John Ceiriog Hughes, the leading Welsh lyric poet of his day. Eleven letters from Parry to Ceiriog, all but one of them from this period, are to be found in the National Library of Wales.[10] Parry had been setting Ceiriog's lyrics for some time – he had made a choral setting of 'Ffarwel i ti, Gymru Fad' around 1863 and of 'Rhosyn yr Haf' in 1867, as well as solo settings of 'Yr Eneth Ddall', 'Y Trên', and others. He commissioned a number of translations from Ceiriog *into* English, explaining, in a letter dated 20 September 1869 from Dowlais, just before he returned to the Academy, that 'My reason for having it in English is that my English songs are much more scarce than my Welsh songs; and I need some English ones very badly.'[11] It seems that Ceiriog was sometimes slow in responding and Parry became a little irritated; in a later but undated letter, also written from Dowlais, he writes:

> Dear Ceiriog,
> I beg you will send me my copy of 'Y Milwr' *at once* as it is needed by a Pianist for a Concert to be [at the] end of this week. I earnestly trust you will send it by first mail. I hope you have it ready, also 'Gwraig y Morwr'. If not, I am exceeding sorry I can wait no

longer as I had two letters from the Pianist for that copy.

Trusting you and family are well as we are and that I shall receive the copy without fail on Friday.[12]

There were similar delays over translating two of the collection of six anthems that Parry published in 1870. Ceiriog's slowness is not surprising; he was at the height of his powers and success and producing regular collections of his poetry, while employed full time as a stationmaster on the Cambrian Railways.

Joseph Parry returned to London to start his second year at the Academy, and by Christmas 1869 he was touring once again, starting in Dowlais on 23 December, then on to Merthyr Tudful, where for the second year in succession, he was the adjudicator and soloist at the Temperance Cymmrodorion Eisteddfod held at the Temperance Hall on Christmas Day. The tour continued with two more concerts in the south – Beaufort *(Cendl)* (27 December) and Cydweli (29 December) – then up to north Wales at the New Year with engagements at Machynlleth (5 January 1870), Holyhead *(Caergybi)* (19 January) before finishing in Beaufort (27 January).

It was at about this time – January 1870 – that Sterndale Bennett received a letter from the Parry Fund Committee in the United States inquiring about Joseph Parry's progress. The Principal replied that Parry had mastered in eighteen months what the majority of the other students took three years to learn. Sterndale Bennett's appraisal was received with joy and pride, fully justifying a continuation of the Fund money that was sent quarterly to Parry in London.

While Parry had, by now, plenty of experience as an eisteddfod adjudicator, in Wales, America and England, he had always been called on to adjudicate vocal competitions.

In the Pontypridd Eisteddfod on 2 May, for the first time, he was called upon to adjudicate a composition competition. Parry the composer was now judging the music of others. A month later, he was wearing his performing hat once again, this time at the Eryri Temperance Union Music Festival held in Harlech castle on 2 June. He had been at the previous year's festival at Caernarfon castle, making such an impression that the Union's Committee had decided to invite him back as soloist. He was a strict teetotaller, and his presence on stage gave the cause added impetus. It was seen as a coup that the Committee had been successful in securing the services of such a personality, especially as his pieces would often contain a temperance message, such as the solo 'Gwraig y Meddwyn' (*The Drunkard's Wife*) or the glee 'Gweddi Gwraig y Meddwyn'.

After adjudicating in an eisteddfod at the Music Hall in Swansea on Whit Monday, Parry returned to London to complete his second year at the Academy, the annual prize giving ceremony being held on 23 July 1870 at the Queen's Concert Room at Hanover Square. Having sat an examination earlier in the month, he was honoured with a bronze medal for musical achievement. The prize was presented for the second year in succession by Mrs Gladstone. Following the ceremony, the Academy was closed until 20 September but once again Parry would have no real vacation, for the following weeks were packed with musical commitments.

Joseph Parry went immediately to Llandeilo for an eisteddfod and concert. Two days later, he conducted a *cymanfa ganu* in Aberystwyth, before travelling further north for the first Ceredigion Musical Temperance Union anniversary – a *cymanfa ganu* and concert held on 27 July. The *cymanfa* and concert programmes show that Parry brought along a co-soloist for this tour, Megan Watts.

Performances were held in Machynlleth (29 July), Llanberis (30 July), Bethesda (1 August), Blaenau Ffestiniog (3 August). Rhostryfan (6 August), Llanwrtyd (22 August), Caernarfon (27 August) and Denbigh on 2 September.

At the end of the month Joseph Parry returned to the Academy to start his final year as a student. Within a month, he had to start preparing for the climax of his academic career so far: the examination for the Cambridge University Mus. Bac. degree.

The procedure for obtaining a degree in music from Oxford or Cambridge in 1870 was very different from what it is today. Essentially the Bachelor of Music – then usually known as Musicae Baccalaureus (Mus. Bac.) – was an external degree; it was viewed as a professional qualification and possessing it did not confer the right to proceed to an MA and become a senior member of the university. Neither university taught a degree course in music and candidates for the degree were not expected to be resident.[13] Both universities had Professors of Music who were expected to devote only a comparatively small part of their time to the post; their formal duties were mostly concerned with examinations. Candidates for the degree of Mus. Bac. at Cambridge had to take examinations in harmony, counterpoint, orchestration and the history of music; they also had to submit an exercise, a setting of biblical words for voices and orchestra. It was to Parry's advantage that he was going for a Cambridge degree because Sterndale Bennett had been Professor of Music there since 1856 and, in 1857, had given the degree of Mus. Bac. the form in which Parry would take it, with examinations in fields similar to the courses taught at the Academy.

On 15 November 1870, Joseph Parry sent a letter to the Reverend Doctor Stephen Parkinson, Cambridge, outlining his intention to arrive in the city on 19 November in order to submit the £15 registration fee and then sit the exam the following day. With his letter, Parry included a certificate from Hugh Reginald Haweis MA, incumbent of St James, Westmoreland Street, Marylebone in London. In order for Parry to become a candidate for the degree he had to be admitted to a college as a 'pensioner' – a student paying his own fees. He had, according to the regulations, to present a reference letter from a person with an MA from Cambridge or Oxford, as quoted: 'I hereby certify that I have examined Joseph Parry and I consider him qualified, both in manners and learning, to be admitted a member of the University of Cambridge.' He also had to submit a letter of his own to prove his identity. Parry was admitted to St John's College, perhaps because it was Sterndale Bennett's college, or perhaps because of its Welsh connection – Bishop Morgan, who first translated the Bible into Welsh, had been a member of St John's.

Joseph duly sat the Cambridge examination on 20 November. He would not hear the results for several months.

The Academy Christmas recess between 23 December and 28 January saw Joseph Parry leave London immediately, as usual. But before crossing Offa's Dyke, he went to Liverpool to appear in the Liverpool and Birkenhead Gordofigion[14] Eisteddfod, held on 26 December at St George's Hall. In one of his adjudications, he praised the eisteddfod committee for including a solo piano competition, stating that it was a pity that 'his fellow countrymen [had] been so neglectful for such a long time on such a matter.' Parry was becoming increasingly aware of the neglect of instrumental music in Wales and it was to be a recurring theme throughout his career. During his time at the Academy, he composed a number of instrumental and orchestral pieces, possibly as a result of Sterndale Bennett's urging him to venture into fields other than vocal music but, after leaving the Academy, he wrote vocal music almost exclusively. In the New Year, Joseph returned to Wales to undertake his usual concert tour, with the usual songs, of which his audience never seemed to tire, suggesting there was something in his performances that struck a chord with his audience every time.

Upon his return to London at the end of January 1871, Joseph discovered that the city's Welsh community had jointly organized musical events with the Liverpool Welsh,[15] as a tribute to him. Two benefit concerts had been arranged, one in London and the other in Liverpool, and as a further compliment, every item in both programmes would be by him. This would be the climax of all the performances of his music during his three years in London.

St George's Hall, Langham Place, was full to capacity for the first concert on 6 February 1871, and among the artists were Brinley Richards, John Thomas (Pencerdd Gwalia), Ellis Roberts ('Eos Meirion'), Edith Wynne and Megan Watts, who all gave their services free of charge, and a united choir of London's Welsh chapels, which performed the glees 'Ar Don o Flaen Gwyntoedd' and 'Gweddi Gwraig y Meddwyn', the anthems 'Yr Arglwydd yw fy Mugail' (*The Lord is my Shepherd*), 'Duw Bydd Drugarog' (*God be Merciful*) and 'Hosanna i Fab Dafydd' (*Hosanna to the Son of David*), as well as Parry's arrangement of 'Gwŷr Harlech' for mixed choir. The only instrumental item was a piano sonata 'in two parts'[16] – probably a selection from the last of the three sonatas that Parry had composed at the Academy. The concert proceeds, £50, were presented to him, a substantial sum that reflected the general respect and admiration felt toward him. The Liverpool concert, held on 11 April, was less successful, however.

Toward mid-March 1871, Parry heard that he'd been

awarded the Mus. Bac. degree from St John's College, Cambridge. Four of the original seven candidates had failed, so Parry had every reason to be proud of his new achievement. He caused much controversy by claiming that he was the first Welshman to receive the degree. This was indeed a rash claim, in all probability made on the spur of the moment, yet he repeated the claim when addressing students as late as 1897 and in his autobiography of 1902. The claim is, in fact, false because several Welshmen over the previous centuries had held Mus. Bac. degrees, although Parry might well have been unaware of this.

Parry was enormously proud of the qualification. He lived in the public eye; he was idolised by the common people of Wales – people who lacked a formal education themselves but, unlike many of the English working class, held education in the highest esteem and revered the idea of a university degree. And here was one of their own, with a university degree (and who would eventually become a University professor). It is no surprise that he reacted in the way he did.

Thomas Levi wrote on open letter to the press outlining Parry's achievements during his three years at the Academy, his family's difficult financial situation, and his exemplary and teetotal character. Levi asked: 'Is it right of us as a nation that we should let our talented and hard-working fellow countryman starve as he leaves us?'[17] He suggested inviting him to undertake a final concert tour before departing for the United States, with the proceeds of every concert be given to him. The response was good and around twenty concerts were arranged during the five weeks between the end of the Academy's year and the Parrys' departure for America on 30 August. But before leaving London, he had to attend two important events: the end of term concert at the Academy, and a testimonial evening hosted by London Welsh.

The Academy's prize-giving ceremony – the third and final one for Parry – was held on 22 July 1871, and, as was the tradition, student compositions were performed, including Joseph Parry's chorus 'Fe Gyfyd Goleuni' (*Light Arises*) – his Mus. Bac. exercise – in an excellent performance, with even the London newspapers such as *The Times, Daily Telegraph*, and the *London Standard* lauding the work. Here was a fitting and praiseworthy end to Parry's three years as a student at the Academy. In the ceremony, Parry was awarded the college's highest accolade, a silver medal, presented once again by Mrs Gladstone, who remembered presenting him with bronze medals in previous years.

A few days later, Joseph and Jane attended the testimonial meeting arranged in his honour. Gohebydd was primarily responsible for organising the testimonial. The meeting was held at the YMCA in Aldersgate Street, London, on 24 July 1871, chaired by Robert Jones, a Welshman who was a city sheriff at that time. Among the dignitaries present were Henry Richard MP, G Osborne Morgan MP, Hugh Owen (the educationalist), Hwfa Môn, Penry Williams (the painter), Joseph Edwards (the sculptor), and the musicians included Brinley Richards, Edith Wynne and Megan Watts among others. William Sterndale Bennett could not attend due to a family commitment, but wrote that that: 'Mr Parry deserves most thoroughly all the friendship and support he obtains. He will go back to America an accomplished musician and enthusiastic artist.'

Parry's song 'Yr Ehedydd' (*The Lark*) was sung by Miss Evans, and 'Yr Hen Ywen Werdd' (*The Old Green Yew*) by Miss Lloyd. These two singers were apparently two of Joseph's private pupils – there was nothing unusual in talented students at the Academy taking pupils. Gohebydd read out letters he had received in reply to invitations to attend the meeting, and Henry Richard proposed a vote of congratulations and best wishes to Joseph and his family. Brinley Richards' wife presented Joseph Parry with a gold watch, and Robert Jones' wife gave Jane Parry a diamond ring. Then Brinley Richards spoke about his long and successful association with Joseph Parry and Hwfa Môn thanked him for his three years of faithful service as *arweinydd y gân* and organist in his chapel. He also read out a poem that he had composed in honour of his friend, of which the following stanza is typical:

> Mae ei fawl twym, a'i foliant – ei dalent
> Handelaidd a'i urddiant;
> A'i gerdd bêr, ar dyner dant,
> I'w genedl yn ogoniant.

> [*The warm praise, and the worship – his*
> *Handelian talent honour him;*
> *And his sonorous music, performed sweetly*
> *Is glorious to his nation.*]

After Megan Watts had sung 'Gwraig y Morwr' (*The Sailor's Wife*) accompanied by Brinley Richards, the meeting ended with general thanks and appreciation of the monetary contributions. Over £20 had been raised in gifts, including generous contributions from dignitaries such as Henry Bruce, the Home Secretary, many Welsh Members of Parliament, London Welsh people and other prominent Welsh exiles.

The testimonial presentation had been a major success. Following the meeting, Joseph left for Wales to begin a two-month concert tour, culminating in Tywyn, where he and Edith Wynne were adjudicators and soloists in the town's grand eisteddfod. He then headed south for a concert in Swansea Town Hall on 26 August, the venue of his first concert in Wales upon his arrival, back in September 1868.

On 28 August 1871 Joseph Parry and his family sailed from Liverpool. According to his autobiography they sailed aboard the steamship *City of Berlin*; again, however, his memory must have been at fault since the *City of Berlin* was not launched until October 1874.

Thomas Levi had written to the Welsh press about Joseph Parry's recent successes, and penned a similar letter dated 6 October 1871 to the Welsh in America, describing Parry as a 'lively young man, with a soul full of fire, and a warm and open heart'. Levi added that the composer had never once wandered off the path of righteousness while in London, and was faithful to his church. The eyes of the Welsh nation had followed his every move for three years. It was now the turn of Welsh Americans, and there was a warm welcome awaiting his return.

Notes Chapter 3

[1] Richard Davies (1833–1877), a noted Welsh poet from Llanbrynmair, Powys. As will be seen in later chapters, Parry set a great deal of Mynyddog's poetry to music and Mynyddog wrote the libretto for *Blodwen*. A translation of one of Mynyddog's poems, 'When comes my Gwen', was set by 'the other Parry', Sir Hubert.

[2] 23 September 1868, p. 10.

[3] Megan Watts Hughes (1842–1907), was a singer from Dowlais. Her performances in and around Merthyr and Aberdare led to a local fund-raising effort that enabled her to study at the Royal Academy of Music. She was a successful singer – she sang duets with Jenny Lind – and also a minor composer.

[4] 23 January 1869, p. 8.

[5] 23 January 1869, p. 5.

[6] Sarah Edith Wynne ('Eos Cymru' – the Nightingale of Wales) (1842–1897). From Holywell (*Treffynnon*), she was a leading London soprano for some ten years, as well as successfully appearing as an actress. She gave up professional performance in 1875, when she married.

[7] *Y Faner*, 21 July 1869, p. 4.

[8] 15 September 1869, p. 4.

[9] 1 October 1869, p. 77.

[10] NLW 10186D/53 to 10186D/63.

[11] NLW 10186D/53.

[12] NLW 10186D/59.

[13] Joseph Parry's part-namesake and near contemporary, Hubert Parry, for example, gained the degree of Mus.Bac. from Cambridge while he was still a schoolboy at Eton.

[14] *Lit* Ordovicians. A Welsh literary society in Liverpool and Birkenhead that flourished during the middle part of the nineteenth century.

[15] In the second half of the nineteenth century and on into the twentieth century, Liverpool had a large Welsh community and the National Eisteddfod was held there on several occasions.

[16] *Y Cerddor Cymreig*, 1 March 1871, p. 21.

[17] *Y Faner*, 14 June 1871, p. 13.

4

Back to Danville

The journey from Liverpool to New York took five weeks. During the voyage Joseph held two concerts on board ship, assembling a choir and singing himself. Upon arrival in America, one of his first tasks was to organize a goodwill concert tour through the north-eastern United States. He had not forgotten the generous contributions that the Welsh communities had made to the Parry Fund that had sent him to London in the first place. He wanted to thank them, and he felt a moral debt to Welsh Americans for their support and faith in him as a musician. But this tour had a double message: not only would he be singing and accompanying himself and others – as he had been doing in Wales between 1868 and 1871 – but he would also be addressing his audiences and announcing a new idea, that of establishing a music college in Danville for Welsh Americans. Once again the financial assistance of the people would be needed.

During his journeys through Wales, Parry had become aware of the lack of musical education in the country and the effect that this had. A similar situation prevailed in America. He was determined to improve it. Like many immigrants to the United States, he combined a fervent attachment to the old country with an equal enthusiasm for his new home. And America was now his home – he had become a US citizen when his father took out citizenship for himself and his family. He would have to start his efforts to improve the condition of musical education in his adopted country but he hoped to be able to extend the initiative to Wales in the future. His ideas of how a music college should operate were based on what he had learned from his time at the Royal Academy, and he set about creating what he hoped would be a similar establishment, albeit not on the same scale, in Danville.

As well as using his concert tour to promote the appeal, Parry sent a letter to the press and to America's Welsh churches. In 1872, the country's Welsh population attended over 380 places of worship; each one was asked to collect an average of $20 (£4)[1] per annum, a possible total of around $7,680 (£1567) toward Parry's dream. In the letter, he expressed his opinion that it was:

> a fact that there is already outstanding musical talent within the Welsh nation but it is also a fact that our musical talents are dying through lack of nourishment ... The French, Italians, Germans and English have had such establishments for centuries, because of this they are in the forefront of the musical world, while we as a nation have failed to breed even one musician ... who can be considered first class ... Remember, this is not due to lack of talent, but to a lack of facilities within our nation.[2]

In order to try to raise sufficient funds to realise his dream, Parry had set himself a tough task: 103 concerts in twelve states – New York, Pennsylvania, Ohio, Illinois, Wisconsin, Minnesota, Iowa, Kentucky, Virginia, West Virginia and Maine. This musical tour took almost a year to complete; he travelled about 2,500 miles and made approximately $20 (£4.08) per concert – a total of over $2,000 (£408) by the end.

The programme for the concert held in the Calvinistic Methodist chapel in Chicago on 22 August 1872 was typical. One of the chapel deacons, Mr John P Jones, sang a solo, followed by songs from Lizzie Parry James, Joseph's niece and daughter of his late sister Ann and her husband, Robert James. Joseph sang four songs: 'The American Star' (an early song, now modified to include references to Welsh heroes as well as American ones), 'Y Trên' (The Train), 'Gwnewch Bopeth yn Gymraeg' (Do Everything in Welsh) and 'Pleserfad y Niagara' (The Niagara Pleasureboat). The last of these had been composed in 1871 on words by the Reverend Thomas Levi; the music dramatically illustrates the difficulties of the boat and the struggle to rescue its passengers. Although the triplets in the accompaniment convey the passengers' initial enjoyment effectively, the opening melody is simply too reminiscent of Handel's 'Dead March' from Saul. In spite of this, and even though the story ends inconclusively – the listener is not told whether the pleasureboat is rescued – the song succeeds.

Parry's repertoire was different to that of his concerts in Wales during 1868–71; he was aware of the need to win the hearts – and money – of Welsh Americans by singing material that reflected nationalistic emotions from a Welsh-American perspective, appealing directly to the emotions of Welsh people about the Old Country but living in the New World.

A concert in Youngstown, Ohio, the town that had started the Parry Fund in 1865, produced the kind of reaction that Parry was hoping for: at the end of the evening, a minister brought his ten-year-old son to Parry and asked his opinion on the boy's musical education. Parry's natural reaction was to encourage the boy, Charles Evans Hughes, to attend his new music college, which was shortly to open in Danville. Small events like this led to the general success of the fund-raising concert tour; and, as he thanked the American Welsh population for their support, he wrote in a letter that 'every church (with only one exception) opened its doors to me; the ministers gave their co-operation and used their influence on my behalf; the musicians at all venues (except for two) helped me with open hearts, doing their best to ensure my concerts were a success.'

By October 1872, after a year of travelling, performing and addressing audiences, Joseph Parry had secured sufficient capital for his family, now five members since the birth in 1872 of William Sterndale (named after the Principal of the Academy in London), as well as extra funding to set up his music college. The Danville Musical Institute opened in about October 1872, probably at his house on S. W. Upper Mulberry Street, although according to local newspaper records, classes were later held on Mill Street. He was fortunate to secure the services of Dr D. J. J. Mason, a Trecynon-born musician who had made a name for himself as a tenor in Wilkes-Barre (a town fifty miles north of Danville) and surrounding areas. Between them, these two musicians got the Institute going, with Mason responsible for teaching the rudiments of music to younger students – ten to fifteen years old – before transferring them to Joseph Parry for tuition in composition, singing, and playing the organ. Gomer Thomas, Jane's brother, also helped with the teaching from time to time, as well as accepting applications from potential students at his music and stationery shop.

The Danville Musical Institute opened with thirty students, mostly local, but with some from far away, for example Quincy B. Williams from Vermont, 300 miles to the north. By February 1873, student numbers had grown to forty-three, and to forty-eight by March.

There were financial – as well as musical and nationalistic – reasons for establishing the Danville Musical Institute. Joseph could not make an adequate living from performing and adjudicating alone, and, although he threw his energies behind his music college, he continued to receive and accept invitations to perform in public and to adjudicate at eisteddfodau. He established a mixed choir, The Danville Welsh Chorus, many of whose descendants were still living in Danville a century after the formation of the choir.

While Parry was concentrating on his Danville college, another new college was being established in Wales. University College, Aberystwyth, was established in 1872 under the leadership of its Principal, Thomas Charles Edwards. He soon realised the need for a Music Department – the first in Wales – and Joseph Parry's name was put forward as the new professor by Gohebydd. This idea was discussed in correspondence between the Principal and Hugh Owen in London. The latter was Honorary Secretary of the College and an influential member of the College Council; in a letter dated 4 September 1872 he describes Joseph Parry as 'a most estimable man, and moreover a man of talent', to which the Principal replied the following day:

> I shall be delighted to have Pencerdd America filling the Chair of Music at the College. It will help immensely to make the Institution popular in Wales. Let us by all means make a strenuous effort to secure such a man.

The next step was to present these informal and unofficial ideas to the University Council, which met on 20 June 1873. Following the meeting, Gohebydd was authorized to offer – there was no talk of advertising – the position to Parry. The new department was expected: 'to lift the standard of music in the nation generally'; the music education it offered was to be a 'stepping stone' for Welsh musicians on the way 'from the village choir to the Royal Academy of Music' (note that getting to the Academy was the pinnacle!); and the new professor of Music was expected to teach singing, composition, organ and piano to the 80 to 100 anticipated students at the college during its second term, from January 1874.

Joseph Parry was duly offered, the post, and accepted.

Parry's return to Wales was greeted with much anticipation, with the nation generally approving of the appointment. The following was typical: 'We expect the big wheel of musical culture to turn faster than ever before in Wales.'3 In Danville, Parry was not as confident as his compatriots back in the Old Country. It was a big step up from running his own little college in Danville to heading a Music Department at the new Welsh University College.

One of Joseph Parry's principal worries was money. Music teachers of lesser status than him were earning $3,000 to $4,000 (£600 to £800) a year in America. He had managed to make ends meet by augmenting his income as head of the college with earnings from his work as an eisteddfod adjudicator, *cymanfa ganu* conductor and organist. Accepting this new post meant 'a great financial sacrifice to myself and family'.4 His salary in Aberystwyth had not yet been finalised, so it was a financial gamble for Parry to take on the post. Eventually, he agreed that this unique opportunity to serve his nation in such a special way was more important than the financial sacrifice.

By agreeing to move to Aberystwyth, Parry made one nation happy while disappointing another. By 1873 – two years after his return from London – his name and status was still growing. America's loss was Wales' gain. A reflection of his popularity was the offer of a $20 (£4) prize at the eisteddford in Church Hill, Ohio, on 4 July 1874, for 'a speech in English praising Joseph Parry's musical work in America and congratulating him on his new post'.

Parry was asked to start in Aberystwyth in January 1874,

but it was not practicable: the weather for crossing the Atlantic was poor, he had music commitments until mid-1874, there were family arrangements to see to, and, most importantly, he had to decide what to do with the Danville Musical Institute. In order to finalize all these arrangements, he decided to stay in the United States until the summer of 1874.

In Wales, the news of his delayed arrival was met with disappointment. According to Gohebydd, the poet Mynyddog had declared that at least a dozen young persons were ready to start studying with the new professor in Aberystwyth 'as soon as Parry arrived' – but now they would have to wait longer until his arrival in mid summer and the re-start of college in the autumn.

Before sailing, Parry placed advertisements in the press for a series of farewell concerts in the eastern states of America, to be given by a vocal quartet consisting of Fannie McAnnall (soprano), his niece, Lizzie Parry James (contralto), Mason (tenor) and himself (bass). The tour schedule was tight, with few free evenings, but every Sunday was set aside for rest and worship. On 4 July, a special, and different, event was held at the eisteddfod in Youngstown, Ohio, an eisteddfod with special memories for Joseph – he was presented with a testimonial on behalf of the Welsh in America. Contributions had been donated following a letter to the press,[5] calling for all the proceeds of the concert tour to be presented to him as a token of Welsh-American respect toward him.

The Danville Musical Institute closed its doors at the end of May 1874 – both of its teachers would be on tour – and it was Mason who returned to re-open the college in August, after Parry had left for Aberystwyth. But the Danville Musical Institute was short-lived: by 1876 Mason had returned to Wilkes-Barre to teach music, before spending 1881–84 teaching at the Academy in London. He then returned to Wilkes-Barre to teach before spending the rest of his life in Chicago.

In Wales, Brinley Richards, encouraged by Stephen Evans of the University College, had decided to raise money toward the 'Music Fund' for the new department in Aberystwyth, in order to establish music scholarships. A lecture on 'The Old Music of the Welsh' was held in the Temperance Hall in Aberystwyth on 28 July, followed by a concert. Items were performed by a local choir, and the soloists Brinley Richards, Lizzie Evans, Mary Davies, and the violinist Caradog.[6] Similarly successful concerts were held in New Quay (*Cei Newydd*), Newcastle Emlyn (*Castell Newydd Emlyn*), and Cardigan, each resulting in substantial contributions to the Music Fund.

The Parry family – now increased to six following the birth of their fourth child, Annie Edna Parry in 1873 – crossed the Atlantic on the *City of Brooklyn*, from New York to Liverpool. Left behind in America were his 69-year-old mother, his brother and two sisters, while Jane left her parents, her brother and a sister. They reached Liverpool on 13 August to find a telegram awaiting Joseph calling on him to go immediately to the National Eisteddfod in Bangor, which was due to start on the 18th. Even before he had regained his land legs, the nation was calling for his services

The three years in Danville had been experimental. From the point of view of Parry the singer, organist, conductor and teacher they were generally successful. But from the point of view of Parry the composer they were less so. He wrote that 'This period [1871–74] is the least productive of *all* my career as a composer, much to my regret, and contrary to my life's ideals.'[7] It had indeed been a relatively unproductive time, especially compared to the periods immediately before and immediately afterwards. Only about fifteen pieces can be definitely dated from this time in Danville, most of them songs and most with English titles such as 'Cheer Up!' and 'Sleighing Glee'.

The unproductiveness of the period 1871–1874 is explained, of course, by Parry's busy schedule, which barely left him any time to devote to composition. In Aberystwyth, even though he would be as busy as ever, the musical floodgates opened once again, and Joseph Parry returned to his old ways as a prolific composer.

Notes Chapter 4

[1] Throughout Parry's time in America the exchange rate for the US dollar was around \$4.90 = £1 and all conversions have been carried out to the nearest pound at this rate. The question of what \$1 'was worth' at that time is more complicated. In terms of unskilled labour, in 1872 \$1 would buy about the same amount of unskilled working time as \$105 would buy in 2003. In terms of household purchases, however, \$1 in 1872 would buy only what about \$15 would buy in 2003.

[2] Parry is guilty of some exaggeration here. The Italian music schools in Venice and Naples were founded in the early seventeenth century but, by the late eighteenth century, mismanagement and corruption had left them moribund. The Paris Conservatoire was not founded until 1795, although its roots go back to 1783. Three conservatoires – Prague, Graz and Vienna – were founded in Austro-Hungary between 1811 and 1817. The Royal Academy was founded in 1823 but the first conservatoire to be founded in modern Germany was Leipzig in 1843, to be closely followed by Munich, Berlin and Dresden. The renaissance of the Italian conservatoires started with Florence in 1861. In other words, no establishment of the type that Parry is referring to had been in operation 'for centuries'. And to describe the English as being 'in the forefront of the musical world' in 1872 suggests a very peculiar vantage point!

[3] *Y Gerddorfa*, 1 January 1874.

[4] Joseph Parry, p. 32.

[5] *Y Drych*, 21 May 1874, p. 161.

[6] Griffith Rhys Jones (1834–97). Born in Trecynon, Aberdare, he started work as a blacksmith in the ironworks but became interested in music early in his life and became a proficient violin player. He later became a successful choral conductor, conducting the South Wales Choral Union, a choir of some 460 voices, that won the first prize at the Crystal Palace competition two years running. In 1920 a statue was erected in his honour on the square at Aberdare.

[7] Joseph Parry, p. 32, Parry's emphasis.

5

Aberystwyth and *Blodwen*

After arriving in Liverpool, Joseph and his family left immediately for Glamorganshire to spend three days with friends. Then, on 17 August, he went up to Bangor in the company of Gohebydd. The National Eisteddfod was to be held there on 18–21 August, and though his name did not appear on the Eisteddfod programme, he contributed to many of the musical activities, adjudicating the solo song and anthem singing competitions along with 'Owain Alaw' and John Thomas ('Pencerdd Gwalia'), and singing such songs as 'Hoff Wlad fy Ngenedigaeth', 'Yr Auctioneer' (*The Auctioneer*) and 'Y Bachgen Dewr' (*The Valiant Boy*) in an evening concert on the Eisteddfod stage. Most of the solos he sang were pieces he had written before returning to Danville, yet another indication of how little time he had been able to devote to composing in the last few years.

In September, Parry arrived in Aberystwyth to take up his post as Professor of Music and head of the newly formed Music Department at the University College of Wales, Aberystwyth. He and his family moved into the house now known as 'Glanbrenig' in St David's Road. The house, which now carries a plaque commemorating the Parry family's residence there, is a substantial semi-detached house, about half a mile from the College building, in an area that was being newly developed in the 1870s.

The college to which Parry came bore little resemblance to a modern university nor, indeed, to the other institutions of higher education in existence at that time. In England, as well as the two ancient universities of Oxford and Cambridge, there were, by the 1860s, a number of nineteenth-century foundations, including Durham, Kings College London and University College London. In Scotland, there were four ancient universities – Aberdeen, Edinburgh, Glasgow and St Andrews – all dating from the sixteenth century. In Ireland, there were two universities, Trinity College Dublin and the recently founded Queen's University Belfast. But the nearest thing to a university in Wales was St David's College Lampeter, an institution whose main purpose was the education of prospective clergymen for the Anglican Church in Wales, a church that had few adherents among the common people of Wales. The case for a university in Wales was clearly a strong one, but although the aspiration can be traced back to Owain Glyndŵr in the early fifteenth century, the movement to establish it began to take shape only in the 1850s.

Years of publicity and fund-raising followed, with money coming in dribs and drabs from the common people ('the pennies of the poor' was a phrase often used) and in generous donations from wealthier benefactors. In 1867, the committee was able to buy the (unfinished) Castle Hotel in Aberystwyth, following the bankruptcy of its developer, for a fraction of the money that had gone into its construction, and start adapting it for use as a college. By 1872, although the College was deeply in debt, it was able to open its doors, with twenty-six students being taught by the Principal, Thomas Charles Edwards, as well as Professors of Mathematics, Natural Sciences and Modern Languages. The College was still a purely private venture, in the sense that it had no official status and received no money from the government; the first government grant would not arrive until 1884 and the Royal Charter that finally confirmed its official status was not granted until 1889. Furthermore, the fees that students could afford to pay were not enough to cover the cost of teaching them. The College was thus reliant on donations even to cover its day-to-day operating expenses.

Nevertheless, shortly after the College opened, the bold decision was taken to expand the subjects offered to include Geography, Chemistry – and Music. When Parry arrived in 1874, there were eighty-six students, a quarter of whom wanted to study music. Joseph Parry's name was a distinct attraction, with three students, Annie Owen, David Davis and Gershom T Davies, coming from the United States, the last of whom had been a student of Parry's in Danville. Another reason for the 'disproportionate' number of music students was the fact that Parry had persuaded the college authorities to admit female students to the music courses. The new professor's argument must have been that forming a mixed choir was impossible without female voices. Although Aberystwyth was one of the first institutions of higher education to admit women, they were not officially accepted as students until about 1884 – a decade after the Music Department was opened.

When he accepted the post, Parry expressed unease about the financial sacrifice he would incur. In September 1874 – after his arrival – there was still uncertainty as to his actual salary. The College Council met on 22 September and decided on £250 a year, an amount comparable to the other department heads, but less than his earnings in Danville. But unlike the other professors, he had alternative sources of income. As a student in London he had adjudicated, sung and conducted around Wales, and here was an opportunity to continue that practice. Even if he had not been in need of additional income, he would probably have been unable to resist the call for his services. From now on, however, the College was in control and he was no longer his own master. The authorities did not realise the implications of having such a well-known musician in charge of the new Music Department nor would they have known that professors of Music elsewhere were given a great deal of freedom to pursue their professional careers outside the academic world. Parry would have seen this at first hand and assumed that he would enjoy the same freedom. Within a few days of arriving at Aberystwyth, he was off to Pentyrch, then a village near Cardiff, as a soloist in a village choir concert. Since his tenure of the Chair of Music did not start until 1 October, he was free to do this, but it was nevertheless the first indication of what would become a source of friction between the College Council and their new Professor of Music.

On 7 October 1874, the University College, Aberystwyth – and its new Music Department – opened its doors for a new academic term. There were twenty-three music students, following courses in voice and singing, piano and harmonium, composition, sight singing and harmony, with most subjects being taught at both elementary and advanced levels. There was extra tuition to improve sight-singing, harmony, part-song and glee singing etc., and conducting; a special effort was made to educate music teachers, organists and choral conductors. The fee for private tuition with the Professor was £1 per term for a lesson a week. It was also possible to hire instruments from the college for 10s. 6d. (52.5 pence) per session. The College also offered a number of exhibitions,[1] and of the four on offer, one was for women only.

In nineteenth-century Wales, music as a subject was rarely, if at all, a part of the day-school curriculum, so the students in Parry's department, although young and enthusiastic, were musically largely uneducated. Parry's aim was to make up for these deficiencies so that they could return home and teach others in the surrounding area. His dedication to his new calling was obvious from the outset; he wrote that he had:

> deep at heart a strong desire to consecrate my life's labours to the development and promotion of the music and of the young musician of my fellow countrymen [*sic*], as a matter of duty, in return for their noble efforts to educate me.[2]

The courses on offer in Parry's department were of a practical nature, designed to instil those basic skills students needed to take the lead in musical activities back in their own communities or to proceed to more advanced studies at the Royal Academy. The lack of any mention of musical history is very evident and reflects what was perhaps a blind spot in Parry's own attitude to music at the time, although he was later to give public lectures on the topic.

Within two weeks of the start of term, the Music Department had its first opportunity to display its talents, with many of Parry's students singing items at the end of the half-yearly meeting of the College held on 21 October. At the end of this first term, on 18 December, a concert was held in the Aberystwyth Temperance Hall in the presence of college officers. The twenty or so items in the programme included songs for one, two and three voices, and choral pieces, many by Parry, as well as piano pieces, mostly arrangements of folk songs and popular operatic pieces. One of the students, David Jenkins, played a composition of his own; he was to become the second Professor of Music at Aberystwyth.

This December concert saw the first performance of Parry's 'Ti Wyddost Beth Ddywed fy Nghalon' (*Thou knowest what my heart is saying*) and the first performance in

Wales of his trios 'Fy Angel Bach' *(My Little Angel)* and 'Sleep, Lady, Sleep'. He composed few pieces for three solo voices, and from the standpoint of style they suffer because of their Victorian parlour-song harmony. 'Sleep, Lady, Sleep' was composed in around 1864 in Danville but not published until about 1871, when it was dedicated to William Sterndale Bennett. It is a substantial piece, and despite the fact that the composer was only twenty-three when he wrote it, parts of it are musically mature.

As well as the musical programme, there was an address by the Principal of the College, Thomas Charles Edwards, in which he spoke of his pride in the occasion, the *first* college music concert ever held in Wales. He called for similar colleges to 'rescue' the music of Wales and praised his new Professor of Music for throwing his 'heart and soul into his work'.

The college vacation began the day after the concert, but there was to be little relaxation for Parry; on Christmas Day, for example, he would be at the Assembly Rooms in Blaenau Ffestiniog adjudicating and singing in a *cyfarfod llenyddol* (literary meeting) – one of many Victorian terms describing an eisteddfod.

At the beginning of the second term, the college had ninety-six students, of whom twenty were in the Music Department. Music was unlike the other academic subjects in that it was possible to enrol in the department without having to study other subjects, and because of this – and the consequent 'disproportionate' number of music students – the College Council decided to impose a 'Music Entrance Examination' on prospective students in order to try to limit the number of music students. In the college's Annual Report of 1874–75, it was stated that this had to be done because 'Professor Parry's time and energies were overtaxed ... He does not spare his students, neither does he spare himself.' Apparently, on Mondays, Tuesdays, Thursdays and Fridays Parry worked as Professor from 9 in the morning until 8 at night. Wednesdays and Saturdays were set aside for his private tutoring. Later he would be described by his student David Jenkins as the 'happiest and hardest worker I ever came across'.[3] Parry asked the College Council to appoint an assistant, even though Gohebydd felt that it would be difficult to convince the authorities to allocate more money to the Music Department. And so it proved, with an impasse developing between him and the Council that would last for months to come.

On 22 January 1875, the Music Department held a public concert, under Parry's direction, in the College examination hall. But the College Council was not supportive when it learnt that the concert would benefit Parry, one of many 'benefit' events through which he would attempt to make up the financial loss resulting from his move to Wales. In a letter to Gohebydd dated 10 February 1875, Hugh Owen – an influential member of the Council without whose tireless efforts the College would never have been successfully established in the first place – expressed his unease: 'We all like Professor Parry, and admire his talent and his wonderful zeal, but exhibitions such as that referred to cannot be tolerated. The Council cannot afford to tolerate them.' An unfortunate situation was developing: firstly, the disagreement over appointing a music teaching assistant, and secondly, the unease over Parry's right to hold concerts for his own benefit. The writing was on the wall and these difficulties were to rumble on and on, with relations between Parry and the College Council gradually deteriorating over the next five years.

Toward the end of February 1875 Joseph established a Choral Union in Aberystwyth, made up mostly of music students but also with some townspeople as members. In Aberystwyth, as in many university towns, relationships between town and gown have always blown hot and cold. Joseph showed an astute awareness of the benefits of good relations between the two, and the town was to repay him by its enthusiastic support in his dispute with the College authorities.

In spite of the College Council's disapproval of its Professor's 'personal' concerts, they continued. At the end of May, Parry held another concert in Aberystwyth, this time with his Choral Union and members of the Music Department taking part. Solos, duets and choruses out of popular operas were sung, as well as the usual quota by Parry himself.

The summer term finished on 19 June, with an opportunity for both the Professor of Music and the College Council to take stock of the rather unusual professional relationship that had developed between them. The basic problem was lack of money – a situation that had existed since the College was established in 1872. A proposal was made that would, it was hoped, relax the tension that had developed between the Council and the Music Department. An important eisteddfod was to be held in Llanarth, some 20 miles south of Aberystwyth, on 29 July. At the beginning of the year, Parry had agreed to be one of the adjudicators, but it was also decided to hold an evening concert, to be repeated in Newquay the following evening, and present the proceeds to the Aberystwyth College Fund. Parry and the Council were in agreement over this until it came to the matter of the concert soloists. Parry, naturally, wanted his music students to have the opportunity but the Council felt that they would not draw enough of an audience and so not achieve the full earning potential of the occasion. Eventually a compromise was reached: some Music Department students would be allowed to perform but there would also be items by Brinley Richards and Parry himself. The concert went ahead, and was successful.

A new academic year started on 6 October 1875, with a decrease of three in the number of music students – possibly a result of the 'Music Entrance Examination'. The dispute over appointing an assistant for Joseph Parry was still rumbling on, with Hugh Owen expressing his opinion that no more music students should be admitted unless an assistant was appointed first. An agreement was eventually achieved by November with the appointment of David Jenkins of Trecastle (*Trecastell*) as 'second' in the department for a fee of £10 per term. He would teach harmony and theory to his fellow students; since he was already considered a 'star' in the department, it was a natural and popular appointment. Unofficially, Jenkins had been assisting Parry for some time – in fact, four months earlier *Y Faner* described him as 'second music professor in the University'.

Joseph and his family spent that Christmas in the company of old friends in Merthyr Tudful, where he adjudicated in an eisteddfod at the Drill Hall on Christmas Day. He returned to Aberystwyth to face a busy term, with appearances in concerts and eisteddfodau across Wales, but a shadow was cast across the period by the death, in March 1876, of Sterndale Bennett, Joseph's teacher at the Royal Academy. As a memorial, Joseph and his students performed Bennett's oratorio *The Woman of Samaria* in Aberystwyth on 28 April.

At the end of the academic year, Parry's appointments diary was full, as usual. The main event of that summer was the Conwy National Eisteddfod held at Llanrwst 13–14 July, with Parry adjudicating during the day and performing in a concert at night alongside 'Eos Morlais',[4] 'Llew Llwyfo'[5] and Edith Wynne. Items were also given by Joseph Haydn Parry and students from the Music Department. (Even though the College was closed for the summer, the

Professor could still call on the services of his students – such was their dedication to him.)

At the end of the 1876 autumn term the Music Department held a concert, with its climax being a performance, with orchestra, of Rossini's *Stabat Mater*, its first performance in Wales apparently – but it was impossible to please everyone. Some of the audience complained that there was too much 'Classical' in the departmental concerts while others regretted the preponderance of Welsh music – particularly by Parry. Another concert was held on 26 March 1877, with University Council members and Aberystwyth townspeople present, to hear a programme that included Beethoven's oratorio *The Mount of Olives* and 'Cantata Tywysog Cymru' *(The Prince of Wales' Cantata)* by Owain Alaw. This work was conducted by the composer – inviting Welsh composers to conduct their own music was one of Parry's innovations. Even though *The Mount of Olives* is not one of Beethoven's greatest works, the choice of this and Rossini's *Stabat Mater* reflect Parry's desire to widen the taste of Welsh audiences.

A month later, in April 1877, there was a serious accident in Tynewydd colliery in the Rhondda, with five miners trapped underground for nine days. Miraculously, they were rescued, and stated that singing the hymn 'Yn y Dyfroedd Mawr a'r Tonnau' *(In the Great Waters and Waves)* had kept their hopes alive during the terrible entombment. Parry's reaction was to compose 'Molwch yr Arglwydd' *(Praise the Lord)*, an anthem that incorporated the hymn sung by the trapped miners. Then on 14 May 1877 Ieuan Gwyllt died, aged fifty-four, and Parry's reaction once again was to compose. His 'Requiem Gynulleidfaol' *(Congregational Requiem)*, more of an anthem than a requiem, was written in memory of his friend, with words by the poet Mynyddog. These two works were sung extensively, and by July 1877 8,000 copies of the 'Requiem' and 13,000 copies of 'Molwch yr Arglwydd' had been published – exceedingly high figures for their time.

The first days of the summer vacation were busy for Joseph Parry because in late June a meeting of Welsh musicians was held in Aberystwyth. Presiding on the first day was John Thomas, Llanwrtyd, followed by Tanymarian on the second. Among the other musicians present were Emlyn Evans,[6] Eos Morlais, John Thomas (Blaenannerch) and Megan Watts-Hughes, as well as students from the Music Department. One positive outcome of the meeting was the establishing of a musical scholarship in Aberystwyth in memory of the late Ieuan Gwyllt, with the proceeds of a series of special concerts across Wales being donated to the fund. General discontent was expressed at the high proportion of English music that was chosen for competitions at the National Eisteddfod rather than Welsh music of equal value, as well as the tendency of the committees to choose the same pieces time and time again.

Barely three weeks after the musicians' meeting in Aberystwyth, on 14 July 1877, Wales was struck by another blow: the poet Mynyddog died, aged forty-four. Parry had set much of his poetry to music, but Mynyddog is best remembered for his libretto for Parry's opera *Blodwen*. Parry was present at the funeral and his contribution to Mynyddog's testimonial fund was five guineas – Brinley Richards had given 10s and Gohebydd 10s 6d.

On 3 August, Joseph Parry with his wife and two eldest sons were present in London at a testimonial ceremony for Gohebydd, and as in Mynyddog's case, Parry's generous contribution was five guineas. But on 13 December, Gohebydd died suddenly, aged sixty. He had led the support for Joseph on both sides of the Atlantic, and his death meant that Parry lost a valuable ally on the College Council. Joseph's reaction to losing such a close friend was to compose a funeral anthem in memory of him – 'Hiraethgan' *(Song of Longing)* – with words by Gwilym Hiraethog.[7] The funeral was held in Fron near Llangollen, Parry's third funeral in 1877: Ieuan Gwyllt, Mynyddog and Gohebydd – three major personal blows to him.

The college term started anew with a benefit concert in commemoration of Ieuan Gwyllt and Mynyddog, the proceeds going to scholarships to be named after them. Then, at the end of March, it was announced that two major new works by Parry were to be performed – the cantata *Jerusalem*, his Mus. Doc. composition,[8] and the opera *Blodwen* – and the Music Department concentrated its energy on preparing and performing these two works. But there were clouds on the horizon. Some members of the University Council thought that the Music Department was neglecting its academic role, and in a letter dated 14 May 1878 to the College Principal, J. F. Roberts declared unashamedly that: 'The Music Department is a loss, if some change could be made there I should be glad ... that the Department be separated from the College.' Here was an early and definite threat to the continuance of the Music Department, and there was worse to come. In the meantime the musical activities continued, giving the impression that the Department was not totally aware of the deteriorating situation between it and the authorities, and besides, *Blodwen* was about to be born!

The opera had been many years in the making. For example, on 1 April 1876 – two years before the premiere – *Y Gerddorfa* reported that Joseph Parry was busy composing, and that the opera would be heard 'before long'. Many dates have been quoted as the composition date for *Blodwen*, but the composer recorded the completion quite explicitly:

It affords me very much pleasure to be able to record the comp[l]etion of this (my first attempt) in a dramatic work, begun in February 1876, continued to write till April 1876. When I suspended its composition till end of Dec 76, from which time I have given this work my leisure hours, and completed this day Wednesday, February the 7th 1877. Joseph Parry.[9]

This information is entirely consistent with the reports in *Y Gerddorfa*, i.e. that Parry was composing it during the three months February to April 1876, even though the opera was not completed at that time; in any case, the background to *Blodwen* is further complicated by the fact that parts such as 'Cytgan y Milwyr' existed before the composition dates noted above.

Although *Blodwen* was completed in February 1877, the complete work was not performed in public until over a year later on 21 May 1878 at the Temperance Hall in Aberystwyth – a milestone in the history of Welsh music. However there is evidence that parts of the opera had been performed before then at Aberystwyth Freemasons' Lodge. Parry's lodge membership was transferred to the Aberystwyth Lodge 1072 on 9 March 1876. His interest in the fraternity crops up occasionally in correspondence, and his letter of 28 October 1878 to W. R. Williams is revealing:

it was in our Lodge's Complimentary Concert to me for acting as the Organist of our Lodge Blodwen was first performed. So that it was the Masons brought out my important work, this [thanks?] to him and his interest.

If this is the case, then it seems that *Blodwen* was first

performed at the Aberystwyth Freemasons' Lodge sometime between the completion of its composition in February 1877 and its first public performance in May 1878. Probably a selection from the opera was performed at the Lodge – the sections for male voices only, without costumes or acting, and with the composer at the organ.

So it was the first public performance that was held at the Temperance Hall in Aberystwyth on that Tuesday afternoon, 21 May 1878 – on Joseph's thirty-seventh birthday. In a speech preceding the opera, the composer explained that even though the singers were in costume appropriate to the period in which the opera was set (fourteenth-century Wales), they would not be acting. The puritan prejudice against the theatre was strong in Wales and, outside of Swansea, which was visited by touring companies from England, opera was virtually unknown, so this premiere was to all intents and purposes a concert performance.

The chorus consisted of college music students and many of the solo roles were also sung by them: Hattie Davies (Blodwen), Gayney Griffith (Elen), Annie Williams (Lady Maelor), Thomas Evans (Hywel) along with William Davies and J. Lucas Williams – the latter of the 'Crystal Palace Concerts' in London – singing the minor roles. R. Cyril Jenkins, an ex-student, sang Iolo the Bard. There was no orchestra; the accompaniment being provided by the Professor's two sons: thirteen-year-old Joseph Haydn at the piano and twelve-year-old Mendelssohn at the harmonium, no mean feat for such young musicians.

The hall was full to capacity with town and college officials as well as local townspeople. These were the first people in Wales to hear an opera in Welsh, and the majority of them did not know how to react. One anonymous correspondent wrote: 'The people waved their scarves in the air, applauding and shouting so loudly that the musician of renown [Joseph Parry] had to beg the people to let the performance continue.'[10]

Apart from the last scene, which is set in Chester Jail, the action of *Blodwen* takes place in and around Maelor Castle in north-east Wales. The opera opens on the eve of the marriage of Ellen, daughter of Lady Maelor, with the Welsh warrior Arthur, of Castell Berwyn. News arrives that Sir Howell Ddu and his beautiful adopted daughter, Blodwen, will shortly be arriving. Lady Maelor sings of her pleasure that they, and others, are coming to the wedding, and prays for peace and God's protection for Ellen and Arthur. A chorus of servants sings of their joy as they decorate the castle walls and Ellen's chamber with lilies and roses; a bard proclaims peace on Lady Maelor and the castle, and blesses Ellen and Arthur. The arrival of Blodwen and Sir Howell is announced and they sing a song of greeting, wishing good luck to Ellen; Blodwen then breaks into a lament that her mother is dead and her father lost in battle but expresses her happiness at being able to make her home in Castell yr Wyddfa (Snowdon Castle), Sir Howell's castle. Lady Maelor sings of Blodwen's father's bravery and assures her that she is welcome to stay in Castell Maelor; Sir Howell urges her to stay because he fears war is coming and he will be away fighting. The bard predicts that the English king's power will be overturned and that 'the morning star of better times is rising in the east', a sentiment in which all join. Ellen's wedding celebrations in the second scene are interrupted by the arrival of three English soldiers, who demand the keys of the castle, in the name of King Henry. They are sent back carrying a defiant message for their master.

The second act opens on the lawn in front of the castle.

A hunting horn is heard and the huntsmen sing a chorus as they leave for the chase. The bard then appears singing of the dreadful portents to be seen in the stars. Sir Howell next appears and sings of his love for Blodwen in one of the best-known arias in the opera. Blodwen is now revealed, out of sight of Sir Howell; in a recitative she reveals that she is in love with him. She then shows herself and teases him that he has not gone hunting, but this rapidly turns into a love duet still enjoyed today. A messenger from the Prince of Wales (Glyndŵr) arrives, asking for the men of Maelor to prepare immediately for battle with Henry's forces. Ellen and Blodwen take leave of Arthur and Howell, each of them pinning a white ribbon on their lover's breast.

The next scene takes place in Lady Maelor's chamber, where a messenger arrives and describes the ferocity of the battle and the achievements of Hywel and Arthur. Lady Maelor calls in the bard to foretell the outcome of the battle. In reply, he urges her to comfort and support Ellen and Blodwen for disaster is at hand.

At the beginning of the third act, Arthur is back in Castell Maelor, mortally wounded. He sings a last farewell to Ellen and dies. Everyone joins in a dead march mourning him. A messenger arrives to tell Lady Maelor of the defeat of the Welsh army and the death of many of its leaders. Sir Howell was one of the bravest of the Welsh but the messenger does not know whether he is still alive. Blodwen then calls on the mountain breezes to bring her news and sings of the loss of her mother, father and brother, and now possibly of Howell. The bard then then arrives bringing the news that Sir Howell has been captured and is in Chester Castle awaiting execution.

The final scene takes place in Chester Castle, where the Welsh prisoners are singing a defiant chorus based on a Welsh folk tune. Lady Maelor, Blodwen and the bard have been allowed to see Sir Howell for the last time before his execution. Sir Howell sings a song of farewell to Blodwen, an aria that remains a favourite with Welsh tenors to this day. An English crowd outside the castle walls is heard singing a chorus of celebration for the victory. A stranger appears, asking for Sir Howell's cell in a recitative accompanied by the Welsh air 'Morfa Rhuddlan'. The stranger turns out to be Rhys Gwyn, Blodwen's father, who was thought to have been killed twenty years before. He announces that King Henry is dead and that, as a consequence, he has been released from captivity and, what is more, he brings a command from the court that all prisoners are to be set free. The work closes with a fugal chorus of rejoicing, into which 'Men of Harlech' is woven.

The success of *Blodwen* is not surprising: it contains much attractive music; it has a romantically patriotic plot but raises no awkward political questions; and it is in Welsh. It has, however, many weaknesses. Musically, its eclecticism often brings a smile, albeit a sympathetic one, to the listener's lips. The servants decorating the castle for the wedding have much in common with the peasant girls strewing flowers in *Le Nozze di Figaro*, the wedding waltz might have been written by Johann Strauss; the final chorus reminds the listener of the *Amen* chorus from Handel's *Messiah*, despite the ingenious interweaving of 'Men of Harlech'; and there are less specific overtones of Rossini and Verdi to be heard throughout the work. Nevertheless, numbers like 'Fy Mlodwen, F'Anwylyd, fy Mhopeth' (*My Blodwen, my Dear One, my All*), the final chorus 'Moliannwn' (*Give Glory to God*), and of course 'Hywel a Blodwen' (*Howell and Blodwen*) are memorable and fit well into the action of the opera, while the final scene of the second act contains some particularly fine music.

The opera is historically inaccurate, but historical

accuracy has never been a requirement for, nor a guarantee of, an opera's success. The dramatic weaknesses are much more serious. While there are many minor improbabilities and inconsistencies, perhaps the most damaging is the sudden arrival of Rhys Gwyn, ten minutes before the end of the opera. The fact that he is still alive, having been believed dead for twenty years, is remarkable enough, but it is still more remarkable that the English court should have entrusted him with the news of the king's death and with the warrant freeing the prisoners. The dramatic damage is caused not so much by the improbability of this but because the action, which seemed to be heading inexorably towards a tragic ending, is suddenly turned around.

The blame for the dramatic weaknesses cannot be laid wholly on Mynyddog. Mynyddog had probably never seen an opera and Parry seems to have done little in the way of planning the plot. The poet was often called upon to write words for Parry's extant music, the duet 'Mae Cymru'n Barod' *(Wales is Ready)* being a case in point. This may also account for the apparently poor word setting in some cases: in the second verse of Blodwen's solo 'O Dywed im Awel y Nefoedd' *(O Tell me, Breath of Heaven)*, for example, she imagines her father dying either in jail or on a bloody battlefield, but does so in the major key with a jaunty 6/8 rhythm.

While no one would claim that *Blodwen* is the equal of the masterpieces of Gounod, Verdi, or Wagner, both musically and dramatically it is at least as good as many of the less well-known French, German and Italian operas of the period. It was a success – a major success – for many reasons: it was new and pioneering, the music was attractive, it had a nationalist plot, but most important of all, it was in Welsh. Given the low status that Welsh enjoyed in the Wales of that time, it might have been possible to compose a successful 'Welsh' opera with a libretto in English (like the majority of Parry's other eight operas) but, from the outset, Parry and Mynyddog had decided that *Blodwen* would be in Welsh, a decision that made it even more of a success with Welsh speakers and created a milestone in the history of Welsh music.

Around this time, Parry decided to try to obtain a doctorate in Music. The requirements for being awarded a Mus. Doc. degree from Cambridge were similar to those for the Mus. Bac. that he had obtained in 1871, that is, registering with the University, sitting an examination, and composing a substantial work – usually a sacred cantata – for voices and orchestra. But unlike the Mus. Bac. degree, the doctoral composition – *Jerusalem* in Parry's case – also had to be performed. Despite the state of his finances, Parry decided to take *Blodwen* as well as the cantata *Jerusalem* on tour through Wales and England, going to London and then to Cambridge for the doctoral performance. For this tour, Parry used soloists from his Music Department as well as 'The Welsh Representative Choir' from south Wales. The high point of the tour was a performance of *Jerusalem* at St John's College Chapel, Cambridge, on 13 June, at the start of the University Congregation. Two days later *Jerusalem* and *Blodwen* were performed at the Alexandra Palace in London. The tour was a musical success but a financial loss for Joseph Parry, costing £800 to stage but with takings amounting to a little over £550. The Aberdare members of the choir decided to redress the deficit and the Cardiff contingent aimed at raising £100 from a benefit concert.

On Thursday 13 June 1878 Joseph Parry, one-time puddler's boy, was accepted as a Doctor of Music of Cambridge University.

By July 1878, *Blodwen* had appeared both in staff and in

sol-fa notation. Joseph Parry himself published the opera, and despite the generosity of the Freemasons and a long list of sponsors, he lost money on the venture, at least in the short term: 'a dreadful blow to my empty bank'.[11] The effort involved in mounting even a concert performance of *Blodwen* is illustrated by a series of letters written by Parry between September 1878 and March 1879 to a friend, Mr William Roderick Williams, a dispensing chemist, who moved from Maesteg to Baglan during the course of the correspondence. The letters were donated to the National Library of Wales by Williams' son, Roderick, in 1936;[12] they concerned projected concert performances in Maesteg and Bridgend, which were to have taken place over Christmas and the New Year but eventually did not happen until the summer of 1879. They show Parry concerned about the size of the chorus – 'A choir of 30 or 50 might well do' is scrawled across the corner of one of the letters – and asks whether the choir will give their services for nothing if he lets them have the copies of the choruses for half price and whether one or two of them would be willing to take on solo roles *gratis*. He is immensely concerned that the choir should learn the choruses properly, in good time.

With his return to Aberystwyth towards the middle of June, Parry put the trip and its financial problems behind him as a new idea came into his head; this was to write a grand oratorio *Emmanuel*. He was to set to music the words of a poem by Gwilym Hiraethog entitled 'Cyfryngdod Emmanuel' *(The Intercession of Emmanuel)*, published in 1860. The words were well suited to sacred music and, although 1878 was the year in which Emmanuel was composed, the work, like *Blodwen*, contains music from earlier periods; the aria 'O Chwi sy'n Caru Duw' *(O ye, who Love God)*, for example, was composed when Parry was a student in London. From the same period come also the chorus 'Fe Gyfyd Goleuni' *(Light Arises)*, his Mus. Bac. exercise of 1871, later incorporated in *Emmanuel*, and the overture and chorus 'O Jerusalem! Ti a Leddaist' *(O Jerusalem! Thou hast Killed)*, from *Jerusalem*. The chorale and choral fugue 'Fy Nuw Cyfamodol a Fydd' *(My Covenanted God shall be)* are based on the hymn tune 'Llangristiolus', which Parry composed in 1869.

Emmanuel is an oratorio in the 'English' tradition (of Handel and Mendelssohn), containing all the usual musical forms: solo, duet, recitative, chorus, and so on. However, it uses hymn tunes in place of chorales, and, at times, the congregation is invited to join with the choir. *Emmanuel* was well received but it was not performed as often as *Blodwen*. It is a long work and is not easy to sing. However, a number of choruses became popular and were later published as individual items.

The 20th of June 1878 saw the end of another academic year. For the Professor of Music and his department the preceding weeks were full, with the tour of *Jerusalem* and *Blodwen*, along with the work on *Emmanuel*, taking up time and energy. But there was a price to pay for this busyness; Parry's latest neglect of his academic duties caused such a stir among the members of the College Council as to cause that body to meet during the summer vacation. It was decided that due notice should be given to Parry, in order to start to make new arrangements between him and the Music Department.

Although Parry had undoubtedly upset a number of powerful people and there were those who wanted to see him taken down a peg or two, it would be wrong to see the action of the Council as being based on malice or a desire to put Parry in his place. The financial state of the College at the time was critical: press criticism, particularly in the *Cambrian News*, was making it increasingly difficult to raise money from the public to cover the running costs and the request for a government grant for the College had just been refused. The appointments of three professors – Grimley (Mathematics and Astronomy), Keeping (Zoology) and Craig (Political Economy) – were terminated in the summer of 1878. There were doubts about the ability of all three and it proved possible to replace each of them with competent men at lower salaries. Parry was not treated in this way. The minutes of the College Council meeting of 29 July 1878 state that it was decided:

> that Dr. Parry should retain his Professorship at a salary to be agreed upon for such teaching as above-mentioned. Dr Parry would be free to give ... teaching, of a public or private nature, at Aberystwyth or elsewhere, ... outside the walls of the College ... during the Sessions of the College Dr. Parry should not give, nor professionally attend concerts in Aberystwyth or in its immediate neighbourhood.

On the face of things this was by no means ungenerous. Parry would be allowed to retain his professorship and to augment his professorial stipend with outside teaching, as much as he wished. However, Parry was primarily a practising musician – singer, organist, conductor and composer – rather than an academic musician, and he was being asked to give up what he most enjoyed. What is more, he saw teaching music students as his mission in Wales, and he would be losing that too. It may be, of course, that the Council realised this perfectly well and intended to force his resignation, but it is more likely that its members simply did not understand Parry.

This was the culmination of a series of unfortunate events that had begun almost as soon as Parry crossed the threshold of the College. The restrictions were not the result of a sudden decision on the part of the Council but its final answer to a situation that had been smouldering since his arrival. The Council recognised that Professor Parry 'has discharged his functions with zeal and ability ... but that the interests of the College in its primary and essential objects should render this modification necessary.' However, Parry was by no means blameless, for he gave more attention to other activities – ones that brought more glory to him personally than to the College – than to his main job of running the only Music Department in a university institution in Wales. And although Joseph Parry took his students from the College to perform in his concerts, the Council saw these concerts as unnecessary and undesirable ostentation. There was a strong prejudice against large-scale public display. Moreover, money was a constant worry for the College, and the fee paid by a student did not cover the extra costs that he or she generated. Thus Parry's success in attracting students actually exacerbated the College's financial problems.

It is clear that Parry's extra-mural activities consumed a great deal of his time, if only because of the difficulties of travelling in west Wales at that time. These difficulties are vividly illustrated by a letter from Parry to Ceiriog in which Parry apologises for failing to turn up for a meeting at Llanidloes. 'I found it utterly impossible to reach Llanidloes in time from Blaenannerch [and] did not reach here [Aberystwyth] till 5 p.m. Had no conception of the inconveniencies of the country of Blaenannerch. I was sorry I failed to come there and also for disappointing you and others.'[13] Blaenannerch is some five miles ENE of Cardigan on what is now the A487, the main road from Cardigan to Aberystwyth. The journey to Llanidloes now takes about an hour and a half by car. In the 1870s, despite the coming of the railway, it could not be completed in a day. Parry had a three-hour wait in Pencader, during which time he wrote a four-part song 'Mi Welaf mewn Atgof' (*I see in Memory*).

At the start of the new academic year, the future of the Professor of Music and his department was uncertain. In the light of the restrictions placed on Parry, it is interesting to note that the department concert on 19 November in the Temperance Hall was in the hands of his deputy, David Jenkins. Parry was present but played no direct part in the proceedings, although a number of his pieces were performed. But in no time he was in trouble again, breaking the Council's conditions by giving performances of *Blodwen* in Maesteg, Bridgend (*Pen-y-bont*) and Denbigh. In May 1879, Parry, along with instrumentalists from Worcester, Gloucester and Birmingham – another indication of the sad state of instrumental music in Wales – performed the work in Ffestiniog and Caernarfon, the first being a concert performance and the second a staged performance. The two occasions were eagerly awaited and their success was inevitable, especially in front of a crowd of four thousand in the recently completed Caernarfon Pavilion.[14] Never had such costumes and scenery been seen nor, especially, *acting*. The opera was sung from memory, but only some parts were acted. Press opinion did not rate the acted parts as highly as the singing. The performance was special also because each solo part was sung *as a solo*; in previous performances the items written as solos had been sung by two or more singers, destroying any sense of characterisation. The quality of this performance led an anonymous poet to write:

> Blodwen! ha, bywiol ydyw – a'i seiniau
> Yn swynol ddigyfryw;
> Haeddodd ein moliant heddiw;
> Eirain ferch wna feirw'n fyw!

Ac at ŵr pur – y Doctor Parri [*sic*] – 'rhed
   Anrhydedd yn genlli,
   A'n hylon fyd yn heli,
   Os aiff y nef â Joseph ni.

Blodwen! ah, she is alive – and her sounds
   So unique and magical
   She deserved our praises today;
   Shining maid who brings the dead to life!

And on that pure man – Doctor Parry – may
   Honours run in torrents,
   And happy our world will be
   If heaven takes our Joseph.

Back in Aberystwyth, 19 June 1879 was the end of another academic year as well as the end of Joseph's period as Professor of Music at the University College of Wales. The Council had finally decided to close the Music Department. Parry's great strength during his time at Aberystwyth had been that he attracted a remarkable number of students, many of whom, David Jenkins and J. T. Rees (Cwmgiedd),[15] for example, were to gain substantial reputations as performers, composers, conductors and teachers. But from the point of view of Parry as a teacher, the comments are rather negative. For example, David Jenkins wrote: 'We did not consider him a good teacher ... he was too lively and wild to explain things carefully, which is what young students need.'[16] And in the judgement of E. Keri Evans: 'Parry was born a musician but he was not born a teacher; although he had the necessary enthusiasm in the classroom and rehearsal room, he was too deficient in other essential characteristics'.[17]

Despite Parry's alleged weaknesses as a teacher, his

students were loyal to him and participated enthusiastically in his concerts throughout his time in Aberystwyth. The relationship between Parry and his students was better than that between him and most members of the Council. He also had the support of the common people and the press. In the pages of *Y Faner* (16 July 1879), there were two letters of support, one from B M Williams, who had been involved with the recent performance of *Blodwen* in Denbigh, and the other by David Jenkins. More practically, Parry's supporters organised a meeting in the Temperance Hall in Aberystwyth on 1 August to defend the ex-professor, and naturally the behaviour of the College Council came under attack.

During September the College Council met again to consider the question of the Music Department but there was no changing of minds; it was confirmed that there would be no successor to fill the vacant post of Professor of Music and that the department would thus be wound up. According to Owain T Edwards in his book on the composer, 'It would have been almost impossible to appoint anyone without losing face and without publicly insulting Joseph Parry, because there was no other Welsh musician at the time who was so highly esteemed'.[18] Not even David Jenkins was considered for the vacant chair and the Council stuck to its argument that the Music Department was being closed for financial reasons not personal ones.

Thus at the beginning of October 1879 Parry did not return to re-open the Music Department in Aberystwyth as he had done in the previous five years. Without the music students, the College was substantially smaller. There were only around fifty students, in comparison with twenty-six when the doors of the college were first opened six years previously. The growth in the number of students thus appeared disappointingly low.

There were two musical scholarships, bearing the names

of Ieuan Gwyllt and Mynyddog, that lay unused and Mr G. E. J. Powell[19] of Nanteos, a country house some three miles outside Aberystwyth, had recently given more than 150 scores and books on music to the College library. Furthermore, Joseph Parry was on the point of establishing his own music college. To this effect he held a public meeting on 10 October 1879 in the Assembly Rooms[20] in Aberystwyth. The venue was full to overflowing. It is interesting that several members of the College, including the Principal and Professor Angus, Professor of Latin and Comparative Philology, were there – whether to show their support or to keep an eye on Parry's doings is not clear. In essence, Parry's idea was to create a music college similar to the Danville Musical Institute that had provided him with a living before he came to Aberystwyth. He addressed the meeting on the state of music in Wales, noting that the Welsh were a musical nation that had never produced more than a handful of singers, performers, conductors and composers. Countries like France, Italy, Germany and America had their own musical institutions but there was nothing similar in Wales. Parry announced his intention of using his own money to ensure the success of the venture and, a week later, on 17 October 1879, the Aberystwyth School of Music – one among a number of names considered – opened its doors. A special meeting was held in the Assembly Rooms with another speech by Parry, this time on the subject of the study of music. There were also speeches of support from some of his former pupils and a programme of musical items including a duet for violin and piano performed by the 15-year-old Joseph Haydn Parry and a Miss Szlumper, and items from *Blodwen*.

According to press announcements, within a year the School of Music would be offering the following: voice training and singing lessons; piano; harmonium (to prepare pupils for work in chapels); harmony; counterpoint and fugue; orchestration; form and composition; various 'educational wants'; and the preparation of pupils for music exams. The courses were similar to those that he had offered in his previous position but some of them were also available as correspondence courses – a new idea. There would be three terms per year, as in the University College, and four classes per week in each course, at a cost of 6 guineas a term or 18 guineas a year. As in the old Music Department, there would be a student concert at the end of each term; the first end of term concert would take place on 16 December 1879. Many of the students from the former University Music Department moved with their professor to the new college, another sign of his personal appeal, and a number of them took part in the concert, for example David Davies and T Cynffig Evans. The October opening evening came to an end with a student choir singing the final chorus from *Blodwen*, 'Moliannwn'.

As far as the state of the School of Music itself is concerned, it is interesting to note that Parry travelled less and concentrated more of his energy on the institution – exactly what the College Council had been trying to make happen by imposing its new conditions on him. Another factor was money; given that the success or failure of his dream would determine his income, we see less of Parry as adjudicator, conductor and soloist. But in the early months of 1880 he nevertheless had to make frequent trips between Aberystwyth and London – a journey that took almost nine hours on the fastest train – for rehearsals of *Emmanuel*, which was to be performed by the London Welsh Choir in St James' Hall on 12 May. Only a selection of the oratorio was performed because of problems with the length of the work. The composer was congratulated on having ventured to produce such a large work, and there were many famous

Londoners present, both musicians and politicians, amongst them Signor García (Parry's one-time singing teacher at the Royal Academy), Brinley Richards, Thomas Weist-Hill (Principal of the newly established Guildhall School of Music), Dr Henffer (music critic of *The Times*), along with four members of Parliament, including Henry Richard. The performance was so successful that a second performance was arranged a month later in the Crystal Palace.

Before the second performance, however, preparations were required for a series of performances of *Emmanuel* across Wales, beginning in Aberystwyth on 1 June. Over the course of six weeks, the composer was responsible for training the choir and conducting each of the twelve performances, trying especially hard to be present at as many rehearsals as he could, from Ffestiniog to Maesteg, and thus compelled to be away a great deal from his School of Music in Aberystwyth. These performances were not on as large a scale as the London one, being accompanied only by piano and harmonium, and with Parry's pupils singing the solo parts as well as making up the choir. Nonetheless, every performance was well received. Half-way through the trip, Parry returned to London for the second performance there. In the Crystal Palace, an audience of 6,000 heard the work performed by the same conductor, choir and soloists as had performed it five weeks before. The concert was part of a great Liberal Party festival, with the excerpts from the oratorio forming the first part of the concert and Eos Morlais conducting a selection of English and Welsh songs after the interval.

On 10 July, Joseph, together with his family and David Davis, the tenor from Cincinnati who had been his pupil in Aberystwyth,[21] landed in New York on the *City of Berlin*, for a three-month visit. It was Parry's seventh Atlantic crossing.

The *City of Berlin* was a large and fast ship: more than twice the size of the ships in which he had made his 1865 crossings, she carried 1770 passengers. In 1875 she won the blue riband for the fastest crossings in both directions, with crossings taking less than eight days.

A welcome meeting was held for Joseph and his family in Danville. His brother-in-law, Gomer Thomas, had announced in the Welsh press in America that Parry was available to take on musical engagements of various kinds during his visit to the states of New York, Pennsylvania, Ohio and Wisconsin, at a fee of $100 for each concert and/or lecture, much of which would go to meet travelling expenses. Over the following weeks, he, Haydn, his niece Lizzie Parry James and David Davis took part in some forty musical events in many of the places that he had visited on his musical tour in 1871–72. In Newburgh, Ohio, on 25 September, the four of them took part in a performance of *Blodwen*, and the next day Parry conducted a *cymanfa ganu* in the Independent chapel. They returned to the town to give a second concert on 6 October but without Joseph, who was taken ill with gall stones in Cincinnati and was confined to bed there. He missed the rest of the tour, including a concert in his brother Henry's academy in Philadelphia. Given the pressures under which he lived and worked, such loss of health was hardly surprising.

On 9 October, after Joseph had thrown off his illness, he and his family returned to Liverpool on board the *City of Richmond*. But back in Aberystwyth, Music was not included in the list of courses for the new academic year beginning in October 1880, and Parry formally resigned from the Chair of Music, thus breaking once and for all his relationship with the College. Parry wrote 'the national success of my tune 'Aberystwyth' ... named after the place, comes as a rebuke to the Council for discontinuing its duties to its nation's most prominent gifts, namely music, since this subject was of no financial burden to them'.[22]

There was one more musical achievement to come in 1880. On returning to Aberystwyth, Parry set to work on a cantata called *Joseph*, based on the familiar story from the book of Genesis, with Welsh words by Rev Thomas Levi, who had provided the libretto for *Cantata y Plant* ten years earlier, and English words by Rev David Rowlands.[23] According to Levi, the text was written, a bit at a time, in great haste at Parry's request. The manuscript[24] states that the cantata was finished at the 'End of the year 1880'. Despite the apparent haste, the cantata did not receive its first performance until a year later, at Christmas 1881, when it was performed at the Temperance Hall in Merthyr, under the auspices of the town's Cymmrodorion Society, with Parry conducting. It was performed 'in full costume'.[25] *Joseph* proved a success and by April 1883 had received forty performances in the USA alone. It was sometimes performed as an opera, with or without costume – a surprising late nineteenth-century reflection of the close links between opera and oratorio in the first half of the eighteenth century. In June 1893, it was performed in Bethesda 'with a magic lantern'.

Joseph is divided into four 'scenes' and follows the traditional oratorio pattern, with recitatives, choruses, and solos. The work calls for six soloists: soprano, baritone, bass, and three tenors, along with a mixed chorus and a male voice chorus representing Joseph's brethren. It was never fully orchestrated and was usually performed with piano or harmonium accompaniment, although strings were sometimes added.

There is no overture; instead, the scene is set by the pastoral opening chorus 'Dewch rhwymwn ein 'sgubau yn rhes ar ôl rhes' (*'Oh! Come let us gather the corn while we may'*), sung by the Israelite reapers. From the freshness of this opening chorus through to the splendid finale for soloists, mixed chorus and male chorus, it is the choral writing that is the most striking. The Ishmaelites' chorus (no 9, in part II) shows Parry using *alla turca* techniques effectively. The writing for the male voice chorus is memorable, particularly in the march-like no 27, in part IV ('Joseph a ganfu ei frodyr' – '*Joseph saw his brethren approaching*').

The work is certainly not without its faults. In the music, there is too much use of descending chromatic thirds and sixths, and similar Victorian clichés, along with occasional reminiscences of *Blodwen*. The English text frequently descends into bathos: 'We fondly expected more leisure to know/In Canaan where olives and pomgranates [*sic*] grow.' (The corresponding lines in the Welsh text[26] are completely different and much better: 'We had expected a better life after coming to our promised land, the land to which our fathers journeyed'.) Nevertheless, the work has much to commend it. By setting out to write what is described on the title page as an 'easy' cantata, Parry created an attractive work in which the music fits the text well and, for once, there is no feeling that the work would have been much improved if he had taken the time to revise it.

Financially, Parry's own School of Music was in no better state than the University College. The price of his musical successes during 1880 was his absence from the School. There was no captain at the helm and no second-in-command who could steer the ship effectively in his absence. In the face of these difficulties, he decided to pull up his roots entirely and to move to Swansea, where he had been offered an opportunity to relaunch his musical career. But before bidding goodbye to Aberystwyth, he gave one last, farewell performance of *Blodwen* in March 1881. The concert took place in the Temperance Hall, which had been the venue for the first public performance of the opera as well as for the regular College concerts. 'Town and country came in their thousands. Crowds waited for the doors to open, hundreds were turned away because there was no room for them and a second concert had to be arranged for them.'[27]

So it was the people of the town and the surrounding district who paid the sincerest farewell tribute to Parry. To them it had been an exciting experience and an honour to have him in their midst for seven years. He left a gap that could not be filled.

Notes Chapter 5

[1] In the British academic system, an exhibition was a financial award to support a student's study; it carried less prestige and less income than a scholarship.

[2] Joseph Parry, p. 32.

[3] *Y Cerddor*, November 1913, p. 117.

[4] 'Eos Morlais': Robert Rees (1841–1892). Born in Dowlais, he entered the steel works at the age of nine. He was a well known tenor whose singing of 'Hen Wlad fy Nhadau' (Land of my Fathers) at the Bangor National Eisteddfod in 1874 did much to establish its popularity.

[5] Lewis William Lewis ('Llew Llwyfo') (1831–1901) was a native of Llanwenllwyfo, Anglesey. He was a poet, journalist, novelist and raconteur, and was an extremely popular public figure as a singer and conductor of eisteddfodau in Wales, Liverpool and America. He was struck by illness at the age of forty-seven and died in abject poverty in Rhyl.

[6] David Emlyn Evans (1843–1913). Editor and critic as well as a composer and a collector and arranger of traditional Welsh tunes.

[7] 'Gwilym Hiraethog': William Rees (1802–1883), Independent minister, poet and journalist. He wrote a number of fine hymns, including 'Dyma gariad fel y moroedd' (*Here is a love like the oceans*) generally regarded as one of the greatest hymns in Welsh.

[8] This should not be confused with Hubert Parry's anthem 'Jerusalem'.

[9] This text, signed and dated, stands alone on a single sheet of manuscript paper in the Parry archive in the National Library of Wales [9297E].

[10] *Yr Ysgol Gerddorol*, July 1878, pp. 50–51.

[11] Joseph Parry, p. 34.

[12] The letters are to be found in case 11720D.

[13] NLW 10186D/63.

[14] Caernarfon Pavilion was built in 1877, to hold 10,000 people; it was demolished in 1962. It was used for all sorts of events from music hall entertainments to opera, from eisteddfodau to political meetings. It was the most important and prestigious hall in north Wales.

[15] John Thomas Rees (1857–1949), and a distant relation of one of the authors, Dulais Rhys.

[16] *Y Cerddor*, November 1913, p. 117.

[17] *Cofiant Joseph Parry*, p. 57.

[18] Joseph Parry, p. 40.

[19] George Ernest John Powell (1842–1882). The Powell family of Nanteos were an ancient family of Welsh landed gentry, tracing their origins back to the 11th century prince Edwin ap Gronow. G. E. J. Powell inherited the estate on the death of his father in 1878. He was a poet and a friend of Swinburne and Longfellow, and he had a reputation as something of an eccentric. The male line of the family became extinct with the death of E. A. L. Powell in 1930.

[20] The Assembly Rooms were built around 1830, at a time when Aberystwyth was enjoying some popularity as a fashionable watering place. After the First World War, they were bought and refurbished by the Old Students' Association for use as a Students' Union, in memory of the founders of the College and of its students who had fallen in the war. The Students' Union started to move to the new site on Penglais Hill in 1970, and eventually vacated the Assembly Rooms in the early 1980s. The Assembly Rooms were then allocated to the Music Department and, subsequently, to Continuing Education. The main hall was christened 'The Joseph Parry Hall' and is still used for chamber music concerts.

[21] It is not clear whether this is the same David Davis as the one who came over to study with Parry in 1874.

[22] Joseph Parry, p. 36. Parry's emphasis.

[23] 1836–1907. Often known by his bardic name of 'Dewi Môn' (David from Anglesey). He was a distinguished scholar and for many years Principal of Brecon College. He collaborated with Parry on many occasions though the results were not always happy.

[24] NLW 19802D.

[25] *Cronicl y Cerddor*, 1 February 1882, p187.

[26] 'Disgwyliem well bywyd 'nol dyfod i'n gwlad, hen wlad yr addewid, gwlad ymdaith ein tad'.

[27] Joseph Parry, p. 106.

6

Swansea and the Musical College of Wales

The Parry family moved from Aberystwyth to Swansea towards the end of March 1881. The Swansea they moved to was, by some distance, the most musically sophisticated town in Wales. Haydn's 'Surprise Symphony' was performed in a Town Hall concert there in 1817, it acquired its own orchestra in the 1820s, and from the 1840s onwards it received regular visits from the English Opera Company. It was the one Welsh town in which opera, performed by touring companies from England, was a comparatively familiar phenomenon.

The man who was responsible for enticing Joseph from Aberystwyth was Dr Thomas Rees, minister of Ebenezer chapel and a considerable specialist in the history of Welsh Nonconformity and congregationalism. He was a great preacher, a hymn-writer and the author of a number of books. Joseph accepted without hesitation the invitation to become the official organist at Ebenezer, for an honorarium of £60 per year, and by Easter 1881 was installed in the position. He had not been in receipt of a regular income since leaving the College in Aberystwyth – and in Swansea he would be free to augment his salary by freelance work. And he still held to his dream of establishing a musical college for Wales, his third attempt at doing so. On the 22 April 1881, a public meeting was held in the Agricultural Hall in Swansea, with the aim of publicising his plans. A number of officials of the town accepted the invitation to attend. The Principal of University College, Aberystwyth, was also there, providing further evidence that he was much more sympathetic to Parry than the majority of the College Council.

Parry made an eloquent speech supporting the setting up of a Welsh music college and reasserting the arguments put before the similar meeting in Aberystwyth two years earlier. He said that Wales needed such an institution in just the same way that she needed a university. After airing the topic of the disagreements in Aberystwyth, he went on to say that there was a real need for 'competent music teachers' to teach people in their own neighbourhoods, spelling out how his college would help to achieve this by offering evening classes and correspondence courses in the elements of music. It was also intended to hold concerts, run examinations and offer scholarships, that is, to open a college similar to the one Parry had established in Aberystwyth.

The 'Musical College of Wales', was one of several different names enjoyed by the establishment, which started in the Parrys' house at 1 Northampton Terrace, Swansea. In an advertisement that appeared in the *Western Mail* of 27 April, Parry 'respectfully begs to inform the Public that he OPENED THE ABOVE COLLEGE on THURSDAY April 21, 1881.' His house was dignified with the name 'Blodwen House'.

The outstanding library of books on music, received as a gift from the Powell family of Nanteos, along with the Ieuan Gwyllt and Mynyddog scholarships, also moved to Swansea. To these were added the Ambrose Lloyd scholarship. The scholarships offered a year's instruction, that is, four lessons per week, together with the right to attend all other classes given by Dr Parry. According to Daniel Protheroe, one of the students in Swansea, the music college offered a national approach to musical education in Wales and the response of the nation was to support the venture.

Parry also had plans going beyond the walls of his college. By mid-1881 he had set up a choral society in the town, under the name of The Swansea Musical Festival Society, following the example of Evan Davies a quarter of a century earlier. Between the choir, the chapel and the college, Parry was busier than ever. He continued to take part in eisteddfodau and concerts across the country.

Since Parry's victories at the national eisteddfodau of the mid-1860s, the National Eisteddfod had been going through a difficult period, with its future in considerable doubt. The 1881 eisteddfod in Merthyr was the first to be organised under new arrangements that were to prove successful in guaranteeing its future stability.

Unfortunately, although the town was Parry's birthplace, this was to be an eisteddfod to forget. Parry's oratorio *Emmanuel* was to be performed with an impressive cast of soloists. He was called upon to conduct at short notice and the performance proved a disaster. He wrote in his autobiography 'The Merthyr National Eisteddfod performances [in fact, there was only one] of my oratorio 'Emmanuel', I should not conduct, the fiasco results!'[1]

But worse was to come. While co-adjudicating the competition for composing a cantata on the text 'Cantre'r Gwaelod',[2] Parry stirred up a hornets' nest through disagreements with his co-adjudicators Tanymarian and J. Spencer Curwen. Parry disagreed with them, placing 'Taliesin Ben Beirdd' third, rather than 'Corelli'. At a meeting to resolve the issue, it was agreed that it would be best to withhold the prize. In the meantime, however, 'Corelli', that is W. Jarrett Roberts (Pencerdd Eifion), had somehow heard of the original judgement of Curwen and Tanymarian, and on this basis had travelled from Caernarfon to Merthyr to accept the prize. The judges, especially Parry, were accused of deceit and things became very sour, with vituperative letters and articles appearing in the press. In the end, the storm blew over, but it was obvious that Parry was shaken by the ferocity of the row.

This unpleasantness did not stay long in Parry's mind, however, because the Prince and Princess of Wales were coming to Swansea on 18 October to open a new dock in the town's port. His contribution to the occasion would be to compose two anthems 'Hoff Dywysog Cymru Gu' (*Dear Prince of our Beloved Wales*) and 'Â Chalon Lon' (*With Cheerful Heart*), on English words by Irvonwy Jones translated into Welsh by Dr Thomas Rees. Silas Evans, *codwr canu* at Ebenezer, was appointed to conduct the anthems but he died suddenly a few weeks before the visit and Parry was asked to take his place. The performance was a resounding success, with a choir of over 2000 voices and three brass bands. Despite this, the members of one local choral society complained about the attention that Parry attracted. He was a newcomer to the town and his choral society had only been in existence for six months, while other local choirs had been toiling away for years. This rivalry was to come to a head more than once during Parry's stay in Swansea.

On 21 December Joseph was in Liverpool as conductor and soloist at a concert in the Park Road Congregationalist chapel. He had had a happy relationship with the Welsh people of the city ever since his first visit, during his period as a student. Over that Christmas he appeared in several concerts in aid of his college; in Llanwrtyd and Llandrindod he succeeded in raising thirteen guineas (£13.65) for the Mynyddog scholarship. By now, however, he was accepting fewer engagements away from home and the college was doing well.

The first exams in Swansea were held on 21 and 22 June 1882, with Ben Davies, D. Emlyn Evans and David Jenkins conducting practical tests. The students were divided up according to age and/or instrument, with scholarships being awarded to the two best – Miss Howells (Mumbles), piano, and Miss Annie James (Llanelli), voice; a third scholarship, for composition was withheld, presumably because there was no candidate of sufficient merit. Medals and prizes were awarded to the best candidates in other categories and age groups. The list of prize winners shows that, although the majority of the pupils were from the Swansea area, there were significant numbers from elsewhere in south Wales. The prizes were presented in a ceremony that took place during a concert given by the students in the Albert Hall, Swansea, the day after the examinations.

During the summer vacation, Joseph and his family visited Germany. This is Joseph's only trip to Europe for which we have reliable evidence. Never able to relax completely, he wrote a number of hymn tunes during the trip. He returned to Wales in time to attend the National Eisteddfod in Denbigh on 22–24 August. There, he addressed a meeting of the Honourable Society of Cymmrodorion[3] on 'Musical Education in Wales', with John Thomas (Pencerdd Gwalia) in the chair. Once again, he emphasised the need for musical education at college level and talked about the Nanteos family's gift of the music library, the need for good conductors, and the lack of appreciation of instrumental music. He also called for the creation of a Welsh Music Society – something that the efforts of Parry and others never succeeded in making happen – for biographies of Welsh musicians, for the opportunity to take music examinations locally, and for the establishment of a National Music Festival in Wales. David Jenkins gave a vote of thanks, supporting Parry's ideas.

In September, the Music College of Wales started on its

new academic year. There were a hundred pupils on the register, receiving instruction either from Parry himself or from his assistant, his eldest son Joseph Haydn. For a fee of between £1.50 and £6.30 per term, they were offered four lessons a week in various fields of music, along with the opportunity to compete for medals, prizes and three scholarships. Despite the general enthusiasm and the high student numbers, the shortage of money was a continuing concern, although Parry did not allow it to affect his musical plans nor did it impair his creative energies.

The year 1883 saw Parry's second opera performed. The American Civil War is the subject of *Virginia*. Unlike *Blodwen*, it is an opera in three short acts. Its mood is that of a 'light military operetta' and it is lighter and wittier than its predecessor. Another difference is that the words are in English only. Their author, Major Evan Rowland Jones, was born in Tregaron but his family moved to Wisconsin when he was a child. He was United States consul in Cardiff and wrote words for Parry on several occasions. The work was performed in the Theatre Royal, Swansea on 19 July 1883, from manuscript copies – Parry dared not risk publishing another opera, after the losses on *Blodwen*. This was the only known performance of the new opera and it was not a success. The libretto was in English and the action set in America; it did not have the same appeal to Welsh audiences that it had to Parry and Jones, who had, after all, lived through the Civil War in America.

By September 1883, Parry had succeeded in putting the finances of the college on a firmer footing, and the list of financial supporters included Henry Hussey Vivian[4] and Lord Aberdare[5]. By now, the college was offering a variety of courses: elements of music, harmony, counterpoint, orchestration, piano, violin, organ, voice training and sight singing. But the growth and success of the college did not prevent him from applying during the summer of 1883 for the post of lecturer in music at the University College of South Wales and Monmouthshire in Cardiff.

There were eleven applicants for the post, including Parry and David Jenkins. In the end, a Mr Clement Templeton, secretary of the Harrow Music School, near London, was appointed. The Welsh press was angered by the appointment, not only because Templeton was an Englishman but also because he had no special musical qualifications. Indeed, the October issue of *Cerddor y Cymry* described him as an 'amateur musician' and could not understand why neither David Jenkins nor Joseph Parry had been appointed. Parry's application was accompanied by over twenty letters of support from well-known and influential people, including professors from the Academy in London, John Stainer (organist of St Paul's Cathedral), John Thomas ('Pencerdd Gwalia'), the Principal and former professors of the Aberystwyth University College, ministers, the Mayor of Swansea, Welsh musicians, Members of Parliament, Lady Llanover and the Marquis of Bute. This was the first time that Parry had competed for an appointment. As was the custom at the time, he canvassed all the support he could, but he was not appointed.

In December 1883, Parry ventured into another new field, that of publishing books in Welsh on the teaching of music. In an article on 'Musical Education' he addressed his remarks to the particular needs of the young people of Wales and the lack of musical resources available to them. He published his intention 'to play my part in meeting the educational needs of my country, not only as a teacher but also by preparing a series of educational books *in Welsh*'.[6] Parry's intention was to fill gaps in the fields of singing, harmony, counterpoint, fugue, orchestration, form, and so on. He noted that there were plenty of books in English and that the Welsh deserved educational resources that were as good, if not better than, those of the English.

By the end of 1883, Parry had come to the conclusion that his college was not fulfilling its duty as a truly national Welsh institution. It was successful in Swansea and district if not in the south more generally, but there were very few pupils from the north. Parry therefore wrote to his friends and supporters asking their feelings about his wish to broaden the geographical scope of the Musical College of Wales so that it would be at the service of the whole nation. A meeting of supporters of the college was held in the Guildhall in Swansea just before Christmas 1883, and Parry called for the setting up of a governing council. He felt that the college was on the threshold of major developments and that, if his dream of a *national* musical institution was to come to fruition, it would need a board of this sort to manage it successfully. It is perhaps ironical that he should have been proposing a system of governance so similar to the one that had given him so much trouble in Aberystwyth. In September 1884, the nominations of Henry Hussey Vivian as President of the college and J. T. D. Llewelyn as Vice-President were announced.

The major part of the first quarter of 1884 was spent in rehearsing *Emmanuel* for a performance in Swansea on 6 March. Parry was the conductor and Haydn Parry played the organ; the orchestra and soloists were local. On the night, although the composer himself was on the podium, the performance was at times weak and uncertain in the quality of the singing and the ensemble. The length of the concert – three hours – was also a cause for complaint. The vocal weaknesses were not entirely unexpected: since Parry had come to Swansea and set up his own choral society, it had been in direct competition with other choral bodies such as the Eos Morlais Choral Society.

Any disappointment over the poor performance of *Emmanuel* was soon forgotten in the excitement of preparing for a performance of Parry's cantata *Nebuchadnezzar* at the National Eisteddfod at Liverpool, in September 1884. This was the first of four works the National Eisteddfod would commission from him over the next fifteen years, and the Liverpool Eisteddfod would be an opportunity for Parry to reassert his influence over the music of Wales, an influence that had been in decline since he left Aberystwyth.

The first performance of *Nebuchadnezzar* took place on 18 September with the composer conducting in front of an enthusiastic audience of ten thousand. According to many reports, the performance was not as good as it might have been but the music critics from London and Liverpool were pleased.

Although not without its imperfections, *Nebuchadnezzar* is one of Parry's finest works. It is described on the title page as 'a short dramatic cantata' and consists of eleven numbers, the whole work lasting less than an hour. The text is taken from chapters 3 and 4 of the Book of Daniel, in the King James version and tells the familiar tale of three Jews, Shadrach, Meshach and Abednego, who refuse to bow down before the idol that King Nebuchadnezzar has caused to be set up. They are cast into a fiery furnace but are protected by God and emerge unscathed.

Although the work calls for seven soloists, their parts are comparatively short and the main burden of the work falls on the chorus. For the elaborate Dedication March, the chorus is divided into four choirs, representing the Babylonians, the Hebrews, the King's Guards and the Musicians. Each choir sings its own contribution before they join together in a contrapuntal chorus. The score includes a diagram showing how the four choirs should be positioned. Most of the choral numbers are long and it is a structurally complex work; although it has traditional solos, duets, and choruses, each part of the work runs freely into the next, giving the soloists and chorus a lot to learn. The work is punctuated by chorales that are reminiscent of hymn tunes but are more sophisticated in their harmonic structure and their part-writing. The fugal finale, while similar to the finale of *Blodwen*, is much more varied and altogether more interesting and mature. The music as a whole shows many of the characteristic features of Parry's style, e.g. chromatic thirds and sixths, fast syncopations and, unfortunately, overuse of the diminished seventh chord for dramatic effect, so that it becomes a musical cliché.

Nonetheless, and despite the high standard and sophisticated nature of the music, the cantata was never a popular work in Wales; according to Ap Mona[7] the reason for this was that 'Joseph Parry had not intended it for his own people, having not provided Welsh words for it'.[8] This may well have been a factor in parts of Wales but in the industrial south it is more likely that it was the difficulty of the work as a whole and specifically the difficulty of assembling and handling the four choirs that made performances comparatively rare.

For Parry, the Liverpool Eisteddfod was one of the high points of 1884. He returned to Liverpool at Christmas-time to adjudicate at the eisteddfod of the city's Welsh community in Hope Hall; he then returned immediately to Swansea to prepare for the first performance of *Nebuchadnezzar* in the town, on New Year's Day 1885. The work proved to be popular over Christmas, with at least four performances in the Merthyr Tudful area alone.

By the end of 1884, Joseph's family had seven members.

A fifth child, Dilys Joseph, was born that year and it is from that period that we have one of the rare photographs of the whole family. Even more scarce are pictures of his wife Jane and the children as individuals.

On 3 January 1885, Haydn Parry sailed from Liverpool for a concert tour of America, visiting the Welsh communities who had supported his father in the past. While his son was overseas, Joseph had to hold the fort at the college. In March, it was announced that the end of term examinations would be held on 29 April in Swansea Guildhall, with Dr Roland Rogers of Bangor as assessor. Details of the latest scholarships and prizes were also announced, leading *Y Faner* to remark perceptively that Parry was to be commended for giving the opportunity to 'the leading talents, many of whom could not hope to receive the benefits of higher music colleges in the capital [i.e. London]'.[9]

Despite the pressures on him, Parry found the time to organise and conduct two full performances of *Blodwen* in the Albert Hall, Swansea at Easter, with costumes and orchestral accompaniment – a rare event in Wales at the time. Despite the large numbers of performances of the opera that had taken place since 1878, one which included costumes, acting and orchestral accompaniment was unusual and, according to the reports, the two nights were very successful.

A month later, the people of Swansea were shaken by the death of Dr Thomas Rees, minister of Ebenezer chapel, a great friend and supporter of Parry. He died on 5 May 1885, at the age of seventy-nine, and a public funeral service was held three days later in the chapel where he had served for close on a quarter of a century. Ebenezer was overflowing (it could hold over 500) and Joseph led the singing from the organ. During the service, his *Requiem*

Gynulleidfaol was performed. Relations between the organist and the minister were close and, according to Parry's autobiography, Rees was mainly responsible for his decision to start work on the Welsh National [Hymn] Tune Book; he also wrote the texts for many of Parry's hymn tunes and other vocal pieces.

Two days after the funeral of Dr Rees, Tanymarian – that is, the Rev. Edward Stephens – died: enthusiastic musician, composer of *Ystorm Tiberias* (*The Storm on Tiberias*), the first Welsh oratorio, and one of the nation's great benefactors. Parry travelled to Tal-y-Bont, near Llanllechid in the far north of Wales, for the funeral, his second within the week, and led the singing along with Eos Morlais.

Haydn Parry returned from the United States in June after a successful musical tour. After reflecting on his future, he decided to move to London to live and work as a composer and musician on his own account. This was a blow to his father's college and a loss to the family generally. Swansea's loss was London's gain and 1886 proved a period of personal and musical success for Haydn. In March, he conducted in a concert in the London Polytechnic. He was appointed first assistant and then successor to Mr Faning, piano teacher at Harrow School. There were 250 applicants for the post, including holders of music degrees, and even a professor from the Academy in London. Then in November, Haydn was appointed organist of Harrow Parish Church and accompanist to the choir of John Stainer, organist at St Paul's. Joseph himself went to London at the beginning of April 1886 to give a lecture-recital entitled 'The Musical Composer and the Development of his Art', to the Honourable Society of Cymmrodorion. Stephen Evans, one of the London Welsh who had supported him in Swansea, was in the chair. Musical examples by Haydn Parry and others were included.

On 11 June 1886, Joseph's mother died, aged eighty-one. Elizabeth Parry spent her last years with her daughter, Elizabeth Lewis, in Ligonia Village, Cape Elizabeth (now South Portland) in Maine, where she was bedridden for the last eighteen months of her life. Of her family in Wales, the last to see her was her grandson Haydn, in June 1885, during his concert tour. In the United States, as well as Elizabeth Lewis, she had a daughter, Jane Evans, living in Kingston, Pennsylvania, and a son, Henry, who had settled in McKeesport in the same state. As with his father, Joseph makes no mention of his mother's death in his autobiography, but he wrote the hymn tune 'Maine' in her memory.

By now, Joseph was travelling less and also singing less but at the beginning of September he attended the eisteddfod at Caerwys in north-east Wales, where he gave the first performance of his song, 'Y Marchog' *(The Knight)*. The song became popular, perhaps because of the spirit of the words and the syncopated military rhythm. The last section, 'Arweinwyr Ffyddlon Cymru' *(The Faithful Leaders of Wales)*, is an adaptation of the folk tune 'Ymdeithgan Caerffili' *(Caerphilly March)* and, since the original tune is a good one, the song reaches an effective musical climax.

Joseph's wife Jane went to America at the end of 1886 for a long visit, arriving in New York on 5 December and staying until September 1887. This was her first visit without Joseph. She spent her time visiting relations and friends. For the college, 1887 was a period of decline. Without Haydn there to help, keeping it going was difficult. Joseph continued to undertake commitments elsewhere, probably because he needed the money. During the summer, he attended the National Eisteddfod in London, the Gwynedd Regional Eisteddfod in Porthmadog, and an eisteddfod in St David's *(Tyddewi)*, where he was one of the soloists in the eisteddfod concert, with Madame Clara Novello, mother of Ivor Novello,[10] at the piano.

The period from 11 June 1887 to 5 May 1888 marked Parry's first serious venture into journalism. During this time he wrote extensively for the *Cardiff Times and South Wales Weekly News*. Almost all the articles were accorded a prominent position on the front page of the paper. It says much about the popularity of music in south Wales at the time that Parry's column and a column entitled 'Musical and Eisteddfod Notes' by 'Maelgwyn' frequently occupied two adjacent columns in the centre of the front page.

During March 1888, the Council of the University College of South Wales and Monmouthshire again found itself advertising for a lecturer in music, the post for which Parry's application five years earlier had been unsuccessful. (Templeton left his post at the end of the 1886–87 academic year and the Council decided not to fill the vacancy, for reasons probably both financial and cultural. However, the Welsh speakers in the College and the Cardiff branch of the Cymmrodorion Society, along with various similar Welsh bodies, put pressure on the Council to change its mind and, in the end, it felt obliged to advertise the post.) Once again, Parry's application was supported by a host of his most influential friends. Twelve applications for the post were received and, on the recommendation of the Senate of the College, Parry was invited to appear before the Council on 2 May to explain how he would approach the job. His presentation was successful and he was appointed on the spot at a salary of £100 a year along with 'two thirds of the fees'. *The Cardiff Times and South Wales Weekly News* reported that 'Dr Parry had testimonials from such authorities as the late Sir G. A. Macfarren, Sir W. S. Bennett, Sir George Grove, Sir F. Ouseley, Professor Stainer, Signor García, and Signor Randegger,[11] while many great singers and musicians, such as Miss Mary Davies, Mr Ben Davies[12] (of *Dorothy* fame), Mr James Sauvage[13] (Carl Rosa), Miss Eleanor Rees, and Eos Morlais, had strongly recommended him.'[14]

Joseph was not the only member of the family to move ahead during 1888. Haydn Parry was appointed a professor at the Guildhall School of Music in London, a post that allowed him to continue his work at Harrow, and Mendy was appointed music master in Llanbrynmair College. Not so much is heard about this second son, whose talents were rather outshone by those of his father and elder brother. Although musical, he was of a quieter disposition and he didn't have the same pioneering spirit and enthusiasm that they had. He had helped his father and brother run the music colleges in Aberystwyth and Swansea and losing him from Swansea was the final nail in the coffin of the college.

Parry's activities in Swansea came to an end gradually, and the implications of the move to Cardiff were considered at length. There was no reduction in his various musical activities. It was around this period that he published the first of his series of educational books. He described 'The Cambrian Series' as 'a series of educational books on music' and Part 1, *The Elements of Music*, carried the following preface: 'Dear young musicians. Are you studying the heavenly art of music?' The elements of music were to be covered in nine books of the series – material that the author was said to have been preparing and using for years. Although they were written in Welsh, the majority of the technical terms were in English.

Looking back on Parry's period in Swansea we must ask how far the college there, or indeed its predecessor in Aberystwyth, was successful in realising his dream of a national music college. In fact, neither succeeded in achieving this goal. If anything, Swansea, perhaps because of its geographical situation, had less national appeal than Aberystwyth. A list of students shows that the majority of them came from the town or the neighbouring districts, extending as far as Pembrey (*Pen-bre*) to the west and Tredegar to the east, with only a few such as Mr D. Manllwyd Jones of Llanberis coming from further afield. Only two of the students at Swansea, Daniel Protheroe[15] and David Vaughan Thomas,[16] were to achieve any sort of musical reputation. This may be because of the large number of local students under the age of fifteen. In contrast, Parry's period at Aberystwyth produced a significant number of students who were to become well-known in Wales and, in some cases, further afield.

Parry must have had mixed feelings about saying goodbye to Swansea: he had had fewer personal difficulties there than in Aberystwyth, but the success of his college had been limited and his ambitious plans for music and book publishing had not progressed very far. As a composer, however, he was satisfied with his work in the Swansea period, writing in his autobiography 'I am there for seven happy years of my life. I here write some of my best compositions.'[17] Certainly, the music of this period is more mature and more original than that of earlier periods and was a portent of better to come. Parry's contributions to the musical life of Swansea were widely appreciated. On 17 January 1889, he returned to Swansea to be presented with a testimonial as a mark of gratitude for what he had done for music at Ebenezer.

Parry left Swansea for Cardiff. Another new period was facing him. The nation's expectations of him were higher than ever – as were his own hopes of achieving his personal and musical dreams.

Notes Chapter 6

[1] Joseph Parry, p. 36.

[2] Cantre'r Gwaelod (the hundred at the bottom) is a legendary land lying under Cardigan Bay.

[3] A learned society established for the encouragement of literature, science and the arts as connected with Wales. It was founded in London in 1751 by the brothers Lewis and Richard Morris and was granted a Royal Charter in 1951. It is firmly apolitical and remains based in London.

[4] Henry Hussey Vivian (1821–1894). An innovative industrialist, MP for Glamorganshire (1857–1885) and Swansea (1885–1893). Created Baron Swansea in 1893.

[5] Henry Austin Bruce, 1st Baron Aberdare, 1815–1895. Born in Aberdare, son of a local landowner. Educated at Swansea Grammar School and called to the bar in 1837. Entered politics as Liberal MP for Merthyr Tudful in 1854. Rose to become Home Secretary and Lord President of the Council. Retired from day-to-day politics after the defeat of the Liberal government in 1876. President of the Council of Aberystwyth University College from 1874 until his death and instrumental in setting up the University of Wales.

[6] *Cerddor y Cymry*, December 1883, pp 78–79, Parry's emphasis.

[7] Owen Gaianydd Williams (1865–1928), a Calvinistic Methodist minister, an able preacher, and a historian of some distinction.

[8] *Cerddor y Cymry*, August 1887, pp. 41–43.

[9] 25 March 1885, p. 10.

[10] David Ivor Davies, 1893–1951, took his mother's maiden name when he entered the acting profession. He wrote a series of very successful operettas, was an immensely popular actor on the conventional stage, and appeared successfully in many films.

[11] Signor Alberto Randegger (1832–1911). Born in Trieste, he came to London in 1854 and made a successful career as a conductor of opera and a professor of singing at both the Royal Academy of Music and the Royal College of Music.

[12] Ben Davies (1858–1943). A popular Welsh tenor, born in Pontardawe, a few miles from Swansea. Like Sauvage, he sang with the Carl Rosa opera company.

[13] James Sauvage (1849–1922), born James Savage in Rhosllanerchrugog, north-east Wales, he became an internationally famous baritone. He and Parry had much in common: he was working in the mines by the age of nine, he emigrated to the United States at the age of 18; he married in the United States and went to London to study at the Royal Academy at a mature age. Unlike Parry, he became wealthy and settled in the United States, where he retired from the stage to become Professor of Singing at Vassar, the socially exclusive women's college in Poughkeepsie, New York State.

[14] 5 May 1888.

[15] Daniel Protheroe (1866–1934) was born in Ystradgynlais and emigrated to Scranton, Pennsylvania, USA, in 1885. He graduated in music in 1890, and was

later awarded a doctorate. He taught music at the Sherwood Music School in Chicago and conducted various choral societies in Scranton, Milwaukee, and Chicago, where he lived. He composed anthems and hymn tunes, some of which are still sung today.

[16] David Vaughan Thomas (1871–1934) was born David Thomas, in Ystalyfera, Glamorgan. He attended Llandovery College in the late 1880s from where he won a scholarship to read mathematics at Exeter College, Oxford. He gained a third class degree in Mathematics, having played a prominent role in university musical life. He took the name Vaughan in 1911 when he became a member of the Gorsedd of Bards. He taught mathematics and music at various schools, including Harrow, before returning to Wales in 1906, where he worked as a freelance composer, teacher and adjudicator. He was also a talented poet and translator. He was the father of the distinguished broadcaster and writer Wynford Vaughan Thomas (1908–1987).

[17] Joseph Parry, p. 38.

7

Cardiff

Joseph Parry and his family settled in Penarth, a small town on the coast some four miles south of Cardiff. It was, as now, a genteel town inhabited largely by professional people who commute into Cardiff by train, just as Joseph did. He started his new job on 9 October 1888. The stipendiary duties associated with the post were comparatively light: he had to spend some five hours a week lecturing to a handful of students. His lectures were on musical form, the history of music, counterpoint and orchestration. In the evenings, he held classes in part-singing, elements of music, and sight-singing for the College Philharmonic Society and the students' Musical Society. This was the foundation of the musical education that Parry provided more or less throughout the time he was in the post. By the beginning of the twentieth century, the courses became more sophisticated, covering topics such as acoustics and eastern music. Students could follow courses leading to the degree of Bachelor of Music. Up until 1893, the degree awarded was from the University of London, but in 1893 the University of Wales was established; Cardiff was a constituent college of the University, as were Aberystwyth and Bangor, and so the degrees awarded from 1894 onwards were degrees of the University of Wales and continued to be so until the beginning of the twenty-first century. It was, of course, necessary to pay for taking courses, and the fee varied from 15s (75p) to a guinea (£1.05) per session.

Even before starting his duties at the University College,

Parry was advertising for private pupils for Mendy and himself, offering "private lessons in singing, composition, pianoforte and the organ", at their home in Penarth and at 'Beethoven Chambers', 2 Newport Road – opposite the University College. By the summer of 1892, these activities had been transformed into the South Wales School of Music, offering instrumental tuition for the violin, viola, cello, clarinet, oboe, bassoon and harp, with six additional teachers to cover these areas, and it had moved to Queen Street. Advertisements for the school appeared regularly until 1897. The last advertisement, on 2 June 1897, described it as having moved to Dumfries School and Cartref, Penarth. Later in the decade Joseph taught evening classes, under the auspices of the 'Technical Instruction Committee' of Cardiff Corporation. His name, and sometimes that of Mendy, also appeared from time to time in advertisements for local schools, such as St Charles School for Girls, Penarth, and others, such as Llandovery College and Liverpool College, much more remote.

In December 1888, Parry accepted an invitation to become organist at Ebenezer Chapel in Cardiff, with an honorarium of £40 per year. His salary as a lecturer was £100 a year, so this was a significant increase in his income. The instrument in Ebenezer Chapel Cardiff was, in fact, a harmonium, a step down in prestige from the pipe organ in Ebenezer Chapel Swansea. He and Mendy shared the work on Sundays, Joseph accompanying one service and his son the other. Following their arrival, the quality of the music in the chapel improved and on Sundays the choir was swollen by the presence of many College students. A concert was held on 13 March 1889 to show off the musical transformation of the chapel. In June, however, he decided to give up the post, largely because of his frequent absences on Sunday caused by his other musical commitments and, as he said in a letter dated 11 September 1889 to E. R. Gronow, a former member of the church, 'I find my Sunday's work is really too much of a strain upon me, and, I also find that I cannot now do what I could 20 years ago.' (he was then forty-seven.) Nonetheless, he continued to attend two churches in Penarth, Christchurch (English Congregational) in Stanwell Road and Bethel Chapel (Welsh Independent) in Plassey Street, and he seems to have been a member of, and occasional organist at, both.

Over Christmas, Parry spoke at eisteddfodau in Bala and Coedpoeth, near Wrexham. The burden of his addresses was that Wales needed a nursery for teachers and instead of sending them directly to London, they should first be sent to places like Cardiff; he had come back from America to Wales to provide this sort of education for his fellow countrymen. By allowing that London should be the final goal, he seemed to want to maintain a delicate balance between pressing his own cause and making a fair and honest judgement about the education of musicians in Wales at the time.

On 10 May 1889, the Cardiff Orchestral Society held its annual general meeting and, following the resignation of the conductor, Mr S. Fifoot, Joseph Parry was unanimously elected as his successor. This was the start of a new chapter in his life as a conductor and, in the Porthcawl Eisteddfod on 22 July, he conducted the Cardiff Orchestral Society in a competition performance of the overture to Auber's opera *La Muette de Portici*. He and the fifty-strong orchestra received a warm reception and easily won the first prize of £25. But the highlight of the year was winning the first prize of £20 for their performance of the first movement of Mozart's Symphony No 40 in G minor at the National Eisteddfod in Brecon.

The year 1890 was to prove remarkably successful for

Parry and his two oldest sons, as well as marking the beginning of a new phase in the development of music in Wales.

On 9 April the Cardiff Orchestra Society, now numbering some eighty instrumentalists, gave a concert in Park Hall[1] in which Haydn Parry appeared as the piano soloist in *Allegrezza*, a work that he had composed the previous year. Father and son appeared together again in a concert in St James's Hall, London on 9 May. The first part of the concert was devoted to music by Haydn Parry, and the second half to music by Joseph, with each composer conducting his own works. The evening began with a performance of Haydn's cantata *Gwen* to words by J. Young Evans of Oxford, based on the legend of Llyn y Fan Fach *(Little Peak Lake)*. This work was given an enthusiastic reception, but the same was not true of the second half, a performance of Joseph's cantata *Nebuchadnezzar*, perhaps because the choral parts were beyond the ability of the choir of London Welsh chapel members. *Gwen* was subsequently performed for an entire week, from 22 to 28 September, in the Albert Hall, Swansea, and on 22 October in Cardiff, with Haydn conducting all the performances.

For some time, Joseph had been working with Llew Ebbwy (John Williams), a former pupil from the Aberystwyth period, and Mr Fletcher, owner of the Theatre Royal in Cardiff, on plans to mount a full week of performances of *Blodwen* and *Arianwen* in the theatre in June. The performances were to be fully staged, with a full orchestra and professional soloists. It was intended to follow this by a lengthy tour through Wales. *Blodwen* was, of course, an old favourite with audiences in Wales but this would be the first performance of the opera in a professional theatre and, so far as we know, the first performance ever of *Arianwen*. Subtitled 'Merch y Pysgotwr' *(The Fisherman's*

Daughter), *Arianwen* is a romantic comic opera set in a fishing village. Its dramatic construction seems, if anything, worse than that of *Blodwen*; the music, however, proved popular. The opera contains a good deal of spoken dialogue and, although the original libretto, by Dewi Môn,[2] is in both English and Welsh, it seems only to have been performed in English.

The marketing of the Cardiff season was good; there were several preview articles in the press, including descriptions of the plot of *Arianwen*; the Great Western Railway ran a special excursion from Swansea for its first night; and the Taff Vale Railway and the Rhymney Railway ran special excursions and offered cheap tickets. According to the press reports, the theatre was full or nearly full for all the performances.

The tour also proved a success. The touring company played under the name of the Welsh National Opera Company. For perhaps the only time, we see opera attaining a similar level of popularity in Britain to that which it enjoyed in Italy. This year was also a success for Joseph's second son: the tour marked the emergence of Mendy as a successful manager. He took the responsibility for organising and running the tour and seems to have demonstrated a considerable aptitude for the job. By the beginning of September, the company had given fifty performances of *Arianwen*, and the cast presented Mendy with a dressing case to mark the occasion.[3] On its second visit to Merthyr, at the end of September, the company gave its seventy-fifth performance, by which time Bridgend, Maesteg, Risca, Neath and Abercarn had all been visited twice. The tour ran until late November, with some venues receiving three visits. According to an interview that Mendy gave some years later to the *Western Mail*,[4] the company gave a total of 116 performances and, from what evidence survives, it seems that the performances were equally divided between the two operas.

The success of the tour demonstrated that the Welsh appetite for music went beyond a taste for choral competitions. The success of *Arianwen* also demonstrated that the taste for opera was not limited to the patriotic and heroic elements that characterise *Blodwen*. Furthermore, the tour showed that the taste for opera was not limited to the Cardiff bourgeoisie but extended to the small industrial towns and to the country market towns. The idea of a Welsh National Opera Company lived on for a number of years. In 1894, following his review of a concert by the Rhondda Glee Party in Park Hall, Cardiff, Parry wrote:

> It has been my opinion for some years that the time must come in Wales, as in other musical countries, to establish a Welsh National Opera Company, and I am glad to make known that this desire of my heart, as a pioneer of Welsh opera, will be soon realised, and also to make known that Mr [Tom] Stephens, the celebrated conductor, [the conductor of the concert Parry was reviewing] will at once proceed to form a syndicate to organise, for the first time in the history of the music and musicians of Wales, a Welsh National Opera Company.[5]

In April and May of 1897 there were productions of *Arianwen* and *Sylvia* in Cardiff, Swansea, Aberdare and Pontypridd, by the Welsh National Opera Company under Mendy's management. But there is no sign of a permanent company being set up and the name went out of use until the present Welsh National Opera was set up after the second World War.

The Cardiff season provoked two heated controversies

that were eagerly reported, perhaps fanned, by the press, in particular the *Western Mail*. The publicity that they gave to the productions probably helped to launch the tour successfully. The first of the controversies may well have been sparked by lengthy and enthusiastic reviews of the operas in the *Western Mail*. The review of *Blodwen* contained the following passage:

> The curtain descended upon the closing scene of Dr Parry's opera, 'Blodwen', last evening at the Theatre Royal, Cardiff, amid remarkable manifestations of enthusiasm ... It marked the breaking down, to some extent, of the barriers of prejudice which have closed the operatic stage to Welsh vocalists; the rapid spread of those more enlightened views which recognise the value of the theatre as an educative and elevating agency. For the first time in the history of modern Wales, the best vocal talent of the land has willingly lent itself to the production of a national opera within the walls of a theatre. Only those familiar with the idiosyncrasies of the Welsh people, their tenaciously-held beliefs as to the evil tendencies of the drama, can fully appreciate the significance of last night's performance.[6]

The review of the final performance of *Arianwen* in the *Western Mail* of Monday 9 June not only praised both productions enthusiastically but also reported at length on the ecclesiastical affiliations of the members of the chorus and the audience. If Parry's conscience was at all worried, his concerns would probably have been allayed by the presence of twelve ministers in the pit section of the audience for the Thursday night performance, and by the fact that his own denomination, the Welsh Congregationalists, seemed to have attended in large numbers. The performances raised the hackles of the Cardiff puritans, and especially of the Rev. F. C. Spurr, a leader of the forces of prejudice that had ensured that the first performance of *Blodwen* was not a fully staged performance. It was not so much the operas themselves that were the bone of contention as the fact that chapel members would be performing in a 'playhouse' – a term that, to strict Nonconformists, carried overtones of opprobrium equivalent to 'tavern' or 'brothel'. The controversy even reached the London Press and the *Pall Mall Gazette* reported that:

> The Rev. F. C. Spurr, pastor of the English Baptist church, Cardiff, before commencing his sermon last night, said he wished to enter a solemn protest against the recent productions at the Theatre Royal of the Welsh operas of Dr. Parry – namely, 'Arianwen' and 'Blodwen.' With the operas themselves and the composer he had nothing to do, but he protested emphatically against daughters of officers of Nonconformist churches taking part in such performances. The principals and chorus were, he understood, drawn mainly from the Christian churches in Cardiff. One of them was the daughter of a Congregational minister, one the daughter of a Church of England clergyman, two or three were daughters of deacons, and a number were members of church choirs. It was a hideous spectacle, that of people who pretended to be Christians going to the theatre to amuse people they ought to try and convert. In a short time he would have left Cardiff, but he washed his hands of the matter, and protested against the inconsistency manifested.[7]

The *Western Mail* itself reported Spurr's speech at length and then, at even greater length, reported on the views of individual Nonconformist ministers who had seen the production and attacked the puritan attitudes of Spurr and those like him. They carried interviews with members of the chorus, all of them pillars of the church or the chapel, who asserted firmly that they had seen no signs of profanity or depravity during the production. In a powerful editorial, it welcomed the productions as an important step forward for Wales: "In one short week we have seen the old prejudice against the theatre visibly melting, prim Nonconformists joining with their more latitudinarian neighbours in seeking instruction and amusement from the stage. The Puritanism which has for two centuries held the Principality spellbound has at last given way under the kindly influences of the Welsh national opera."[8]

The Cardiff productions of *Blodwen* and *Arianwen* led to a second, albeit very different, controversy in the columns of the *Western Mail*. The music critic of the *Western Mail* was Gould Thorne, who wrote under the pseudonym 'Zetus'. On 13 June, the newspaper published an interview with Zetus, which was strongly critical of aspects of the operas and also, more generally, of the development of music in Wales. On 16 June, it published an interview with Parry and, on 17 June, a letter from William D. Rees, a strong supporter of Parry, and a final rejoinder from Zetus on 20 June.

Zetus' most specific criticism was that much of *Blodwen*'s music was plagiarised, albeit unwittingly. He cited two specific examples, the Huntsmen's Chorus, which he said 'savoured strongly of *Der Freischütz*,' and the Dead March, which he asserted was a crib from 'Quis est homo' in Rossini's *Stabat Mater*. He further asserted that 'in my intercourse with musicians – many of whom are Welsh to the core – I have frequently heard charges of plagiarism preferred against it [*Blodwen*].'

The specific allegations are easily rebutted. The Huntsmen's Chorus in *Blodwen*, as Parry said when interviewed, uses the traditional huntsman's horn call in a way that any composer writing a hunting scene might do. In fact the Huntsmen's Chorus in *Der Freischütz* is so different from the one in *Blodwen* that no question of plagiarism can be seriously entertained.

There is undoubtedly a similarity between the Dead March and Rossini's 'Quis est homo' but it is on the same level as the similarity between the main themes of the last movements of Brahms' first and Beethoven's ninth symphonies. We know Parry had conducted Rossini's *Stabat Mater* not long before he wrote *Blodwen* so it is quite likely that he was unconsciously influenced by it, but this hardly amounts to plagiarism. Parry himself rebuts the charge rather disingenuously by pointing out that the Dead March is, in fact, modelled on (but not, of course, copied from) the Dead March from *Saul* by Handel.

It appears that Zetus was unaware of the difference between plagiarism and imitation. That *Blodwen* was derivative was never in dispute; that it was copied, which is what the term plagiarism implies, has never seriously been suggested by anyone other than Zetus. (The report of the interview does imply that it was the *Western Mail* reporter who introduced the word plagiarism into the conversation, so there could have been an element of mischief-making.)

In the original interview and in his final rejoinder, Zetus seemed to go out of his way to offend the Welsh musical world. He asserted that 'nearly all the Welshmen or Welshwomen of today who have attained to any eminence outside Wales would probably have remained in obscurity had they not been brought under English influence'. He also asserted that a Welsh school of music is impossible because the life of Wales is 'so interwoven with that of England'. He further asserted that the audiences for the Cardiff productions 'knew less of opera than a periwinkle; people whose patriotic impulses would not allow them to think, let alone speak, unkindly of anything Welsh.' When asked the question 'Do you regard Dr. Parry as the greatest musician in Wales?' he responded that 'He is undoubtedly very clever and a prolific composer but as a pianist and writer of delightful melody I don't think that Brinley Richards has yet found an equal.' If this was seriously meant, it calls into question Zetus' musical judgement but it might well have been a deliberately mischievous remark.

The controversy petered out, having presumably helped to boost both the *Western Mail*'s circulation and the audiences for Welsh National Opera Company's forthcoming tour. In print, at least, Parry and Zetus, who both lived in Penarth, seem to have studiously ignored each other for the remaining nine years that Zetus continued as music critic of the *Western Mail*. When he left to return to London, a presentation was made to him by local musicians; Parry's name was not on the list of subscribers.

By now, the pattern of three concerts a season by the Cardiff Orchestral Society had been established and at one of them, in November 1890, the celebrated Madame Adelina Patti appeared in Cardiff for the first time. The concert on Easter Monday contained a suite written by Parry for the orchestra, subtitled *Three Tone Statuettes*; the individual movements were called *Regret*, *Mirth*, and *Courage*.

At about this time, Parry started his campaign to establish a 'Cardiff Musical Festival'. For years, he had been writing letters to the press arguing for Welsh music festivals and appealing to the Welsh not to concentrate completely on eisteddfodau, despite the strength of that tradition. The editor of the *South Wales Echo* called a meeting at the end of

September 1891, at which it was decided to go ahead with a festival in September of the following year. Cardiff was chosen as the venue because of the availability of suitable halls, but Parry was clear that it should be an occasion for the whole of south Wales. Argument continued in the press for and against the idea. There were many problems about the arrangements, especially regarding the appointment of a conductor. Mendelssohn's *Elijah*, Mozart's *Requiem*, Handel's *Messiah* and Parry's *Saul of Tarsus*, a work commissioned for the National Eisteddfod in Rhyl, were chosen for the programme. The first performance of the last of these would be during the first week of September – the same month as the intended festival in Cardiff.

But the preparations were interrupted by a traumatic shock to the family. Around the end of March 1892, the youngest son of the family, William Sterndale Parry, came back from London unexpectedly because he was ill. His condition worsened and he died on 5 April, at the age of twenty. As a child, his health had not been good but the loss of one so young came as a terrible blow. His father's feelings, as expressed in his autobiography, may sound overly rhetorical to modern ears, but they give a real sense of his loss: 'Oh Time! Oh Time, Thou art a cruel mother, giving birth to sad and sorrowful incidents and events, that ye this year send thy servant death into our quiet and happy family circle.'[9] Willie had decided to follow in the footsteps of his father and his two talented brothers: he was a singer and a pianist and had recently started to learn the elements of harmony and counterpoint. He was described by David Jenkins as always having 'an innocent and amiable smile', and D. Christmas Williams said of him: 'His gentle temperament, his gentlemanly behaviour, and his spotless character won him many friends and admirers.' The funeral was held in Penarth and on his gravestone in the churchyard of St Augustine's church are carved the words 'Blessed are the pure in heart for they shall see God.' Joseph cancelled his musical engagements for the following weeks and, at the annual general meeting of the orchestra on 31 May, resigned as conductor; T. E. Aylward was appointed his successor.

At the beginning of June, Joseph's friend Eos Morlais died suddenly at the age of fifty-one. The two were the same age and had been friends since Parry's time at Ebenezer Chapel in Swansea, where Eos Morlais was the *codwr canu*. Joseph gave an address at Eos Morlais' funeral in Neath on 10 June.

Press reports from around this time show that Joseph and his son Mendy were intending to set up a music college to be called the 'Music School of the South'. However, despite its grandiose title, little was heard of it, even in Parry's autobiography, and, to the extent that it existed, it must have been on a small scale. Both father and son had been offering private music lessons in Beethoven Chambers since coming to Cardiff, and in 1890 they appointed D. Christmas Williams as their assistant.

On a happier note, Parry was in the midst of preparations for the National Eisteddfod in Rhyl, from 6–9 September, with the first performance of *Saul of Tarsus* as one of the main musical events of the week. *Saul of Tarsus* was his second oratorio; there is a gap of well over a decade between it and its predecessor *Emmanuel*. It depicts Saul's life in four scenes: Damascus, Philippi, Jerusalem and Rome, following the Biblical tale of Saul's conversion to Christianity. The text is in English. Much of it is scriptural but some sections, for example, 'The Christians' Morning Hymn', have words by the ubiquitous Dewi Môn. The work is scored for soprano, tenor, and bass soloists, chorus, organ, and orchestra.

Saul of Tarsus is less rigid in form than *Emmanuel*, with smooth transitions from one part or scene into the next. By now, the Handelian element had all but disappeared and Parry unifies the work via a system of *Leitmotifs*, even naming and numbering them in the score. Unlike Wagner's, Parry's *Leitmotifs* are merely musical identifiers; he does not vary them according to the action or emotional context, although he skilfully combines them, at times creating complex polyphonic textures and climaxing with a polyrhythmic combination of four *Leitmotifs* close to the end of the work.[10]

The score is almost operatic at times with many stage directions. For example: 'They all kneel in solemn prayer.' At the beginning of the Temple scene, there is a trumpet fanfare and the score states:[11] 'The actual notes blown by the Priests at that time, also the very psalms chanted on the occasion, authority Edershime.' Although the orchestra is mostly subservient to the singers, the instrumental links between sections are one of the work's strengths.

The oratorio successfully combines Victorian melodrama with the composer's religious sincerity and dramatic polyphonic textures – for once these do not go on for too long. Parry includes two Welsh hymn tunes, sung by the choir (unlike in *Emmanuel* where the audience was invited to join in) in textures reminiscent of chorale preludes and often combined with the *Leitmotifs* played by the orchestra. Stylistically, the music is less derivative than most of his earlier works. However, he still cannot avoid the occasional over-use of diminished seventh chords for dramatic effect, as in the threatening chorus of Roman guards[12] in Philippi or the earthquake during the Prisoners' scene.[13]

Parry's creativity is at its height in this highly emotional and religious work. It is certainly as good as any nineteenth-century oratorio written in Wales, England or Scotland until *The Dream of Gerontius* appeared in 1900, and it more than deserves a revival.

Although Parry tried in places to make provision for performers' limitations, *Saul of Tarsus* remains a difficult work that can only be tackled by experienced and competent choirs, with professional soloists. Nevertheless, the first performance was a great success. So great was the applause at the end of the performance on 8 September that Parry was called upon to address the crowd. But once more, as in the case of *Nebuchadnezzar*, the Welsh language press was critical because the text was in English: 'If the words had been in Welsh, we would have felt more proud of the work'.[14]

The performance of *Saul of Tarsus* at the Cardiff Festival two weeks later received a mixed reception and it was generally agreed that the thrill of that first performance in Rhyl was missing. The audience was smaller, the composer did not conduct the work with the same spirit, and the choir had not learned the work so thoroughly. The performance lost money; nevertheless, a second Park Hall performance of the work was immediately arranged for 3 November. This proved to be a better performance than the Festival one but still no match for that glorious night in Rhyl.

Parry spent Christmas 1892, as so often in the past, in Blaenau Ffestiniog, adjudicating and singing. Christmas Eve to Boxing Day were spent in the town's Assembly Rooms, where the Annual Eisteddfod of the Welsh Independent chapels was held, with concerts in the evening. That year the leader of the Eisteddfod spoke publicly of Parry's Music School in Cardiff, of the advantages to young musicians of going there, and of the fact that entrance scholarship examinations would be held in January 1893. Over the years, Ffestiniog and the surrounding area gave Parry enthusiastic support and, if more communities had promoted his ideas in the same way, perhaps his academic career as a teacher of music would have shone more brightly.

In March 1893, Mendy married Hannah Jones, a singer, and daughter of a Swansea builder, and it was in that town that the wedding took place. Like her father-in-law, she had received her musical training at the Academy in London, and she made her first appearances as a singer at the National Eisteddfodau in Denbigh and Cardiff. From then on, she was in great demand as a professional singer and won considerable acclaim.

Between 5 and 9 September 1893, an eisteddfod was held as part of the World's Fair in Chicago. The National Society of Cymmrodorion in America was responsible for arranging the eisteddfod, as the contribution of the Welsh-Americans to the grand occasion. Joseph Parry and David Jenkins were invited to adjudicate but in March 1893 it was announced that neither would be attending after all. Nevertheless, the Festival was a proud occasion for Parry because his 'Cytgan y Pererinion' *(Pilgrims' Chorus)* was one of the test pieces for male voice choirs of between fifty and sixty voices. Several choirs from Wales went over to Chicago for the competition, and the generous first prize of $1000 was won by the Rhondda Glee Society.

On 25 October, Parry and some of his pupils gave a concert in Merthyr Tudful, in the presence of Anthony Howells, the American consul in Cardiff, successor to Major Evan R. Jones. Howells was from the Welsh community in Youngstown, Ohio that had supported Parry in his 1868 efforts to raise the money to study at the Academy in London. The purpose of the concert was to launch a fund for scholarships to Parry's Music School. He explained his ideas and invited support for the venture but little was heard of the scholarships after this and it appears that the response was disappointing.

In the same year, Parry suffered a serious loss as a result of a fire, which destroyed the printing plates of *Blodwen*, *Emmanuel* and *Nebuchadnezzar*, worth between £800 and £900. '... lost in the *Western Mail* fire, without a penny's compensation, though they [the *Western Mail*] were morally responsible', according to his autobiography.[15] There is, however, no report in the press of a fire at the offices of the *Western Mail*, and the paper itself reported[16] that the plates were destroyed in a fire at the premises of Messrs Daniel Owen and Co, printers. There is no sign of Parry's relationship with the newspaper having suffered and he continued to write regularly for it for several more years.

On 7 March 1894, the fifth annual concert of the University College of South Wales and Monmouthshire Musical Society was held in the Lesser Park Hall in Cardiff. Parry led his students in a programme that included in the first half his *Cambrian Rhapsody* for orchestra, and vocal and instrumental music by Mendelssohn, Rossini, Meyerbeer and Henry Bishop.[17] *Nebuchadnezzar* was performed in the second half.

Three weeks after the concert, on 29 March 1894, came the devastating news that Joseph Haydn Parry had died, at the age of twenty-nine. After going out to dinner in London, he caught a cold and his condition quickly worsened. He left a widow and two small children. This was the second heavy blow the family had suffered within two years. The funeral was held on 2 April 1894, in West Hampstead Cemetery in London. The chief mourners were Joseph senior (there is no mention of Jane having been present), Haydn's widow, Mr and Mrs Watkins (his parents-in-law), Mendy and his wife, and many musicians from Wales and London. He was buried between George MacFarren (1813–87, former Principal of the Academy) and Walter Bache (1842–88, former Professor of Piano at the Academy). On the gravestone are inscribed the words 'His sun is gone down while it was yet day'.

During the weeks of mourning that followed, Joseph decided that a trip to America would be of benefit to the family; their last trip as a family had been in 1880, although Jane and Dilys had made a visit without Joseph in 1887. Before leaving, at the end of June, Joseph conducted *cymanfaoedd canu* in Llanelli and in his old chapel, Ebenezer, in Swansea, at both of which the hymn tune 'Haydn', which he wrote in memory of his son, was sung. Joseph, Jane, and their ten-year old daughter Dilys, sailed for America on 22 June, on board the *Etruria*[18] – Parry's ninth crossing of the Atlantic – leaving Mendy, his wife, and his sister Edna at home in Penarth.

The Rev. Thomas Edwards ('Cynonfardd'),[19] of Edwardsville, Pennsylvania, publicised the forthcoming visit in the Welsh press and invited the Welsh communities to contact him if they wished Parry to speak in their area. He emphasised Joseph's connections with America and how a warm welcome would help the family forget their recent tragedies. Welsh America responded well to the appeal, and Cynonfardd began to arrange a timetable for the tour. The Parrys arrived in New York on 1 July, after a nine-day crossing, and were warmly welcomed by many relatives and old friends. The next day they arrived in Scranton. Judge H. M. Edwards, one of the notables of the American Welsh, was there to meet them at the station and take them to his house where they would lodge for the first three weeks of their stay. Cynonfardd had arranged a timetable that gave Parry some rest periods and avoided the need to travel every day – he was, after all, over fifty. These rest periods also gave him more time to spend with his family and old friends. He led *cymanfaoedd canu*, adjudicated in eisteddfodau, and delivered lectures to Welsh communities across north-eastern America. On many occasions he sang 'Make New Friends but keep the old' ('*Y Cyfaill Pur*'), a solo he composed in 1886, whose text sums up his feelings towards the people of the country where he passed his formative years.

On 26 July there was a special meeting of welcome in the Congregational Chapel in Elm Street in Youngstown, Ohio. One of the speakers was Joseph Aubrey, who had been a member of the Youngstown Eisteddfod Committee in 1865 when they had decided to set up the Parry Fund. He read out the original circular letter that was sent to the Welsh communities in America in that year, and a copy was presented to Parry for the Cardiff Museum. At the end of his speech of thanks, Parry spoke of his intention to return in 1895 with an opera company to perform *Blodwen* and his other operas there – an idea that had been simmering in his mind for a long time.

The 1894 trip was enjoyable and successful. Joseph had had three months which were busy without being overloaded, and his lectures were warmly received. Joseph's response to the warm-hearted reception they had received was to publish a letter of thanks in the Welsh press there. He and his family left America on 29 September. While they had been in America, two Welsh musicians in London – Charles Coram and Frederick Griffith – had organised a memorial concert for Haydn Parry, which had raised a substantial sum of over £187.[20]

Parry's most important musical engagement in 1895 was a performance of the oratorio *Saul of Tarsus* on 19 February in Newcastle-upon-Tyne – a city that had enjoyed a varied musical life of high quality for over two hundred years. The Harmonic Society of the city invited him to conduct the performance. Such was the enthusiasm of the audience that several parts had to be repeated. The oratorio enjoyed a rather warmer reception than it had in Wales two and a half years earlier – perhaps because the English did not have the same prejudices and were readier than the Welsh to accept the work for what it was, without the shackles of the eisteddfod and chapel traditions.

It had been decided that Joseph's services to the music of Wales should be recognised during the 1896 National Eisteddfod by presenting him with a 'National Testimonial'. The Eisteddfod would also commission a third work from him. The general content of the commission for 1896 had already been decided, a cantata on a libretto by O. M. Edwards, which would contain 'telynegion' (a type of lyric poetry) by John Morris Jones, Bangor, and Dewi Môn. There would be three parts to the work: 'Wales Past', 'Wales Present', and 'Wales Future'. It was composed during the rest of 1895, so that rehearsals could start in Llandudno over New Year.

On 29 June 1895, a concert in aid of the Parry testimonial fund took place in Cardiff. 'Unforgettable' was the word the composer used in his autobiography to describe the occasion. Around 9,000 people packed the Rosebery Hall to enjoy a male voice choir selected from the eight or nine best male voice choirs in Wales, famous soloists, the Glamorgan brass band, and a local orchestra. An attempt to repeat the success in Swansea, later in the year, proved a failure, however.

On 19 August in the Theatre Royal, Cardiff, there took place a performance that the composer later described as the most important musical event of his life, a performance of the opera *Sylvia*, which he had been working on intermittently for four and a half years.

The English libretto for *Sylvia* was written by Mendy who had, by now, followed in the footsteps of his late brother and moved to London, there to establish

169

'Mendelssohn Parry's Concert and Operatic Agency' during the second half of 1895. There was an element of the poet in both father and son, although the father was more inclined towards sentimental song lyrics and flowery description. Fairies are the subject of *Sylvia* and Mendy's words were criticised as being too serious for a story of such lightness, magic and enchantment. However, *Sylvia* has been described as Parry's best opera, mainly because it avoids the traditional Italian plan – one of the weaknesses of *Blodwen* – and the plot therefore moves along more smoothly. It is also innovative for Parry because it contains ballet.

On 28 January 1896, Joseph Barnby, Principal of the Guildhall School of Music in London, died. He was a versatile musician and had some connections with Welsh music – he had conducted the Cardiff Festivals of 1892 and 1895 and had written words for some of Joseph Haydn Parry's compositions. In February, Parry decided to apply for the position. We can only speculate about the reason for this decision. Certainly, he was not unsuccessful in Cardiff, even though he had yet to fulfil his ambition to see a real music college for Wales there. He was a staunch Welshman but still, many great musical Welshmen had moved to London over the years and achieved success there, among them Brinley Richards. Also, success had come to Joseph Haydn Parry and to Mendy there, and it is possible that a desire to raise his musical status in the eyes of the Welsh was the main motivation for their father. Nor should we forget his emotional ties with the Guildhall through his late son – nor, of course, the fact that the salary would be considerably higher. There might also have been the temptation to be part of an established music school.

There were thirty-eight applicants for the post and Parry's application was backed by dozens of letters of support; among them were letters from the mayor and thirty-two Cardiff councillors, the Principal and twelve staff of the University College, Cardiff, dozens of Parry's students and former students, the committee of the Cardiff Orchestral Society, and well-known musicians such as Sir George Grove, first Principal of the Royal College of Music, and Sir John Stainer, now Professor of Music at Oxford. By the end of May, the selection process had taken a step further with the original list of applicants being reduced to ten on the first vote, with Parry's name still included. A second vote took place shortly afterwards to produce a short list of five; Joseph Parry's name was not on it. In the end, on 4 June, William Hayman Cummings was appointed.

How realistic was Parry's candidature? The fact that it was supported by Grove and Stainer must have meant that it would be taken seriously. As a composer, he was clearly well ahead of Barnby. Barnby was a prolific and fluent composer but his output is largely liturgical. Little of his music survives today except the hymn tune *Perfect Love* used for the wedding hymn 'Oh Perfect Love'. Even in that specialised genre, he cannot compete either in popularity or quality with Parry's best tunes such as 'Aberystwyth', 'Dinbych' or 'Sirioldeb'. Cummings made no claim to be a composer; he was a singer, an organist and a scholar of distinction, and had been professor of singing at the Royal Academy of Music for the previous fifteen years. As an organist and conductor, Parry was – or had been, because we hear little of him giving organ recitals in later life – probably of the same standard as Barnby and Cummings. If anything, the range of his experience was wider than theirs, even if it did not include the music of the Anglican church. Overall, as a musician Parry was better qualified for the job than Cummings was or Barnby had been. However, to be head of a major music school, such as the Guildhall, requires much more than musical knowledge and ability; in particular, it requires administrative skills and a wide knowledge of the world of music. Although his various ventures had given Parry administrative experience, none of them had been so successful as to provide convincing evidence of his skills as an administrator. And he had limited knowledge of the musical world of London, let alone Europe.

Although his failure to be appointed Principal of the Guildhall School must have been a great disappointment to Parry, he scarcely had time to fret over his failure. The National Eisteddfod was fast approaching. It was to be in Llandudno during the first week of July, and the chief events for Parry would be the performance of the commissioned cantata, *Cambria*, and the presentation of the testimonial.

During the ceremony to present the testimonial, Anthony Howells spoke of Joseph's early years in Danville. He recalled meeting him in Youngstown in 1865, spoke of his musical career in the United States, of the Parry Fund, and of sending him to the Academy in London, and he presented the National Testimonial, worth £581.2s.6d. (By the fund's closing day, the total of the gifts was £628.4s.1d.[21])

The ceremony was followed by a successful first performance of *Cambria*, with the composer conducting the orchestra and a choir of 450. In contrast to the earlier large-scale works, the text of *Cambria* is in Welsh, and it was well received, with Parry having taken advantage of the broad stage of the National Eisteddfod to create a work for soloists, chorus and orchestra. There is also a part for a speaker, who recites words in a notated rhythm written on the stave, with accompaniment.

The weakness of *Cambria* is the imbalanced form: Part I is long and Parts II and III are short, and Parry should have responded to criticism and lengthened the later sections. As with *Saul of Tarsus* and *Nebuchadnezzar*, there were few performances of *Cambria*, mostly because its sophisticated style made it difficult to perform and appreciate.

Parry spent the first half of 1897 travelling through Wales rehearsing various choirs for the annual Welsh Music Festival of the Tonic Sol-fa Association in the Crystal Palace on 17 July. Parry conducted a united choir of 2,500 voices, as well as an orchestra and four brass bands. The programme included many pieces by Parry but the only memorable points were 'Cytgan y Pererinion', 'A dream' and three hymns. The audience was disappointed by the otherwise generally untidy performances. In his autobiography, Parry blames the choirs for not having learned the music thoroughly,[22] despite the amount of time he had spent travelling hither and thither across Wales to rehearse them.

Parry's spirits were raised by an invitation to adjudicate at an Eisteddfod in Salt Lake City, Utah at the beginning of October 1898. He sailed from Liverpool on 30 July – without Jane and the family – aboard the *Campania*. Cynonfardd, who had been responsible for arranging his previous visit and who spent much of his life in America, travelled with him. As on previous voyages, Parry entertained his fellow passengers with impromptu concerts.

Joseph arrived in New York on 12 August and travelled to Danville to visit relations and old friends. On 21 August he played the organ at a *cymanfa ganu* in the Mahoning Presbyterian Church, where he had once been organist. Many of his hymn tunes were sung, he addressed the audience in Welsh and English, and the occasion was recorded on phonograph discs by the Edison Bell company.

He visited the Welsh communities in Ohio and Tennessee, some of which he had last visited when raising money to finance his time at the Academy. Then he started on a week of train travel that is described in detail and with great enthusiasm in his autobiography. He travelled through Louisville, St Louis, Kansas City, Denver and Colorado Springs, before reaching Salt Lake City on 25 September. A committee from the local Welsh community and eisteddfod officials came to the town's Rio Grande station to meet him. They took him to the Kenyon hotel, where a three-room suite was waiting for him. During the ten days before the eisteddfod, he was given a warm welcome and was taken to visit the Great Salt Lake and the countryside around, as well as the town of Ogden to the north, where he was fêted by the mayor and corporation with a picnic in the mountains. In Salt Lake City itself, he was treated as an honoured guest, his picture was displayed all over the town, and a visit to the opera house was arranged. He also had the moving experience of meeting two old couples from Bethesda Chapel, Merthyr, who had known his parents and the rest of the family.

The eisteddfod was held in the Mormon Tabernacle. There were twenty-four competitions and around fifteen hundred people had come to compete in front of an audience of ten to fifteen thousand. Among the test pieces were many of Parry's compositions and he himself delivered his adjudications from the stage. He sang 'Hen Wlad fy Nhadau' (*Land of my Fathers*), was President of the day, and delivered a lecture/recital on 'The Masters: Mozart, Schubert, Beethoven, Schumann and Chopin'. On 9 October, he said farewell to Salt Lake City at the end of an outstandingly successful visit and on 15 October sailed from New York, again on the *Campania*.

Parry returned to America a year later for a tour lasting from August to October. This time he took a vocal quartet with him: Ashworth Hughes, Hannah Jones (Mendy's wife), Maldwyn Humphries and Meurig James, the last two being former pupils of his; Mendy went with them as general administrator and official accompanist. This visit had been under consideration for five years and, by 1899, practical considerations had dictated a programme of excerpts from *Blodwen, Sylvia,* and *Arianwen,* all in costume, rather than a complete opera.

Between 5 September and 6 October 1899, the group gave over twenty-five concerts, right across the states of Wisconsin, Illinois, Ohio, Indiana, West Virginia, Pennsylvania, Vermont and New York. This was a much more extensive trip than Parry had ever undertaken previously. As on previous visits, the group received a warm reception. Joseph, Mendy and Hannah returned around the middle of October, while Maldwyn Humphries and Meurig James stayed in America until the beginning of November.

On his return to Wales, Parry received several invitations to present his lecture/recital on 'The Masters', he conducted a few *cymanfaoedd canu,* and he adjudicated at the 1899 National Eisteddfod in Cardiff. One of the test pieces in the competition for male voice choirs was 'Iesu o Nazareth' *(Jesus of Nazareth),* a piece he had written especially for the competition. It became almost as popular with male voice choirs as 'Cytgan y Pererinion'. The work was described by the editor of *Y Faner*[23] as being like 'cool waters to the thirsty soul'.

At the turn of the century – 1 and 2 January 1900 – Parry was in the north of England, to celebrate the twenty-fifth anniversary of the annual Workington Eisteddfod under the chairmanship of Ivander.[24] Later in the year, he went to the National Eisteddfod in Liverpool where his fourth National Eisteddfod commission, *Ceridwen,* was performed in the first half of the evening concert on 20 September. It had not been intended that the composer should conduct but, as a result of some disagreement, he was asked to take over at the last minute, without the time to prepare and with just one hurried rehearsal. Despite this, the performance was a success and, according to his autobiography, three thousand people had to be turned away because the Pavilion was filled to capacity.

The plot of *Ceridwen* concerns the druids, the Roman invasion, and the coming of Christianity. Parry indicated that the work could be performed either as an opera or as a cantata. It was in the latter form that it received its first performance. The same fate awaited *Ceridwen* as had overtaken his three previous Eisteddfod commissions: initial success but with very few performances thereafter, perhaps because of the elevated nature of the music. Possibly learning from past experience, Parry may have tried to make *Ceridwen* more popular by including his hymn tune 'Aberystwyth', to be sung by the audience and the performers together. Traditional tunes are the musical basis of the work and the composer uses them skilfully, as shown by the treatment of 'Toriad y Dydd' *(Daybreak)* and 'Aberystwyth'.

Just like the previous year, 1901 began with a trip to Workington to adjudicate in Ivander's eisteddfod on 1–2 January. Long journeys like this[25] were becoming less frequent now, as Parry was drawing nearer to sixty and his health was not what it was. Back home in Penarth, however, he was working diligently on a new project, *The Maid of Cefn Ydfa*. This would be his seventh opera, this time using words by Joseph Bennett, a London music critic who had been interested in the music of Wales ever since attending the National Eisteddfod in Carmarthen (*Caerfyrddin*) in 1867. But Parry had to wait while the words arrived sporadically from London. Meanwhile, he wrote two other operas, his seventh and eighth, *His Worship the Mayor* and *Y Ferch o'r Scer (The Maid of Sker)*. *His Worship the Mayor* makes fun of civic life, petty politics and the self-importance of local government officials. A light and amusing opera, not unlike the works of Gilbert and Sullivan, it was never published and possibly never performed.

Christmas 1901 was to see performances of *Ceridwen* and *Nebuchadnezzar* in Pontypridd; unusually, both works were performed as operas, in costume. Parry conducted the United Male Voice Choir of mid-Rhondda, to the accompaniment of piano and harmonium. In spite of extensive preparatory work, the performances were only adjudged 'fair' – a situation that occurred only too often according to Parry's observations in his autobiography.[26] Indeed, writing his autobiography (in English) attracted much of Parry's attention during the first half of 1902, and he went at it with enthusiasm – and haste. The whole work is only around 10,000 words; there are substantial gaps in its coverage of his life; the style is uneven; and the ordering of the material is untidy. The limitations of the work demonstrate the extent to which Parry's inability to write good English may have been a disadvantage to him in his profession. Despite all this, it gives a valuable picture of Parry's thoughts as his life of musical and cultural service on two continents was drawing to a close. He began the work, on 1 January 1902, with the poetic invocation 'O thou; unseen, and ever moving time!' [Parry's punctuation], and went on to mention that his sister Ann and his brother Henry had died but that his two sisters Elizabeth and Jane were still alive and living in America. From then on, the first part tells the story of his life with more detail or less detail, depending on the vagaries of memory, reaching 20 May 1902 sixty pages later.

In the second part of the work, Parry listed – at excessive length – the musicians he had seen, heard or met, ranging from Manuel García and Sterndale Bennett to Wagner,

Liszt, Grieg, Dvořák, Hallé, Richter and Verdi. Unfortunately, he did not distinguish between those whom he had met, those whom he had heard, and those whom he had merely seen. He then listed, with many spelling mistakes, over seventy operas that he had seen – including works by Verdi, Mozart, Puccini, Rossini, Weber and Sullivan – along with the American states and European countries he had visited.

The third part of the autobiography has only the grand heading 'Wales as it is, Wales as it needs be, and Wales as it might be'. Unfortunately, the rest is blank. Parry was interested in the Cymru Fydd (Wales of the Future) movement and wrote a song with that title. This movement was started by T. E. Ellis in 1886 with the aim of encouraging a renaissance of Welsh culture, and gaining self-government for Wales. It was led for a period by Lloyd George, but declined rapidly following Lloyd George's failure, in 1896, to get the South Wales Liberal Federation to support the movement. It is a great pity that Parry did not complete this part of the autobiography because it would have given us a better insight into his attitude towards Wales and the Welsh language.

The musical epilogue to 1902 was the completion of the score of *The Maid of Cefn Ydfa* and the arrangements for five performances in the Grand Theatre, Cardiff, starting on 15 December, by the Moody Manners[27] Opera Company. It was a great success – indeed, in the autobiography Parry describes the first performance as 'the greatest success of my life [sic] labours'[28] – with all the resources of the theatre, full orchestra and the opera company working splendidly together. Madame Fanny Moody, who was the prima donna in the Carl Rosa Opera Company for three years, sang the part of Ann Thomas, the main character in the opera. Mr Manners promised that he would try to include the opera in the repertoire of his A company, which toured in England (companies B and C were the ones that most often came to Wales) and Joseph Bennett promised to provide Parry with the libretto for another opera.

Like his previous opera *Y Ferch o'r Scer*, *The Maid of Cefn Ydfa* tells a story based on a legend, using unaccompanied dialogue. It quotes many folk songs, especially 'Bugeilio'r Gwenith Gwyn' *(Watching the Golden Wheat)*. This time, however, instead of using the tune and varying the accompaniment, Parry uses 'Bugeilio'r Gwenith Gwyn' as the musical basis of the opera. It is heard played by the orchestra in the prologue – there is no conventional overture – and in a 'cerdd dant'[29] version with the character Will Hopcyn singing the counter melody, beginning, in accordance with tradition, after the start of the instrumental tune (Example 3).

Musical Example 3
'Bugeilio'r Gwenith Gwyn'

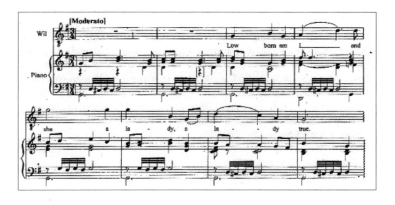

The opening of Wil Hopcyn's cerdd dant aria from 'The Maid of Cefn Ydfa'

Parry had grand plans for 1903. He was intending to visit Australia for a lecture/recital tour and to adjudicate at the Ballarat Eisteddfod on 9 October. He would then sail for San Francisco, touring, lecturing, giving concerts, and conducting *cymanfaoedd canu*, before leaving for home in early 1904.

In January 1903, Parry wrote to the Music Committee of the National Eisteddfod asking whether there was any possibility of performing his oratorio *Jesus of Nazareth* at the National Eisteddfod in Rhyl in 1904. He intended this joint effort between himself and the bard Elfed[30] to be the greatest work of his life, and although the oratorio had been in his mind for over five years he did not begin composing it in earnest until 1902. He said that half the work was ready and that it was 'a splendid piece, and one of my best works. Will this be the last thing I do?'

Notes Chapter 7

[1] A fine concert hall built in 1885, with a Father Willis organ. It was later converted into a cinema and was destroyed by fire resulting from bombing in 1941.

[2] Reverend David Rowlands (1836–1907) 'Dewi Môn'. He was born near Amlwch on Anglesey and, after studying at Brecon College and graduating from the University of London, he served as a Congregational minister in Llanbrynmair, Weshpool and Carmarthen. He returned to Brecon College as tutor and subsequently became its principal. He wrote prolifically on educational, social, national and religious topics, as well as writing opera libretti for Parry and lyrics for many of his songs.

[3] *Western Mail*, 5 September 1890.

[4] *Western Mail*, 21 April 1897.

[5] *Western Mail*, 22 March 1894.

[6] *Western Mail*, Tuesday 3 June 1890.

[7] *The Pall Mall Gazette*, Monday 16 June 1890.

[8] *Western Mail*, 9 June 1890.

[9] Joseph Parry, p. 44.

[10] Joseph Parry, score, *Saul of Tarsus*, p. 274 onwards.

[11] *Ibid.*, p. 120.

[12] *Ibid.*, p. 35 onwards.

[13] *Ibid.*, p. 79 onwards.

[14] *Cerddor y Cymry*, October 1892, p. 116.

[15] Joseph Parry, p. 44.

[16] *Western Mail*, 6 June 1893.

[17] Sir Henry Rowley Bishop (1786–1855). Professor of Music at Oxford and prolific composer of undistinguished operas. Remembered today as the composer of 'Home Sweet Home'.

[18] The *Etruria* according to Parry's autobiography but the *Umbria* according to the report in the *Western Mail* of 6 August 1894.

[19] The Reverend Thomas Edwards (1848–1927), 'Cynonfardd'. Independent minister born in Landore (Swansea). The Dr Edwards Memorial Church in Edwardsville, Pennsylvania, is named after him and has continued to hold an annual Cynonfardd Eisteddfod to this day.

[20] Worth £15,263 in 2007.

[21] Worth £52,119 in 2007.

[22] Joseph Parry, p. 48.

[23] 2 August 1899, p. 2.

[24] William Ivander Griffiths (1830–1910), 'Ivander'. Choirmaster in Pontardawe, nr Swansea. Moved to Workington around 1870 to set up a tinplate works. Established the annual Workington Eisteddfod, which subsequently became the Workington Music Festival.

[25] Cardiff to Workington would have taken at least nine hours by train in 1900.

[26] Joseph Parry, p. 58.

[27] Formed in 1897 by the singer Charles Manners (1857–1935) and his wife Fanny Moody (c1886–1945). The company disbanded in the 1910s.

[28] Joseph Parry, p. 62.

[29] See chapter 8.

[30] The Reverend Howell Elvet Lewis (1860–1953), 'Elfed'. From 1904 to 1940 he was minister of the Welsh Tabernacle Chapel in King's Cross. He won the crown at the National Eisteddfod in 1888 and 1889 and the chair in 1894. He wrote an extensive study of the Welsh Revival of 1904–05 as well as a number of other books about religion in Wales. The National Museum of Wales has a portrait of him by Henry Jarman, painted in 1934, but it is not currently on display.

8

'The harp has been broken ... '

There was to be no performance of the oratorio and no trip to Australia: the last question in the letter proved unfortunately prophetic, because Joseph Parry died within a month of writing it. The end came suddenly: he was taken ill at the beginning of February, had an operation on the fifth, and there was every sign that he would get better. However, he developed blood poisoning and underwent another operation, but his condition continued to deteriorate.

Joseph Parry died at half past nine on the evening of Tuesday 17 February 1903, at the age of sixty-one.

The funeral, held on 21 February, was an enormous event and it was estimated that about 7,000 mourners – including Spencer Curwen[1] from London – gathered in Penarth. The funeral service was conducted by the Reverend J. Gwilym Jones, Penarth, the Reverend H. Elvet Lewis, London, and the Reverend D. Charles Davies, Cardiff. After the service in Christ Church Congregational Church, the funeral cortège went on to the cemetery of St Augustine's Church, where the coffin was laid in the same grave as Joseph's son Willie. The music at the funeral service was in the hands of Mr Norman Kendrick and included the hymns 'Oh God, our Help in Ages Past' (sung to the tune 'Dundee') and 'Now the Labourer's Task is o'er', along with Mendelssohn's anthem 'Happy and Blest'. There were addresses in English and Welsh. In his address, in Welsh, Elvet Lewis ('Elved') said:

It is not possible to bury a musician; you can bury a poet, or a painter, or a preacher, but never a musician, because the musician's songs stay alive in the mind of the nation through the ages, and the music of Joseph Parry will live in the memory not only of this age but of all the ages of the earth, and thus they will preserve his name and immortalize his memory.

The funeral procession was led by the ministers of religion and the deacons of Christ Church; they were followed by local councillors, members of the governing body of the University College, members of staff of the College, Parry's former students, representatives of the National Eisteddfod, and so on. The end of the cortège was marked by the united choirs, followed by the hearse and the family mourners. The singing in the procession was conducted by Tom Stephens, an old friend of the family. 'Aberystwyth' was sung twice, once to the English words, 'Jesu, Lover of my Soul' and once to the Welsh words 'Beth sydd i mi yn y Byd' *(What is there for me in the World)*. 'Cytgan y Pererinion' was sung at the graveside.

In the evening of the following day, a memorial service was held in Christ Church. It seems to have been largely in English. Psalm 39 was chanted, 'Jesu, lover of my soul' was again sung to the tune 'Aberystwyth', there were anthems by Parry ('Oh! Lord Abide with me') and Stainer ('What are these?'), Mendelssohn's 'Song without Words No 27' was played as a voluntary, and the service concluded with Guilmant's 'Marche Funèbre and Chant Séraphique', the last a remarkably enterprising choice[2] in the light of the conservative nature of all the other music.

Services, meetings and concerts were organised in Parry's memory across Wales, his music was sung in special *cymanfaoedd canu*, and laments were written for him. The following stanza from an anonymous lament is typical:

> Joseph, fy mhlentyn mwyn,
>   Collais dy siriol wedd;
> O! gresyn oedd dy ddwyn
>   Mor gynnar i dy fedd;
> Lluniaist alawon penna'th wlad,
> A'i chysygredig donau mad.

> *Joseph, my tender child,*
>   *I miss thy cheerful smile;*
> *O! pity that thou were taken*
>   *So early to thy grave:*
> *Thou created the best music*
> *And sacred songs in thy country.*

On 16 March in Youngstown, Ohio, a special memorial meeting was held. 'Aberystwyth' was sung and addresses were given by Joseph Aubrey and Anthony Howells. There were tributes in verse from Mathrafal, J. B. Lodwick and D. J. Hughes. Joseph Aubrey talked in detail about the Youngstown Eisteddfod in 1865, the Parry Fund, and Parry's years at the Royal Academy. Many similar meetings and memorial services were held across America.

Joseph Parry's minister during his teenage years in Danville was the Reverend John B. Cook, whose reaction to the loss of one of his flock was to write (in Welsh) that:

> goodness was part of his make-up, kindness and generosity were part of his nature. The death of Dr Parry, faithful citizen, high-principled patriot, helpful neighbour, and honest friend, is a loss to the world.

His death was news as far away as Salt Lake City:

No name is held in greater honor in Welsh-American circles than his ... Dr Parry was a man of superior type. He was the embodiment of conscientiousness, and he sought diligently to be just to all men, regardless of creed or nationality.[3]

There were musical tributes as well, a number of composers composing memorial pieces, such as 'Drylliwyd y Delyn' ('The Harp has been Broken') by David Jenkins – 'a simple anthem in memory of my teacher Dr Joseph Parry', on words by Elfed. By March 1903, Alaw Ddu (W. T. Rees) had composed 'O! Alar Ddu' (O! Dark Grief), a 'Requiem in memory of Joseph Parry and so many other Welshmen recently lost such as Isalaw'. A Remembrance Festival for them was held on 26–27 December 1904, and the competition works included a variety of pieces by Welsh composers with Parry prominent among them. Writing memorial works to Parry also became popular as an eisteddfod competition.

Joseph Parry left a family of four: his wife, Jane, and three of the original five children – Mendelssohn, Dilys and Edna. Mendy died in 1915 at the age of fifty; he and Hannah had two daughters, Elsie and Viola. Hannah was friendly with Clara Novello Davies and, like their mother, the girls went into the world of light opera. After the death of her father, Dilys married George Smith, and they had one daughter. Dilys and her mother ran the Music School of the South for a period, concentrating on teaching the piano. Dilys also led the Cymru Fydd Glee Society in Penarth for a time, and continued to follow in her father's footsteps until her sudden death on 4 August 1914. She is buried in Star Cross cemetery in Devon.

Jane travelled to America during August and September 1904, visiting relatives such as her great-nephew Haydn

Parry Evans – who was still alive and coming up to his century in the 1980s – in Wilkes-Barre, Pennsylvania and staying with Anthony Howells, in Masillon, Ohio. She died in Penarth on 25 September 1918, aged seventy-five, and was buried beside her husband in the cemetery of St Augustine's church. On the gravestone are the words 'He is waiting and watching for me.' Amongst the mourners were D. Christmas Williams and David Evans, two of her husband's former pupils.

Edna lived the longest of Joseph Parry's children, dying around 1940. She and her husband, Wilkie Waite had one child, a daughter Doreen born on 1 March 1898. The family was living in Barry (*Y Barri*) at the time but spent many years in Wolverhampton. They returned to Barry and it was from there that the manuscript of Parry's autobiography was sold to the National Library of Wales in 1935. Doreen Waite married Sam Widgery and died on 4 July 1979.

At the time of Joseph's death two of his sisters, Elizabeth and Jane, were still living in America and he had five nieces there. There were distant relatives of his mother living in the area of Mynyddygarreg, Cydweli, in 1903. Gomer Thomas, Joseph's brother-in-law and his American publisher, died in Danville on 12 October 1903.

One of Parry's great-grandchildren survived into the twenty-first century and is still alive at the time of writing. Mhari Elizabeth Forbes Parry is the daughter of Arthur Haydn, the son of Joseph Haydn Parry. Of all Parry's descendants, she has had the longest and most successful musical career. At the start of the Second World War, she turned down a place at Oxford in order to become an ambulance driver. She toured as a soloist with the Staff Band of the Royal Army Medical Corps, as well as broadcasting extensively. She became a 'Forces Sweetheart'. After the war, she joined the English Opera Company, making her debut at Glyndebourne as Lucia in Britten's *The Rape of Lucretia*. She also set up and, for two years, ran the Wigmore Hall lunchtime concerts. However, her great achievement was the founding, in 1950, with Phyllis Thorold, of the Opera Players (later the London Opera Players). She sang extensively with the company and continued as its Managing Director until 2001. She remained Artistic Director of the company until it was forced to close, for financial reasons, in November 2006.

After Parry's death David Evans was appointed to Parry's post at University College Cardiff. He was a talented musician, who composed the familiar Welsh carol 'Tua Bethlem Dref' (*Towards the Town of Bethlehem*); in 1908, his post was upgraded from Lecturer to Professor, so that he was the first Professor of Music in University College, Cardiff.

Joseph Parry left a personal estate worth £440.[4] Remembering the financial difficulties that he had had during his life, a comparatively small sum such as this is not unexpected. However, it was necessary to ensure that there was an income for Jane, his widow, and with this in mind, public meetings were held in Penarth and Cardiff following the funeral. A committee was formed from musicians, academics and journalists in Cardiff, which decided to establish 'The Dr Joseph Parry Memorial Fund'. The interest from the contributions would be paid annually to Jane Parry. Funds were raised through a variety of musical activities, such as a concert given by Parry's former pupils in the Cory Hall, Cardiff, a performance of David Jenkins' opera *Enchanted Isle* in Aberystwyth and the Barry Island Eisteddfod held soon after the 1903 National Eisteddfod in Llanelli. On 26 November 1903, the fund stood at £1,089.19s.2d, and, despite the fact that the published closing date was 15 January, contributions continued to flood in, the fund reaching £1,246.6s.5d on 16 April. The sum of £100 was presented directly to Jane Parry, various expenses were paid, and £1,099.2s.7d was transferred to the coffers of the Trust. After Jane's death in 1918, the fund was used as the basis of the 'Dr Joseph Parry National Scholarship Trust' for young musicians wishing to study at the Academy or the Royal College in London, or any similar establishment within the University of Wales. Management of the scholarship fund was transferred to the National Eisteddfod of Wales and the prize was worth around £70 in 1976, according to the official programme of the Eisteddfod.

By any reckoning Parry's professional life had been successful. He had risen from a poor background, with little education, to a position of esteem in Britain and America. His music was widely appreciated and widely performed. His adjudications were sought and respected. His writings on musical matters were taken seriously, and he had enjoyed great popularity as a conductor and performer. On a personal level, he had been fortunate in his marriage and family life, despite the premature death of two of his sons, and he had enjoyed the friendship and support of many outside his family.

In the second part of this book we explore Parry, the man, the musician, and his music in greater depth.

Notes Chapter 8

[1] John Spencer Curwen (1847–1916). Son of one of the inventors of sol-fa notation, Principal of the Tonic Sol-fa College, and head of the publishing firm J. Curwen and Sons, later the Curwen Press.

[2] Alexandre Guilmant (1837–1911) was a member of César Franck's circle and a composer and organist of some standing; he was one of the founders of the Scuola Cantorum in Paris and Professor of Organ at the Paris Conservatoire.

[3] *Desert Evening News*, Salt Lake City, 28 February 1903, p. 3.

[4] Worth £33,874 in 2007.

Part Two

9

Joseph Parry – the Man and the Musician

Our knowledge of Parry the man is decidedly limited. It is largely filtered through the words of others. Although plenty of Parry's public writing has survived, in the form of articles and letters to the press, we have only a few business letters and almost no personal letters. While many members of the professional classes and the landed gentry would routinely keep personal letters, this practice was rare among other sectors of society. Neither Joseph's family nor Jane's family would have thought of keeping personal letters on the scale that, say, his part-namesake Hubert Parry's family did. A particularly unfortunate consequence is that we have very little idea of Joseph's relationship with his wife, who was at his side for forty years and bore him five children.

Nevertheless, there are a number of features of Parry's background and character that we can readily identify and which clearly influenced him and affected his behaviour throughout his life. His Welshness, his humble background, his lack of formal education, his profound if unsophisticated religious beliefs, his child-like naivety and his ambition, all these are well attested in the writings of his contemporaries and indeed in his own writings and his actions. It is on sources such as these that we have to rely to form a picture of the man and his private and public life. In doing this, we must realise that, although he is best remembered today as a composer, much of Parry's time was spent in more ephemeral activities – performing, conducting, adjudicating, journalistic writing, teaching, and so on – and that through these activities he may well have had as much influence on musical life in Wales as he had through his compositions.

Parry's pride in his Welshness needs to be seen in the historical and social context of the nation. Of the four nations that made up the United Kingdom in the nineteenth century, Wales was educationally and culturally by far the poorest. Albeit Henry VII (Henry Tudor) was partly Welsh, Wales had been effectively under the rule of English kings since the time of Edward I and had been absorbed into England by a series of acts imposed by the English parliament between 1536 and 1543. As a result there was no separate administration for Wales; English was the language for all official matters; and the predominantly English-speaking Church of England was the established church. Until the foundation of the college in Aberystwyth in 1872, higher education in Wales was limited to St David's College, Lampeter, intended for educating Anglican clergymen, a few teacher training colleges such as Bangor Normal, established in 1858, and a few colleges for training Nonconformist ministers.

In contrast to Wales, Scotland had been completely independent of England until the Scottish king James VI became also King of England in 1603. Scotland had enjoyed a cultural golden age in the first half of the sixteenth century, when the four universities of Aberdeen, Edinburgh, Glasgow and St Andrew's were established. When Scotland was united with England by the Act of Union in 1707, the international reputation of these universities – certainly of Edinburgh and Glasgow – was on a par with that of Oxford and Cambridge, and her capital, Edinburgh, was a cultural and intellectual centre, as Glasgow also increasingly became during the eighteenth century. The tradition of public concerts in Edinburgh goes back to at least the end of the seventeenth century and in Glasgow to the 1720s. Although there was a branch of the Church of England in Scotland, the established church was the (Presbyterian) Church of Scotland, which was very much the church of the people. There was a great respect for education among all classes in Scotland and a long tradition of poor but able Scottish students studying at the Scottish universities. The ministers of the Kirk provided encouragement and support, and had the contacts to help such students. If Parry had been born into a humble Scottish family, it is very likely that he would have received full schooling and proceeded to study at one of the universities. This was beyond the realms of possibility for the son of an iron worker in Wales.

The educational and cultural poverty of Wales was recognised in London and in 1846, a Royal Commission was appointed to investigate the state of education in Wales; its three members were all Anglicans and none of them spoke Welsh. Its reports, published in 1847 in three volumes bound in blue, laid the blame for the poor state of Welsh education – and, indeed, the poor social conditions in Wales – on the use of the Welsh language and the prevailing religious nonconformism of the population. These reports became known as Brad y Llyfrau Gleision: 'the Treachery of the Blue Books'. The following quotation demonstrates considerable ignorance on the part of at least one of the commissioners, along with a remarkable willingness to give offence.

> The Welsh language is a vast drawback to Wales, and a manifest barrier to the moral progress and commercial prosperity of the people. It is not easy to over-estimate its evil effects. It is the language of the Cymri [sic], and anterior to that of the ancient Britons. It dissevers the people from intercourse

which would greatly advance their civilisation, and bars the access of improving knowledge to their minds. As a proof of this, there is no Welsh literature worthy of the name.[1]

To be fair, the report as a whole is much more factual and less biased than this, and it must be said that many Welsh people at the time held the view that education in English was what they wanted and what they needed. Nevertheless, the direct consequence of the report was that no Welsh was taught in state schools in Wales until the twentieth century, and the indirect consequence was to further the trend to avoid the use of Welsh in higher education and in all sorts of formal situations apart from the chapel – English was even the official language of the National Eisteddfod until 1950.

Like most of his contemporaries, Parry was romantically attached to his native Welsh language, and loved to use it for worship, in music and in the family. But for other purposes, he expected to use English, even when his interlocutors and correspondents were Welsh-speaking. English had become, to a considerable extent, the language in which educated Welsh people communicated with each other. It was not just Parry's lack of fluency in written Welsh that led him to write to Ceiriog, the leading Welsh lyric poet of the day, in English; even Owain Alaw, a Welsh writer and composer, wrote to Ceiriog in English.

* * *

Until Parry arrived at the Academy in London, most of his musical education came from amateurs. Subsequently 'he developed little if at all in any direction other than a musical one'.[2] His innocence and naivety were widely acknowledged, and are reflected in the way he named his children and in his choice of pseudonyms. This element in his character is confirmed by the observations of Asaph in *Y Faner*:

> Dr Parry was, to a great extent, a child of nature. There was a childishness and an innocence that we couldn't help but like. Not for a moment did he conceal his true feelings; nor could he, his character was too innocent and simple for that. He was often misunderstood or falsely accused because of the lack of deceit in his nature. So different from others.[3]

His writing often reflects the same thing. When he finished scoring the orchestral accompaniment to *Emmanuel*, he wrote:

> News! NEWS! NEWS!!! Ye fowls of the air – ye creatures that *growl, groan, and puff* in the mighty deep; ... Thus the herald screams as he rushes through the universe bearing the glad tidings of some little man who resides at a remote corner of our world, having this day completed the score of his last work 'Emmanuel'. So intense is the news that all things are *dumb* with *astonishment and fright*, even *paralyzed* as the herald's tones and vibrations *roll* onward through space. So now for a while, my poor and feeble brain, nerve and hands may pause awhile and wonder what such a pause means, being so unusual ... *News!* NEWS!! GLORIOUS NEWS!!![4]

Despite the apparent arrogance, there are also occasional signs of insecurity. Looking back in his autobiography to the time in 1865 when the Eisteddfod Committee in Youngstown, Ohio, suggested that he should embark on a career in the world of music, he said that he was 'much afraid of my non-success.'[5]

A more serious example of the mixture of naivety and arrogance arose when Parry, in his reponse to Zetus' criticisms, attacked Zetus for his lack of qualifications, in contrast by implication with Parry's Mus. Doc. This was in 1890, by which time Parry should have known better. Indeed, Joseph Barnett, the highly regarded music critic of the *Daily Telegraph*, who was a great supporter of Parry, had no formal qualifications. Barnett wrote, and allowed Parry to publish, an extended technical analysis of *Nebuchadnezzar*. Zetus was quick to point out that many distinguished critics, composers and musicians in general had no formal qualifications.

Perhaps Parry's feeling of insecurity was responsible for his failure to venture outside 'greater Wales': Wales, the Welsh communities in America, and the Welsh in England (London, Liverpool, Manchester and Workington in particular). Throughout the whole of his life, he stayed within its perimeter. And, despite the successful performance of *Saul of Tarsus* in Newcastle-upon-Tyne in 1895, it was within 'greater Wales' that his music received the vast majority of its performances. He may also have been afraid of competition. He gave up competing in the National Eisteddfod in 1866, while his contemporaries such as D. Emlyn Evans, continued to do so regularly. Possibly, there was also an element of pride, the feeling that by 1866 he had become too 'important' a musician to need to prove his creative talents in eisteddfod competitions. Certainly, he was prone to appear self-important and he was very proud of his degrees, especially his Mus. Doc. Despite this, he considered that J. Ambrose Lloyd had written the best Welsh hymn tune ('Eifionydd'), the best Welsh part-song ('Y Blodeuyn Olaf *(The Last Flower)*)), and the best Welsh anthem ('Teyrnasoedd y Ddaear' (*The Kingdoms of the Earth*)).

Parry's was a complex personality and, according to David Morgans: 'he had the Celtic temperament strong within him. He was hasty and indiscreet at times; he would allow his feelings to come between him and his judgement, and offended a number of his best friends'.[6] He had no political or diplomatic instincts and said exactly what came to him – whether or not it was right – and as a consequence brought many a hornet's nest down on his head.

When the National Testimonial was presented to Parry at the National Eisteddfod in Llandudno in 1896, the trustees preferred to invest the £630 raised in a new house for Parry in Penarth, rather than hand over the sum in cash. It may well be that they were aware that Parry had earned quite a lot of money during his musical career – from winning competitions, performing, adjudicating, conducting, and so on – but that he had little inclination to save his earnings, and that his personal life suffered as a result.

The public did not see such aspects of his personality. 'Y Doctor Mawr' (*The Great Doctor*) was an idol of the people and he sailed on a sea of warm appreciation. He had grown up to become one of the nation's leading musicians, while yet staying close to his humble roots. He was not a member of the gentry, nor a Member of Parliament, nor a dignitary of the University of Wales, but soon became equally celebrated. He was not afraid to show his feelings and his nature was so open that he wept publicly on hearing a performance of 'Cytgan y Pererinion' at the Swansea National Eisteddfod in 1891.

Joseph Parry the man was a reflection of his music: full of inconsistencies and contradictions. In September 1885, following a rumour that the Music Department in

Aberystwyth was to be revived, he wrote to Stephen Evans – a member of the College Council – asking whether there was any hope of his returning to the Chair he had held. In view of the unhappy relations between him and the authorities in Aberystwyth, this was the act of a remarkably naïve character. Yet when he wrote 'I feel that silence may produce the very essence of Music',[7] he anticipated the philosophy of the twentieth-century experimentalist composer, John Cage.

The same contradictions are not, however, apparent in Parry's religious views. Throughout his life, he remained a faithful Congregationalist and an uncompromising teetotaller. His parents had been Congregationalist and he had grown up in one of the most zealous families in Bethesda chapel in Merthyr. The early habits he learned there were to remain an important part of Parry's life, be it in Wales, London or America, and at times he travelled many miles in support of his church. From the days of his youth, the temperance movement was also very close to his heart, as evinced by the title of his winning entry in the Danville Eisteddfod of 1860, 'A Temperance Vocal March'; he followed this success with a series of other temperance pieces, especially during his period as a student in London.

A substantial number of Parry's works are on religious subjects: hundreds of hymn tunes and anthems and a variety of other sacred pieces, a number of which have remained popular to the present day. According to contemporaries such as David Jenkins and Daniel Protheroe, Parry's music was at its best when his head was on his knees, that is, in prayer. And Jack Jones puts into the mouth of one of his characters the words 'The foundation of the best work you [Joseph Parry] have done is the chapel and the Bible.'[8]

Parry had firm views on sacred music. These views are well expressed when he wrote that the church was the appropriate place for sacred music and that the Nonconformists 'are too narrow and restrictive in the use of music in their worship: ... We accept only the short tune, thus depriving ourselves of higher and much deeper forms and effects on men's hearts.'[9] He suggested there was a need for more psalm tunes and congregational anthems, as well as a perfect understanding between the minister and the *arweinydd y gân*, to make sure that the choice of music matched the text of the sermon. A choir should be formed in every church, not to supplant the congregational singing but to support it.

Parry never lost his religious beliefs, and the following quotations are a testimony of his faith: 'I hope that He who holds all power in His hand will in his wisdom keep us under his divine wings and that we shall meet again.'[10] '*To God*. The whole universe worshipping God.'[11] 'During all we have had the *guidance* and *support* of a *Heavenly Father*.'[12]

Life was not easy for Joseph Parry and his family. Two sons died, and there were daily financial difficulties. Nevertheless, he overcame these troubles and lived a successful musical life in the public eye – convincing evidence of the steadfastness of his faith and the inner strength of his personality.

* * *

From the point of view of performance, Parry's first 'instrument' was the voice; he sang alto and then tenor in choirs in Merthyr Tudful and Danville. In America he learned the melodeon before moving on to the harmonium, the piano and the organ. At the beginning of his musical career, Parry's reputation was due as much to his talent as a singer as to his achievements in the field of composition. He won further popularity by singing his own songs, a simple and effective way of advertising his music – people flocked to hear Parry the singer and they were presented with Parry the composer at the same time. While, at the time, Parry was probably unaware of the precedents, this was a long established practice and he was following in the steps of Mozart, Paganini and many others in using his popularity as a performer to promote his own compositions.

His performances on stage were perceived as something special. For example, when he sang at a concert in Cwmaman, in 1869, an anonymous journalist wrote that one of the things that would make him world-famous would be:

> His powerful and expressive way of singing ... he puts over so much of the nature of the song, in his facial expression, his gestures, and above all his correct and creative enunciation of the words; the words are not half swallowed or half whistled through the teeth as some singers do ... Mr Parry can infuse more life into his performances than other singers ordinarily do.[13]

At the end of Parry's period as a student, the London Welsh held a gathering in his honour and among the testimonials that were received was one from Manuel García, who remembered his voice as:

> [a] good Baritone of extended compass and good flexibility, and your [Joseph Parry's] knowledge of the different styles of voices extends to you the career of either singer or professor – the former in my opinion is the more profitable and the more pleasant.[14]

Because Parry sang so many of his own songs, he also accompanied himself (on the harmonium rather than the piano, because it was the harmonium that was usually available in chapels and local halls). The accompaniment to solos like 'Y Trên' and 'Gwraig y Morwr' is complex and technically difficult so it was no mean feat to accompany himself in these songs. He could also play the organ, having taken lessons in the Academy with Dr Charles Steggall, the famous London organist, who was professor of the organ at the Academy from 1851 to 1903 and one of the founders of the Royal College of Organists. Parry must have had a fair talent for the keyboard: while at the Academy he wrote a number of pieces for the piano, including three sonatas, and they are pieces that require significant technique. After his move to Aberystwyth in 1874 he reduced his public appearances as vocal soloist or pianist, although he continued to accompany throughout his career. As an organist, apart from his period playing at the Freemasons' Lodge in Aberystwyth, it was worship that called him, whether in London, Danville, Swansea or Cardiff. However, it seems that he more or less gave up the organ in 1889, according to a letter he wrote just befor his death.[15]

There is no evidence that Parry received any lessons in conducting; his great popularity as a conductor suggests that he was able to add something special to the music performed under his baton, whether in a concert or a *cymanfa ganu*. In an article in *Yr Ysgol Gerddorol*, he expressed the view that conductors ought to do more to explain the basics of music to the singers – notation, scales, tempi, tonality – because 'too much singing and too little familiarity with the music are common'.[16] Several contemporary reports bring this situation to life, for example, according to W. Afan Evans:

> During rehearsals, he [Joseph Parry] goes almost wild; he expects the members of his choir to read

correctly at sight. Even when the piece is classical and of the greatest difficulty, if they don't come up to his expectations he uses words that cut to the quick. But when he is conducting in public, he is much more contented.[17]

The article went on to remark that Parry usually sat, but rose to his feet when he wanted a special effect. He would gesture to the section of the choir that would be most prominent in the musical texture, he knew about the orchestral instruments, and he would insist on the appropriate tempo in a performance, 'possibly the best [conductor] I ever saw'. Furthermore, an article in the *British Weekly*[18] was to mention him as one of the most popular conductors in the whole of Wales – his charisma was manifest in his conducting.

Because of the uncertain state of his income, financial as well as cultural obligations probably forced Parry to accept every call for his services as conductor. At the beginning of 1889, he was coming up to fifty and he had moved house and job only a little before, but he nevertheless continued to travel. On 6 March he was in Tabernacle Chapel, Bangor, conducting the annual *cymanfa ganu* of the Calvinistic Methodists, where over 600 turned up to sing. Then, on 1 April, he was in Soar chapel, Merthyr, conducting three *cymanfa* sessions for the chapels of the area. And on 19 April, Good Friday, he conducted two *cymanfaoedd* in Cardiff, one for the Independents, in Wood Street Chapel, and the other for the Methodists in Pembroke Terrace Chapel.

Parry was in North Wales on 25–26 May 1889 to conduct *cymanfaoedd canu* in Blaenau Ffestiniog and Maentwrog. Then he returned to Cardiff to conduct the Ebenezer Chapel Choral Union in his cantata *Joseph* in Park

Hall. He had just been appointed conductor of the Cardiff Orchestral Society and his first rehearsal with them was on 8 June, he conducted a *cymanfa ganu* in Cardiff on the 10th, and another in Caernarfon on the 25th. There were 3,000 members of the Caernarfonshire Independents in the town Pavilion for the morning session and 7,000 for the afternoon and evening sessions. Parry then travelled back to the south for another *cymanfa ganu* in Rhymney on 1 July, where the three sessions were completely devoted to his hymn tunes and anthems.

This sort of musical activity was characteristic of Parry's life and reflected the demand for his services as a conductor. The evidence of those who saw him confirms his popularity, one man especially – John Evans who was 112 years old when he died in 1990 – remembering him conducting the Independent *cymanfa* in Ebenezer Chapel, Swansea, is reported as saying 'A man of authority he was, and he knew what he was talking about'.[19]

As well as Parry the performer and Parry the conductor, Parry the adjudicator was much in demand and he spent a lifetime contributing to *eisteddfodau* great and small, in Wales, England and America. He first performed the duty of an eisteddfod adjudicator in 1862, in Hyde Park, Pennsylvania, barely two years after his first success as an eisteddfod competitor, at Danville in 1860.

After Parry took up his post as Professor of Music at Aberystwyth in 1874, his compositions became rapidly more popular as competition pieces in all kinds of eisteddfodau, and the natural next step was to invite the composer of the test pieces to judge the competition. While in Aberystwyth, he received a letter from Gwilym Cowlyd of Trefriw in Snowdonia asking for details about the charges for his services at an eisteddfod. His reply has survived:

Adjudicating at the eisteddfod = £12/12/0[20]
[£12.60] for one day
+ Concert soloist = £20/0/0 for two days
£26/10/0 for three days
Soloist = Joseph Parry + his son [Haydn] for violin
solos, piano solos and duets with his father.
And for £30, a 'lady vocalist from here [Aberystwyth
Music Department]' can be added.

While there is some ambiguity in this reply, it is clear that
Parry's services did not come cheap. However, there was no
lack of demand for them.

Parry was paid £31 for a week's adjudicating in the
National Eisteddfod in Merthyr in 1881. On the face of it,
this suggests that Parry was not asking for higher fees,
despite his growing popularity. On the other hand, Merthyr
was his old home town, he could travel there and back in a
day from Cardiff if he wished, and it was the *National*
Eisteddfod. All of these considerations mean that he was
likely to be prepared to accept a smaller fee than for a small
eisteddfod in a little-known and remote part of north Wales.
This was the year of the disagreement and bad feeling over
the adjudication. But as usual, the extrovert nature of his
personality was responsible for this public squabble, not his
musical judgement in adjudicating the competition.
According to David Jenkins, Parry confided to him that he
preferred to see his work performed in a concert than to
have to adjudicate performances of it in an eisteddfod,
because that could create hostility and personal persecution
– something Parry was to experience during his music
career.

It seems that Parry eventually became too demanding.
On 14 March 1895, the *Western Mail* carried a report of a
meeting of the executive committee for the 1896 Llandudno

National Eisteddfod, at which it was decided that, having ascertained Parry's terms for adjudicating, the committee unanimously decided not to appoint him.

*   *   *

Parry's decision to publish *Blodwen* and many of his subsequent works himself appears at first sight unusual, but it was probably inevitable. The most obvious course would have been to approach Hughes a'i Fab, Wrexham, who were far and away the best-known and the most active of music publishers in Wales in the second half of the nineteenth century. They had published 'Ar Don o flaen Gwyntoedd', as related in Chapter 2. In 1871 they had published a collection of six of Parry's anthems, as his opus 9, and they had subsequently published some fifteen of his anthems and songs, as well as some arrangements of Welsh airs. They seemed to have had a monopoly on Parry's work up to 1876, when they published his song 'Y Bachgen Dewr' as his opus 19 no 1.

The publishing policy of Hughes a'i Fab was, however, driven by commercial considerations[21] and it is unlikely that the firm would have wanted to take on a project of the magnitude of *Blodwen*. The longest of Parry's works that Hughes a'i Fab published was *Cantata y Plant*, at forty-four pages substantially shorter than *Blodwen* and a great deal simpler. They had not published any music of the size and complexity of *Blodwen* before; they would have had to subcontract the printing and the cost of doing that would have been substantial; and they could have had no idea whether there would be a market for the work.

There was perhaps one other Welsh publisher who might have taken on *Blodwen*. William Hughes of Dolgellau published a great deal of congregational music, as well as, in

1886, Tanymarian's oratorio *Ystorm Tiberias*, a score of 137 pages. (The first edition of *Blodwen* runs to 156 pages.) However, Hughes was a chapel deacon and, even if he had thought that publishing *Blodwen* was commercially and technically viable, he might well have been unwilling to be involved in publishing such a controversial and secular work.

It is unlikely that Novello or Boosey or any other English publisher would have been prepared to take the risk of publishing *Blodwen*. Novello had published Parry's 'Maesgarmon', a fantasia for piano, as his opus 24, in 1875, and were subsequently to publish *Nebuchadnezzar* and *Ceridwen*, as well as some shorter works. But choral works were one thing, operas quite another. The only operas by a native composer to have achieved commercial success in the previous fifty years were the operas of Balfe, an Irishman deeply immersed in the Italian operatic tradition. Regardless of the merits of the work, an opera in Welsh, by a Welsh composer, would not have seemed commercially attractive.

There is, however, nothing to suggest that Parry approached any of these firms, whether because he realised that there was little likelihood that they would agree to publish the opera or because he felt that he would be better off financially publishing it himself.

Welsh composers in the latter half of the nineteenth century generally sold all the rights in a piece of music to the publisher, usually for a fairly small sum. No matter how successful the work proved to be, they had no right to any further payment. This was the arrangement between Parry and Hughes a'i Fab. In 1875, Parry sold the rights to six pieces, for two pounds each, to Isaac Jones, a blacksmith turned printer and publisher in Treherbert,[22] who saw in music publishing a promising commercial opportunity.

Jones published the pieces as a collection entitled *Telyn Cymry*. Included among these pieces were the successful anthem 'Pebyll yr Arglwydd' (*The Tabernacles of the Lord*) and 'Myfanwy'. It is very possible that Parry realised how much potential income he had lost and that this led him to the decision to publish *Blodwen* himself.

In contrast to composers, authors in Wales normally retained the copyright in their works, simply paying the printing costs and then taking on the responsibility of distributing and selling the work – printers were reluctant to run any risk and preferred to leave the responsibility for publishing a work to the author.[23] It was common practice for Nonconformist ministers with a reputation for preaching to publish books and then arrange extended preaching tours, selling copies of their books after the service. It may well be that Parry saw this as a model that he could profitably adopt.

The practical difficulty for the composer of a work of the size of *Blodwen* was that the work had to be printed and paid for before it could be sold. This meant that the composer needed access to a considerable amount of capital. The solution Parry adopted was the traditional one of inviting individuals or organisations to subscribe, that is, to pay in advance to receive copies of the work. Some 230 subscribers are listed in the first edition of *Blodwen*; allowing for some ordering of multiple copies, this amounted to 262 copies.

Parry tells us in his autobiography that the cost of printing *Blodwen* was £400. It is by no means clear what this figure covers and, anyway, we know that Parry's memory was unreliable. The work was available in three types of binding – paper covers, cloth boards and extra cloth, with gilt edges. The prices were 5 shillings, 7 shillings and 10 shillings and 6 pence respectively for staff notation copies, and 2 shillings, 3 shillings and 6 pence, and 5 shillings for sol-fa copies. Sol-fa would have been much more popular than staff notation; almost certainly no more than 20 per cent of copies would have been in staff notation. We can expect that subscribers would all have subscribed for the luxury binding, so that we can estimate the income from subscriptions as £78. If we assume sales of 500 board, staff notation copies and 2,500 paper, sol-fa copies, this would have produced a profit of around a £100. Given the success of *Blodwen*, it is likely that, in the long run, sales substantially exceeded this and that consequently it earned Parry a lot of money. However, we know from correspondence regarding projected performances of *Blodwen*[24] that in 1878 and 1879 he was having to sell copies at half price and that there were severe financial problems with some of the productions.

Parry never attempted to publish another opera himself but he continued to publish substantial choral works – *Emmanuel, Nebuchadnezzar, Joseph*, and *Caradog* all appeared over a Parry imprint – as well as many shorter pieces. The music published by Parry and his sons carries a variety of imprints – 'J. Parry & Son' (the commonest), 'J. Parry & Sons', 'J. Parry & Co', 'J. Parry', and 'D. M. Parry'. The place of publication appears as Aberystwyth (or, in a number of cases, Aberystwith), Swansea or Penarth. *Nebuchadnezzar* is particularly interesting in this regard because the sol-fa edition appears over the imprint 'Swansea: J. Parry and Sons' but the staff notation edition has the imprint 'Novello, Ewer and Co. London and New York; Swansea : J. H. Parry'.

From 1890 onwards, Parry seems to have been less keen to publish his music himself. In 1891, however, he published the third movement of his orchestral suite *Three Tone Statuettes*, the only instrumental work he published himself. *Saul of Tarsus*, a massive publishing task, since the vocal score runs to 305 pages, was, however, published by Patey and Willis of London, in 1891; the only other work by Parry that they are known to have published was the song 'Y Melinydd' *(The Miller)*, written around 1869 but not published until 1892. *Cambria* was published by D. Trehearn of Rhyl in 1896, who also published a number of Parry's shorter works. *Iesu o Nazareth* was published in Caernarfon by the Welsh National Press Company, which published several of Parry's pieces in the late 1890s. The choice of publishers in these last two cases was probably dictated by the National Eisteddfod Committee, which commissioned the works.

It is surprising *Arianwen* was never published. Given the success of *Blodwen* and the fact that, according to Mendy,[25] *Arianwen* had received at least 116 performances, it might have been expected that a publisher would readily have been found. We do not know whether Parry tried unsuccessfully to find a publisher or whether he decided that it would be more profitable to restrict performances. The result, however, was that performers could not easily obtain copies and individual items from the work were not therefore performed. In the event, the failure to publish may well have been the main factor that led to such a successful work being so quickly forgotten. A sol-fa edition of the choruses was eventually published by Snell in 1931.

In one respect at least, Parry's decision to publish his work himself proved to be wise. In 1916, Snell, the Swansea music publisher, bought from Jane Parry the stock and copyrights of the works Parry published himself, for £1150[26]. This was a considerable sum at the time, more than the capital of the Dr Joseph Parry Memorial Fund, and must have made a lot of difference to Jane's financial position. In 1910, Snell had acquired the stock and copyrights of the Swansea music publisher, Benjamin Parry (no relation to Joseph), which included the cantata *Joseph* and the two anthems that Parry composed for the visit to Swansea of the Prince and Princess of Wales in 1881. In 1930, Snell acquired the stock and copyrights of Isaac Jones, thus acquiring the copyright of 'Myfanwy'. During the interwar years Snell reprinted many of Parry's better-known pieces and many of these are still available from Snell and Sons today.

* * *

Although Parry was, in his time, Professor of Music and Head of the Music Department in Aberystwyth and lecturer in the Music Department at Cardiff, he did not give lectures in the usual way. He organised his day-to-day teaching more in the form of seminars or practical tutorials, although he sometimes gave more formal sessions, for example, delivering a series of lectures on the 'Masters', from Bach to Wagner, in the Cardiff Music Department during the 1897–98 academic year. By then, his collection of lectures included: 'The Nationalism of Music', 'Our Present Musical Needs', 'Musical Education', 'The Musical Composer and the Development of his Art', 'The Science, Art and Language of Music', 'The Music and Musicians of the Christian Church', 'Music – its Masters, Styles, and Forms, of the Classic, Modern and Romantic Schools', and 'Hanes Caniadaeth y Cysegr' (*A History of Sacred Music*). They were usually given outside his academic work in the College; sometimes he played the musical examples himself and sometimes used other soloists.

The 'lecture-recital', a genre invented by his teacher Sterndale Bennett, was frequently used by Parry when he was on tour in America. He gave the first lecture-recital of his 1894 visit on 6 July in Scranton, Pennsylvania. The topic was the history of music and the lecture, which was delivered in English, was split into two parts, the history of music in Europe outside Wales, and the history of music in Wales. A number of pieces were performed by local soloists. In 1897, he gave four public lecture-recitals in Cardiff, under the general heading 'Music and the Masters'.

The Honourable Society of Cymmrodorion frequently sought Parry's services as a lecturer. On 24 August 1882, he addressed a meeting of the Society during the National Eisteddfod in Denbigh. 'Musical Education', one of Parry's favourite themes, was the topic, and he emphasised musical education at college level, along with the need for the Welsh to nurture conductors who *understood* their work, whether in a *cymanfa ganu* or with a choir. Once again, Parry publicly expressed his disappointment at his nation's lack of interest in instrumental music, saying that a performance of an opera or a cantata was incomplete without orchestral accompaniment; that a 'Welsh Musical Society' ought to be formed straightaway – there had already been a number of attempts to do this, including efforts by Parry himself; that the National Eisteddfod should offer a prize for a scholarly biography of Welsh musicians of the past (this became a reality at the National Eisteddfod in London in 1887, with the prize going to M. O. Jones); that music examinations should be offered on a local level in convenient centres. Lastly, he called once more for the setting up of a 'National Music Festival' in Wales. Lecturing was a comparatively small part of Parry's musical activities but it is important for the light that it throws on his opinions and ideas on Welsh musical matters. Although his ideas were praiseworthy and creative, public apathy stopped them coming to fruition in his lifetime.

Parry was also fond of airing his ideas on paper and he published several of his lectures – 'Hanes Caniadaeth y Cysegr', for example, appeared in the July 1879 issue of *Yr*

Ysgol Gerddorol. At times, he used the press to waken the nation's conscience: in September 1879 he published an article on the composer J. Ambrose Lloyd, who had died in 1874. Parry believed that the composer had been too soon forgotten and called for the establishment of some sort of movement of admirers of Welsh music – yet another praiseworthy idea that never came to fruition.

Parry also wrote as a music critic. In the 25 December 1878 issue of *Y Faner*, for example, he reviewed 'Caniadau y Cysegr a'r Teulu' *(Songs of the Sanctuary and the Family)*, a collection of 450 hymn tunes, and in *Yr Ysgol Gerddorol* in September 1879, he reviewed a solo by Seth P. Jones, 'Rwyf yn Cofio'r Lloer' *(I Remember the Moon)*. His reviews combined praise with constructive suggestions for improvement. It is ironic that he seemed unable to critically view his own compositions in the same way.

Parry's journalistic activities continued through the 1880s and 1890s. He wrote a series of over thirty weekly articles published on the front page of the *Cardiff Times and South Wales Weekly News* between 1887 and 1888. These articles covered a range of musical topics, both Welsh and international, many of which he had previously addressed in lectures, such as 'Welsh Music and the Eisteddfod', 'The Doctor's Ideal Eisteddfod', 'Choir Leaders' Evening Classes', 'Yorkshire Singers', 'The Concert Room', and 'Our Musical Needs'. By 1893, he was writing regularly for the *Western Mail*. He wrote reviews of concerts and more general commentaries on events in the world of music. It is indicative of how the musical world in Wales had developed that he wrote reviews of two chamber concerts given by Joachim and one given by Paderewski. Some of these reviews also included a section 'By our lady correspondent' describing the ladies' fashions to be seen at the concert and, on one occasion, regretting that the dirty condition of Park

Hall discouraged women, both performers and audience, from wearing their best dresses. During his trip to America in 1894, he wrote lengthy letters to the paper, which were turned into four substantial articles.[27]

* * *

It was common for the Welsh in Victorian times to take a pride in being Welsh and a pride in being British. This often led to inconsistency, typified by Parry writing the opera *Blodwen* to a Welsh libretto, with a plot that is based on conflict between the Welsh and the English, but dedicating it to the Princess of Wales, who was English. What is more, all the material in the score apart from the libretto is in English (apart from the Italian tempo indications). Not only are the title page, the preface and the synopsis in English but, in the index to the vocal numbers, the first line of each is given in English and not in Welsh.

Parry's feelings of nationality were further confused by his having spent seventeen years of his life in the United States and holding American citizenship. His bardic name Pencerdd America reflected this and helped to ensure a warm welcome for him in America, but his feelings for America were not understood by the people of Wales and his opera *Virginia*, on an American Civil War text, was coolly received.

During the Liverpool eisteddfod in 1884, Parry's oratorio *Nebuchadnezzar*, which had been commissioned for the occasion, was condemned for being in English. Parry did not see anything wrong in setting English words in a Welsh work intended for performance at the National Eisteddfod, although this might make the music less 'Welsh' and more like a work produced by an English composer.

There was no consistency about Parry's choice of

language at the National Eisteddfod – English was the official language at that time – but he made a misjudgement when he used English to give his adjudication for the psalm-tune writing competition at the Liverpool Eisteddfod. He defended his action by stating that neither his fellow adjudicator nor some of the competitors understood Welsh. In the 1887 London Eisteddfod, he gave an adjudication in English for the competition to compose a Welsh-language cantata. In the Tywyn Eisteddfod two years later, however, he refused to give his adjudication in English and, when he was asked by a journalist from an English newspaper for a translation of his comments, his response was to tear up his notes and say that the adjudication was in Welsh because the eisteddfod was in a Welsh-speaking town and the test piece 'Mor Swynol ydyw'r Nos' *(How Lovely is the Night)*, by Emlyn Evans, was in Welsh.

But it was not a matter of delivering his adjudications in English in England (London and Liverpool) and in Welsh in Wales (Tywyn). In the National Eisteddfod in Swansea in 1891, English was the language of his adjudication, and in the main choral competition in the Rhyl National Eisteddfod in 1892, he delivered his adjudication in Welsh while his fellow adjudicator, John Thomas, gave his in English.

The relationship between Parry and the National Eisteddfod was mixed: he adjudicated regularly and he received four major commissions, but in a letter to D. Emlyn Evans dated 8 July 1898 he called the music of the National Eisteddfod concerts 'retrogressive'. Had he said that publicly, he would have created a furore.

As well as mixing with the ordinary people at local Welsh eisteddfodau, Parry mingled with the 'great and the good' of Welsh and of English culture in London. On 21 June 1892 he was at the Mansion House, at the invitation of the Lord Mayor, for the annual musical evening of the Honourable Society of Cymmrodorion. Although the landed gentry kept themselves somewhat apart, the upper middle classes in Victorian England approved of those who had come from humble backgrounds to make good. So, despite the poor circumstances of his upbringing, Parry was accepted in such circles in London as easily as in the eisteddfod establishment in Wales. On the night in question, much of the music performed was by Welsh composers, with Parry prominent, and there are many other examples of his music being performed for the gentry and members of the royal family. On 8 February 1894 the Welsh Ladies' Choir, conducted by Madam Clara Novello Davies, performed his patriotic song 'Cymru Fydd' in front of Queen Victoria at Osborne House on the Isle of Wight. The Treorchy Male Voice Choir sang before her at Windsor Castle on 29 November 1895; their programme included Parry's 'Y Derwyddon' (*The Druids*), 'Cytgan y Pererinion', and 'Aberystwyth'. Then, on 9 May 1902, his 'Rhyfelgan y Myncod' (*War Song of the Monks*) was sung in the Caernarfon Pavilion at the installation of the Prince of Wales as Chancellor of the University of Wales.

Throughout his musical career in Wales, Parry zealously supported the idea of establishing a 'Society of Welsh Musicians'. At one of the meetings to establish the Society, in Shrewsbury[28] on 27 December 1888, it was he who proposed inviting the Prince of Wales to be President of the Welsh National Musical Society. The suggestion was accepted, another reflection of the readiness of Welsh musicians to display their pride in being British alongside their pride in being Welsh.

A more definitely Welsh nationalism characterises Parry's dream of establishing a 'Music College for Wales'. He tried four times to turn his dream into reality, but despite his enthusiasm he never succeeded in setting up a national music college. He tried every time to set up a music college on the pattern of the Royal Academy in London, possibly a mistake since major changes were taking place in musical education in England. Around 1870 a report commissioned by Prince Alfred, Duke of Edinburgh,[29] *The Report on Musical Education in England,* called for big changes in English musical education. One consequence of the report was the opening of the National Training School for Music, in London in 1876, with Arthur Sullivan as its first principal. The institution proved moderately successful and in 1882–3 George Grove undertook a lecture tour of England in order to publicise it and appeal for money. The National Training School closed its doors in 1883 but at the same time the Royal College of Music opened its doors under Grove's directorship. Parry had no means of achieving this sort of status and he was almost the only Welsh musician who was enthusiastic about the idea of a Music College for Wales. If he had succeeded in winning the support of his musical contemporaries, there is a chance that the dream might have become reality.

* * *

The real indicator of Parry's Welsh nationalism was his music. In the middle of the nineteenth century Welsh music was heavily influenced by musical life in England. Although every town and district had some sort of musical society or choir, there was little Welsh music that was better than mediocre. There was certainly no Welshman writing music of the same quality as contemporary composers on the continent. The situation in England was not much better. There were, of course, plenty of Welsh composers on a local scale but their education was narrow and their chances of winning fame outside their locality small. There was something new in Parry's music that seized the hearts of the people. He was also among the first to publish more widely than his local area and perhaps the fact that he spent his teenage years in the sprawling state of Pennsylvania rather than in the confines of the industrial valley of Merthyr contributed to his national success.

In the 1860s Parry was composing and singing in Welsh. The musical content of many of his concerts in this period reflects the sad state of music in Wales at the time. Two examples from 1869 will suffice. Parry and two local choirs gave a concert in Porthmadog. Parry sang in Welsh but the choirs sang mostly in English. In his review in *Y Faner*, 'GE' observed 'We can scarcely approve of the way they so often choose to sing English words'. The story in the south was similar – when the choir of Capel Als in Llanelli sang in a concert with Parry, only one of their pieces was Welsh and that was Parry's glee 'Ar Don o Flaen Gwyntoedd'.

Although this glee spread like wildfire through musical Wales, the practice of including so much English music in musical occasions that were completely Welsh was difficult to break. Six years after GE's complaint, Parry, in a letter to D. R. Hughes, called for the best performers in Wales to perform more music produced by Welsh composers, remarking that 'We are now very short of concerted music (Welsh) and no wonder'. The point was discussed at a meeting of musicians in Aberystwyth in June 1877, and the general complaint was that too many English pieces were being chosen as competition pieces in Welsh eisteddfodau, at the expense of Welsh music; the committees were choosing the same old pieces time after time.

The Welsh nation needed worthwhile Welsh music of quality and it was Parry's output that filled the breach, offering a new and exciting musical experience to ordinary people with no musical education. As early as 1878, when reviewing Parry's 'Hiraethgan', one of the journalists of *Yr Ysgol Gerddorol* wrote that Parry's purpose was 'to give the people something practical, and in this he is usually remarkably successful'. That test pieces for hundreds of eisteddfodau were and are by Parry demonstrate his influence on the musical life of Wales, not only directly through his own music but also indirectly in the choice of other pieces by the great masters: in the Llanfyllin Eisteddfod in 1893, the set piece for the main choral competition was the Hallelujah Chorus, not from *Messiah* but from Beethoven's *Mount of Olives*, while the set piece for the village choir competition was 'Ar Don o Flaen Gwyntoedd'.

Parry was a man of the people and it was for the people that he wrote his music. As he matured as a composer, his musical aspirations became more sophisticated – consider his late operas, for example – but his main aim was to serve the musical interests of his people, and the popularity of his music showed that he had succeeded.

One aspect of Parry's approach to music remains difficult to explain, and that is his attitude to sol-fa. This was, after all, the notation read by the people for whom he wrote. Yet there is no evidence that he used sol-fa as a choral conductor, nor that he had any great interest in the system. His musical manuscripts are in staff notation except where the sol-fa has been added by someone else, for example a publisher wanting to print both notations in a single copy. There was more demand for copies in sol-fa than in staff notation, the sol-fa was often published first, and the system was as popular in London as it was in Wales. Indeed, Parry's music owed a lot of the attention it received in England's capital to the concerts of the Tonic Sol-fa Association. Despite the importance of the sol-fa movement as a way of getting Parry's music performed and what he earned through it, his attitude was negative. On Christmas Day 1889, while adjudicating in an eisteddfod in Bala, he was asked to say some words to the children who had been successful in the first sol-fa examination. He made three points:

1. It was a pity that staff notation was not being learned with the same enthusiasm as sol-fa.
2. Sol-fa cannot displace staff notation.
3. Proponents of sol-fa should not pretend to greatness until the system produces a Mozart or a Handel.

Staff notation was Parry's composition medium, so it is possible that he saw sol-fa as a stumbling block. If he had supported the two systems equally, his aim of spreading musical education across the nation might have had more success. Nevertheless, his lukewarm attitude to sol-fa took away nothing of his popularity as the national composer of Wales and the musical hero of the nation.

Another aspect of Parry's musical nationalism is his choice of texts or titles. Works inspired by nationalist themes (in the cultural or historical sense rather than the political one) flourished in the second half of the nineteenth century, in Scotland and Ireland as well as in Wales. 'Llys Arthur' (*Arthur's Court*) by J. D. Jones, 'Y Ci Gelert' (*The Dog Gelert*) by John Thomas, and 'Gwarchae Harlech' (*The Siege of Harlech*) by Edward Laurence (Cerddor Tydfil) were amongst the most popular Welsh examples. Perhaps Parry was inspired by works such as these, since some fifty of his works have a nationalist title or text. These works fall into three categories: works that are Welsh by virtue of their title (e.g. *Peredur*, for orchestra) or their texts (e.g. *Blodwen* and many other vocal works); Welsh-American works (e.g.

his opera *Virginia*); and works that refer to Wales as part of Britain, such as the solo song 'Sons of Britain'.

Parry's musical nationalism shows itself more directly, however, in his use of traditional melodies and traditional forms. Vocal and instrumental (mainly harp) melodies had been part of the culture of the people of Wales for centuries, although it was not until the end of the nineteenth century that they became the object of academic study. Both his family background and the wider environment of his life in both Wales and America must have made him familiar with this tradition and he was to make use of it in many ways during his composing career.

Parry made direct use of folk songs in many of his works that have a Welsh theme. *Blodwen* uses 'Gwŷr Harlech' in the overture and in the finale; 'Llwyn Onn' (*The Ash Grove*), 'Cwynfan Prydain' (*Britain's Lament*), 'Toriad y Dydd' and 'Morfa Rhuddlan' (*Rhuddlan Marsh*, a lament for those fallen in a battle there). This does not make it into a ballad opera like Pepusch's *Beggar's Opera*. Pepusch more or less restricted himself to arranging popular ballads and composed little original music for the work. Most of the music in *Blodwen* is original and the folk tunes are but a small part of it.

Parry uses folk songs and hymn tunes in his cantatas – *Cambria*, for example, makes use of 'Gwŷr Harlech', 'Rhyfelgyrch Capten Morgan' (*Captain Morgan's War March*), and 'Codiad yr Haul' (*The Rising of the Sun*) – and in other choral pieces, as well as in many solo songs.

The Welsh tradition of *cerdd dant* uses folk melodies in a sophisticated way. In *cerdd dant*, the harp plays a harmonised melody while the singer sings a counter-melody, often improvised, above it. Parry uses traditional melodies in *cerdd dant*-like textures in at least four of his works. Early in *Blodwen* the messenger sings a counter-melody against the tune 'Llwyn Onn' in the accompaniment, and at the close of the work, Rhys Gwyn sings a counter-melody against the tune 'Morfa Rhuddlan'. In *Y Ferch o'r Scer* he uses the eponymous melody as the base for *cerdd dant*; in *The Maid of Cefn Ydfa* Will Hopcyn sings *cerdd dant* against 'Bugeilio'r Gwenith Gwyn'; and he uses 'Llwyn Onn' again in a *cerdd dant* tune in his *Fantasia of Welsh Airs*. Less happily, in 1870 he composed the song 'Gwraig y Morwr', quoting 'Home Sweet Home' (composed by Henry Bishop in 1852, to words by John Payne, but it had almost become a folk song) at the end of the piece. The tune is played in the accompaniment while the voice sings a counter-melody, in a way that creates something of the effect of *cerdd dant*.

Parry was something of a pioneer in his use of folk tunes in major works. Chopin, Liszt and Brahms, among others, wrote works based on folk dance rhythms but made little use of folk tunes as such, although Brahms used them occasionally in some of his songs. Russian composers made use of folk songs, most notably Tchaikovsky in his Second Symphony. It was not until the turn of the century, however, that English composers and the composers of Eastern Europe began to make systematic use of folk material.

As well as quoting Welsh songs in his works, Parry would sometimes use the term 'Welsh Air', or its Welsh equivalent 'Alaw Gymreig', to describe a song that he had composed, for example 'Dangos dy Fod yn Gymro' (*Show you're a Welshman*) or 'Y Fenyw Fach a'r Beibl Mawr' (*The Little Lady and the Big Bible*). And the instruction at the start of Part II of the cantata *Cambria* says 'In the simple style of Welsh National Airs'. These were not folk tunes but pastiches, written in the style of traditional music, in much the same way that Stanford wrote effective pastiches based on the style of Irish folk song.

Parry's greatest contribution to Welsh national song was the publication of *Cambrian Minstrelsie* between 1893 and 1895, in six luxurious volumes. It contained Welsh traditional tunes for various combinations of voices, set to Welsh words, with paraphrases in English by Dewi Môn, his co-editor. The piano accompaniments, written by Parry, are interesting, varied and effective, but the vocal line is unvaried. Side by side with the folk melodies, Parry included a number of original songs along with some 'national songs' written by other composers. 'Gwŷr Harlech' appears twice in *Cambrian Minstrelsie*, and in the Preface Parry and Dewi Môn describe it as 'the finest specimen of martial music in the world'.

Although a number of collections of Welsh national songs had appeared during the course of the nineteenth century, *Cambrian Minstrelsie* was the richest in both form and content. The volumes were published in hard covers, with coloured illustrations, by the Edinburgh company of Thomas Charter and Edwin C. Jack, as a Welsh companion volume to the *Scots Minstrelsie* that appeared at around the same time. (Confusingly, two of the volumes were published by the Caxton Publishing Company of London.) It is likely that the publishers were responsible for the unusual name of the collection. In 1899, the company published the *British Minstrelsie*, a selection of national tunes from the countries of the British Isles; it included eleven of Parry's arrangements, perhaps the ones that he or the publishers considered the best, but it did not include any of his original songs.

From the point of view of popularity, *Cambrian Minstrelsie* was a failure – the volumes were too big and expensive. It was perhaps a mistake on Parry's part to include his own songs, although Brinley Richards had not been criticised for doing exactly the same thing in his *Songs of Wales* published twenty years before. From the musical point of view, *Cambrian Minstrelsie* demonstrates Parry's talent for adding accompaniments to simple tunes so as to enrich the original. Many of the songs, both English and Welsh, had words by Dewi Môn rather than the better-known traditional words, which may also have worked against them.

Joseph Parry the nationalist was a complex character. Although the music of Wales was important to him, he also wanted to succeed outside his native country, if not on an international level. In a letter dated 31 December 1902, to Mr T. W. David, Cardiff, he thanked him for his efforts to find a place for the opera *The Maid of Cefn Ydfa* in the repertoire of the 'Moody Manners' company, 'so as to carry out to the full your primary object of introducing my works into England.' But this aspiration was to prove a failure, and Parry's music was to remain popular only within Wales and amongst the Welsh communities of England and America.

Notes Chapter 9

[1] *Reports of the Commissioners of Inquiry into the State of Education in Wales.* Presented to Parliament, 1847. Part 2, p. 66.
[2] Joseph Parry, p. 248.
[3] 25 February 1903, p. 11.
[4] Joseph Parry, p. 76, excerpted, with Parry's italics.
[5] Joseph Parry, p. 24.
[6] *Music and Musicians of Merthyr and District*, p. 102.
[7] Joseph Parry, p. 76.
[8] *Off to Philadelphia in the Morning*, p. 350.
[9] *Yr Ysgol Gerddorol*, July 1879.
[10] Open letter to *Y Drych*, 1868.
[11] Note at the end of an untitled hymn tune, 8 May 1898.
[12] Letter to Jane Parry, 26 May 1901. NLW GTJ01605.
[13] *Baner ac Amserau Cymru*, 15 September 1869, p. 4.
[14] 17 July 1871.
[15] NLW GTJ01604.

[16] April 1879, pp. 37–38.

[17] *Cerddor y Cymry*, December 1886, pp. 10–11..

[18] 31 March 1898.

[19] *Y Cymro*, 29 July 1980, p. 6.

[20] The equivalent of £877 in 2007.

[21] Jones and Rees, p. 175.

[22] Rhidian Griffiths, 'Isaac Jones: music printer and publisher'. *Y llyfr yng Nghymru: Welsh book studies No 5* (2003). National Library of Wales. Available on the website of the National Library.

[23] Paper read to a Library Association meeting in Cardiff by W Eilir Evans, in 1895. Available on the web at http://library.oxfordjournals.org/cgi/reprint/s1-VII/1/391.pdf

[24] NLW MSS 11720D.

[25] *Western Mail*, 21 April 1897.

[26] Rhidian Griffiths, 'Swansea's "Mr. Music": the career of D. J. Snell, music publisher', *Y Llyfr yng Nghymru: Welsh Book Studies 1* (1998), pp 59–90 National Library of Wales. Available on the website of the National Library.

[27] *Western Mail*, 6 August 1894, 5 September 1894, 6 October 1894, 22 October 1894.

[28] Shrewsbury is in England but the constraints that geography imposed on the railway system in Wales meant that it was the most convenient location for meetings which were expected to be attended by people from all over Wales. For many years, committees of the University of Wales used to meet there.

[29] The second son of Queen Victoria, Alfred (1844–1900) was created Duke of Edinburgh in 1866. He made a career as a successful and well-respected naval officer, eventually becoming Admiral of the Fleet. He was fond of music and said to have been an excellent violinist.

10

Parry's Music

Joseph Parry was a prolific composer. Leaving aside his hymn tunes, at least 400 pieces can be attributed to his name. In his autobiography he struggled to record how many he had written in each year but the result is incomplete and sporadic. Nor are there any details of what the numbers cover. Despite the large total, only a tiny percentage get performed today and these few pieces are not a fair representation of his output.

Reviews of Parry's work during his lifetime cannot be relied on. High-flown comments, like the following, were often to be found; to the modern reader, they are laughable or inappropriate as a musical judgement:

> Were we to be dragged by the hair on our heads to the furthest ends of the earth, and hear a chorus of cannibals around us singing the cantata *[Ceridwen]*, and never heard it before, nor even heard it spoken of, we would be able to say at once, 'That's the work of Dr Parry'. From beginning to end, the work is filled with delightful signs and characteristics of the composer's work.[1]

Parry composed incessantly over a period of some forty-five years and his music must be judged in the social, educational, cultural and geographical contexts of its period.

Joseph Parry was brought up in a poor working-class home where he received little in the way of general education and only sketchy musical training from teachers who were enthusiastic amateurs. Culturally he was brought up as a Welsh-speaking, Nonconformist Welshman, which is what he remained even after moving to America. He spent seventeen years in that country, three in London, and the rest of his life in Wales. The composer who composed in America does not reflect any American influences. The America of the nineteenth century was a troubled land from a social point of view and had yet to settle down culturally. Numerous musicians had been imported from Europe, especially from Germany, and there was no specific American tradition or the like, except for folk music. Dvořák was unusual in trying to study and assimilate American folk music during his three year stay there; despite his much longer sojourn in America, Parry made no such attempt and his work was European in spirit.

Parry's compositional style was much influenced by the years he spent at the Royal Academy of Music in London, taking composition lessons from William Sterndale Bennett, who was described by Ernest Walker as 'the most prominent early Victorian composer'.[2] Sterndale Bennett's music exhibits the influence of the masters: Handel in his early work, Mozart and Beethoven in his orchestral pieces, and Mendelssohn, under whom he studied in Leipzig, in his general style. Parry's music also looks back to these masters, the natural consequence of studying under a composer who was himself under their influence. Sterndale Bennett believed that his pupil had a special talent, and Parry idolized his teacher. It can be seen in the Parry manuscripts how he accepts Sterndale Bennett's every criticism, suggestion, change and musical improvement, and the three years he spent under his tutelage were of great benefit to his composing technique. This period at the Royal Academy marks the end of his early period. The rest of his composing life divides itself naturally into a middle period (1871–1881) in Danville and Aberystwyth, and a late period (1881–1903) in Swansea and Cardiff.

Musical education was scarce for the people of Wales in the nineteenth century and music lessons in schools were the exception. The musical channels in Wales were the chapel, the Sunday School,[3] the *cymanfa ganu* and the eisteddfod. Nowhere in the country were there real concert halls or opera houses, and there was a great ignorance of orchestral music and of opera, although singing flourished. The works of the masters, such as Handel's *Messiah*, were performed but there was no vocal music of a worthwhile and lasting standard written in Wales until the coming of Parry.

In England, in the first half of the nineteenth century, as well as Sterndale Bennett there were a number of active, if run-of-the-mill, composers, such as Balfe, Benedict, Goss, Hullah, Smart, Ouseley and Steggall. Although, they are remembered now only for a few hymn tunes and ballads, they were professional musicians who had been educated musically to professional standards. In contrast, such composers as there were in Wales were self-taught amateurs and their compositions reflected this.

Not only was Parry's music superior to that of his Welsh contemporaries, it was as good as the best that was written in England until the arrival of the so-called English renaissance, with composers like Hubert Parry, Charles Villiers Stanford and Arthur Sullivan. And *Blodwen* was arguably the best opera written in Wales, England, Scotland or Ireland in the whole of the nineteenth century, albeit the competition is not strong. The people of Wales had no awareness of musical standards outside their own square mile, so Parry gave them what they needed. He served the people – the Welsh in Wales, the Welsh in England and the Welsh in America – in a direct, appealing and attractive style that was usually successful. As a result, he was accused of sacrificing originality for popularity by exploiting too far the style of the day rather than trying to raise musical standards in Wales by composing in a more original and experimental way.

However, when we compare Parry with his contemporaries in continental Europe, we see how far he and all other British composers were from European standards; until Elgar there was no-one who could stand comparison with Parry's continental near-contemporaries such as Dvořák (1841–1904), Fauré (1845–1924), Grieg (1843–1907), Rimsky-Korsakov (1844–1908) or Tchaikovsky (1840–1893).

Sterndale Bennett was amongst the best of the many composers writing in Britain in the first half of the nineteenth century. His output and style were derivative and the vast bulk of his music has by now been forgotten. A musical comparison of Parry and the English composers before the so-called English renaissance, that is, up to around 1875, shows that Parry's style is as good as that of his contemporaries on the other side of Offa's Dyke, while his works are superior to theirs. However, Hubert Parry (1848–1918) and the Irishman Charles Villiers Stanford (1852–1924), who are usually considered the harbingers of the renaissance, changed the scene dramatically. Stanford's operas, now forgotten, were successfully performed in Germany, as were some of Hubert Parry's orchestral works. Joseph Parry's contribution was barely acknowledged in books on musical history and his music was rarely performed outside the Welsh communities, let alone penetrating continental Europe. As Cyril Jenkins wrote, 'He failed ... to stamp his personality on the music of the world'.[4]

A number of factors contributed to Parry's failure on the international stage but an important one was his lack of self-criticism. As his former pupil David Jenkins wrote, 'once he had put his thoughts on paper, that's how they were going to be, and this proved damaging to many really excellent pieces he had composed'.[5] And one of his contemporaries, Alaw Ddu (W. T. Rees), added this blunt observation, 'If he had composed less, he would have achieved more.' After finishing a piece, he would not weigh up its value in musical terms. There are remarkable musical touches in his compositions but he didn't go to the trouble of recognising, pruning and developing them. If he had realised what it was that gave a special character to his style, and had used it more consistently, his music would have been more personal and individual.

One of the consequences of Parry's lack of self-criticism is that his style is eclectic; he was too ready to let the style of the masters influence his own style and could not withstand the influence of whoever was his musical idol at the time. Handel, Rossini, Mendelssohn, Verdi and Wagner each in their turn left their mark on his work. There is no evidence that he set out deliberately to copy them. He had an exceptional musical memory; indeed, Daniel Protheroe believed this was at times a disadvantage because Parry would think he had composed something original when he had, in fact, re-created music from his own work or from someone else's. When studying counterpoint with John Abel Jones in Danville, the young Joseph Parry used a tune by Cherubini as a subject for a fugue, thinking that the tune was his own. Only when his teacher proved that he was wrong did Parry remember singing, as a boy, the alto part in the Cherubini. On the manuscript[6] of 'Yr Ystorm ar Fôr Tiberias' is written: 'Copied June 1867, from memory'. There is a similar observation dated 1882 on the manuscript of 'Y Milwr'[7] – thirteen years after he composed the song in 1869.

Parry would also quote from his own music, although it is clear that this was usually unintentional and there was usually no musical reason for his doing so. Examples 4A and 4B show him doing this early in his composing career and other examples can be found throughout his creative life.

Musical Example 4a
'Y Chwaon Iach'

Musical Example 4b
'Myfanwy'

Parry quoting (probably unintentionally) from an earlier work

The most notable consequence of all this is stylistic inconsistency. Even in the more mature music of his late period there is no consistency in his output from the standpoint of originality or quality. This becomes obvious when we look in more detail at the development of his musical language.

A substantial number of manuscripts from the period in Danville and London (1854–71) have been lost, especially those from Danville, but over a hundred have survived.

Parry was learning his trade during this period: the basics of music and composing technique with John Abel Jones and John M. Price in Danville, from 1858 to 1868, and then composition with Sterndale Bennett at the Academy from 1868 to 1871, the latter having a particular influence on his style.

Among the earliest of the pieces to survive is the anthem 'O, Give Thanks unto the Lord' (*c.* 1860). The work ends with a typically Victorian chromatic cadence – the type of saccharine harmony that Parry never succeeded in avoiding.

One of the songs of this early period is 'The American Star' (1862), which was later reworked as 'Baner ein Gwlad' *(Our Country's Flag)*. This is in through-composed form[8] and is an early example of Parry's use of fast syncopated rhythms. In this case, the rhythm adds musical sprightliness to the spirit of the words, a characteristic not often to be found in the sacred music of the Welsh. Parry used rhythms like this consistently and they continue to be effective today.

The motet with which Parry was victorious at the National Eisteddfod in Swansea in 1863, 'Gostwng, O Arglwydd, dy Glust', was a great step forward; it is the only motet by him that has survived. It is a long piece and closes with a five-part choral fugue. The composer speaks in his autobiography of his 'close study in working out the Cherubini and Albrechtsberger contrapuntal and fugal exercises',[9] as well as of singing great choral works like *Messiah* as a child. The influence of Baroque counterpoint on Parry's motet is evident. But, unlike Handel's, his counterpoint is dull and academic. It goes on too long (over 120 bars), the writing for the voices is uninspired, and Parry seems unsure when to bring the piece to an end. However, the interweaving of the parts is inventive, there are sufficient changes of key, and it leads to a climax – the main subject of the fugue in octaves – then there is a slower, homophonic coda. The work was composed for a choir with two soprano parts, alto, tenor and bass, and we can find other examples of unusual combinations in Parry's early works, for example 'Y Chwaon Iach' (alto, tenor, baritone, bass), 'Sleep, Lady, Sleep' (alto, tenor, bass), and the middle part of 'Mor Hawddgar yw dy Bebyll' *(How Beautiful are Thy Dwellings)* (alto, tenor, baritone). Like 'Gostwng, O Arglwydd, dy Glust', the epilogue of 'Mor Hawddgar yw dy Bebyll' is contrapuntal, but it is much more concise and the writing for the individual parts is more interesting.

One of Parry's early favourites as a singer was 'O give me back my childhood dreams'. The solo is in simple strophic form and, although full of imploring musical sentimentality, it has a beautiful melody that raises it to a higher level than the composer's other songs of the same period. Another favourite with audiences of the period was 'Hoff Wlad fy Ngenedigaeth'. Although it is a typical Victorian parlour song, there are some beautiful touches in it but, unfortunately, the effective harmony he uses here is rare in Parry's early work.

During his first term at the Royal Academy, Parry concentrated on instrumental music. He had produced a little organ music in Danville, and in London Sterndale Bennett seemed to want him to forget about voices for a while and to concentrate on composing for instruments. The piano pieces from this period are heavy with classical influence, especially from the standpoint of form, for example 'Rondo' (1868) and the three sonatas. The harmony belongs more to the Romantic period, and the melodies often remind the ear of Mozart or Beethoven, see for example the start of the 'Adagio Cantabile' (1868) (Example 5).

Musical Example 5

*The opening of Parry's Adagio cantabile, later used as the slow movement
of his Piano Sonata No.1, in C minor*

In 1869, Joseph Parry composed a string quartet. Again, the
form is a classical pastiche, but with an unconvincing fugue
as the finale. The counterpoint suffers from the same
weaknesses as the choral fugues at the end of the anthems
from the early period in Danville, that is, the writing is
academic and uninteresting.

'Gwraig y Meddwyn' was composed around 1867, on
lyrics by Ceiriog, and is on a larger scale than Parry's
previous songs; it ventures to remote keys, for example G
flat, and the accompaniment is more important. There is
also more variety between piano and voice, but only
occasionally is there any form of dialogue between the voice
and the piano.

Vocally, one of the popular pieces of the period was the
anthem 'Yr Arglwydd yw fy Mugail', which was said by
David Jenkins in 1903 to be 'so brilliant that no composer,
English, foreign or Welsh, could succeed in doing so well.'[10]
Thirty years before this it was said that the piece was:

> from the point of view of style and form, one of the
> best examples of an anthem in the Welsh language. It
> could be argued against it that its style is not *Welsh* ...
> The truth is that even now [1871] no Welsh style has
> been formed, except in our old songs ... [11]

The anthem is comparatively simple from the point of view of form (ABA) and style (largely homophonic) but there are some fine dramatic touches, and syncopation is used effectively.

One of the best of Parry's early pieces is 'Cantata y Plant' *(The Children's Cantata)* (1871). Certainly, it is attractive and effective, and it has lost none of its original sprightliness even today. The composer kept the style deliberately 'simple' because the work was intended for the Sunday School, and especially children, and it can be considered as a piece that exemplifies fittingly Joseph Parry's early music. 'Cân y Robin Goch' *(The Song of Robin Redbreast)* is still as lovely as ever.

The years after his return to Danville were comparatively barren from the point of view of composition. The Danville Musical Institute and extensive concerts filled Parry's time, and he said that this was the least productive period of his career. One of the few pieces he composed in Danville during this period was 'Lady Mine!' *(c.* 1873), a simple song with a good tune, without too much sentimentality, despite the nature of the words.

A year later, in Aberystwyth, Parry composed 'Cytgan y Morwyr' *(The Sailors' Chorus)*, a piece that made a deep impression right across Wales. It is unaccompanied and lasts only a few minutes. Written in a hornpipe style, its nautical spirit is dramatic. Its texture is homophonic with modal touches, the flattened leading note (F) contrasting effectively with the sharpened leading note (F sharp) of the key of G minor.

The most brilliant of Parry's pupils in Aberystwyth, David Jenkins, in paying homage to his former teacher, said 'Cytgan y Morwyr' was 'the first indication in his work of a movement towards the Italian school'.[12] This tendency would be heard more clearly in *Blodwen*: it is Italian both in form – recitative, aria, duet, chorus, and so on – and in harmony: much use is made, for example, of the dominant 13th as the penultimate chord of a cadence, *à la* Verdi. The singable melodies reminded Daniel Protheroe of Verdi's *Il Trovatore*, but sometimes echoes of Rossini can also be heard, as for example in the repetition and build-up of a phrase.

However, *Blodwen* contains fewer eclectic elements. The duet 'Hywel and Blodwen' remains an operatic gem, full of life and musical invention. The remarkable popularity of the duet, after a century and more, bears witness to this. In general, however, it is the choral parts of the opera that are the most effective, and although the 'Cytgan y Briodas' *(The Wedding Chorus)* is nothing but a pastiche of Johann Strauss, it demonstrates the same sort of technical assurance as is seen in the more original and dramatic choral parts of the work, for example the end of Act 1, where the Welsh (the chorus) demand that the foreigners from England return their king. Jerky, syncopated rhythms push the music forward to a climax that compares well with the final act of plenty of foreign operas. The finale to Act 3 is not as good. Parry decided on a choral fugue and, despite the skill with which he combines this in counterpoint with 'Gwŷr Harlech', the music suffers from the same weakness as the final sections of the anthems he wrote in the 1860s, that is, uninteresting writing and lack of musical depth.

Another great work of the period is the oratorio *Emmanuel*, which depends heavily on the popular oratorios of the period, such as Mendelssohn's *Elijah* and *The Hymn of Praise*, for its form and general style, and Handel for its counterpoint. But the hand of the master is evident in *Emmanuel*, especially in the handling of complex textures such as double chorus, choral fugue and so on, where he uses Welsh hymn tunes, 'Bangor', for example, in place of the chorales of Baroque oratorios.

On arriving in Swansea, Parry completed the cantata *Nebuchadnezzar*, which can be regarded as the first work of his final period. From the point of view of form, it is less dependent on Italian 'numbers' (for example, recitatives and arias) than *Emmanuel*, and is a more accomplished and generally successful work. The spirit of the music matches the drama of the text, and Parry relies more on Wagnerian *Leitmotifs* for the musical unity of the work. Romantic chromatic harmony is used to depict the king's dream at the start of Part II, and the work comes to an end with the expected counterpoint but with homophonic choral passages between the polyphonic sections. As a result, the counterpoint is not as laboured and directionless, and *Nebuchadnezzar* comes to an effective and dramatic end.

Parry was never adventurous when it came to modulation, but in the music of this period we see signs of a willingness to experiment. 'Cymru Fydd' (*c*.1887), for example, changes from the tonic E major, through G major and E minor before finishing in the dominant, B major.

One of the best small-scale pieces of this period is 'Cytgan y Pererinion' (1886), for male voice choir and baritone solo with piano and harmonium accompaniment. In four sections, the work depicts the feelings of a band of pilgrims on their way to the Cross, at the Cross, and on their return.

The dramatic opening section, setting the scene for the work, is in the minor and based on a pulsating rhythm; it comes to a climax as the pilgrims approach the Cross. The second section, 'At the Foot of the Cross', is a prayer for salvation and forgiveness, with the baritone soloist and the choir singing alternately. This is followed by a hymn of rejoicing as the pilgrims rise at the Cross. In this hymn Parry exploits his favourite quaver-crotchet-quaver syncopated rhythm to fine dramatic effect. The final section is more contemplative; it begins with a declamatory passage sung by the soloist expressing confidence in the heavenly life to come, answered by the full choir and accompaniment, leading to a rousing climax in F major, the predominant key of the work.

'Cytgan y Pererinion' has rich and beautiful melodies, varied textures, interesting writing for voices, dramatic picture painting through the use of syncopation and unusual rhythms, chromatic harmonies, and unexpected modulations. The accompaniment is interesting in that it is for piano and harmonium; the two instruments are not alternatives – they are used in contrasting ways and complement each other. Most importantly, the work sounds uneclectic.

Parry was regularly successful when writing for male voices and when setting sacred texts, so that it is not surprising this piece became, and remained, a favourite with male voice choirs into the second half of the twentieth century. It is one of his best and most original works. This is not Parry imitating Mendelssohn or Rossini or Sterndale Bennett, but Parry writing music through which his own distinctive voice sounds. The work was unusual among Parry's compositions in achieving some recognition outside Welsh and Welsh-American circles. It was performed at the World's Fair of 1893 in Chicago, before Queen Victoria in Windsor Castle, in a Tonic Sol-fa Society concert in London, and in the Paris Exhibition, when the composer Saint-Saëns was in the audience. It deserves to be heard more often today.

The songs of Parry's late period continue, on the whole, to be in the manner of the Victorian 'parlour song', especially in their harmony. Original touches can be found but, in general, the musical content of the songs is weak, for example 'Suo-gân' *(Cradle Song)* (1893), where it is difficult to understand how the composer – or, for that matter, the publisher – could be satisfied with a piano introduction that quotes the beginning of 'Hen Wlad fy Nhadau' along with a tune (bars 8–12) that is similar to 'In Dublin's Fair City'. 'Hen Wlad fy Nhadau' is also quoted in the song 'Llywelyn Ein Llyw Olaf' *(Llywelyn, Our Last Prince)* but there the quotation is clearly intended to summon up national emotion; there is no such reason in the case of 'Suo-Gân'.

'Iesu o Nazareth' *(Jesus of Nazareth)* is a worthy successor to all the pieces that Parry had composed for male voices in the quarter of a century since 'Cytgan y Morwyr'. The work was written as a test piece for the Cardiff National Eisteddfod in 1899. The words were written by Elfed (Rev H Elvet Lewis), with whom Parry had collaborated on a number of occasions. It is written for male voice choir with organ and piano accompaniment, with a bass soloist singing the part of the Narrator. It is divided into three sections: 'Bethlehem (Christmas)', 'His Life' and 'Calvary', of which the last is much the longest. It is a substantial and difficult work, lasting some twenty minutes, and demands considerable musical ability to be performed successfully.

The work starts with the Narrator briefly setting the scene. There follows a remarkable passage in which the tenors and basses are each split into three parts, singing *pianissimo* and wordlessly as a chorus of angels, with the first tenors called on to sing a high chromatic falsetto line. After an interlude in which the choir sings as a chorus of shepherds, the chorus of angels returns to conclude the first section. Through much of this section, the Narrator's recitatives are intertwined with the singing of the chorus.

The second section does not try to recount the events of Jesus' life but, rather, to describe its essential qualities. It is a march for choir and organ and is linked to the finale by a bass recitative. The finale is a dramatic account of the events leading from Gethsemane, through Christ's scourging, up to the freeing of Barabas and the devils rejoicing in hell at the crucifixion; it contains some of the finest music that Parry ever wrote. The opening music returns and leads into a chorus of joyful hosannas celebrating the resurrection.

The work is one of Parry's best and achieved great popularity in Wales, with the final chorus becoming particularly well known. However, unlike 'Cytgan y Pererinion', for all its success in Wales, it was scarcely heard outside the country.

Also written in 1898 was Parry's fine setting for male voices of Edgar Allan Poe's poem 'Annabel Lee', composed for the Rhondda Glee Society. This was conducted by Parry's friend Tom Stephens who had won the first prize in the Cymmrodorion Society of America's Eisteddfod at the 1893 Chicago World's Fair, singing Parry's 'Cytgan y Pererinion'. The subject of Poe's poem is thought to be his wife (and cousin) Virginia, whom he married when she was thirteen and who died of consumption at the age of twenty-four, to Poe's great distress. The theme of the poem, the death of a beautiful woman, was a favourite of Poe's and common in that period. While the poem may not be to modern taste, it is a fine one. Parry's choice of male voices is appropriate and the setting is sensitive; he avoids the sentimentalism into which he was too often inclined to fall.

Parry's oratorios and cantatas, although usually religious in character, were intended for public performance in any suitable location and on any appropriate occasion. While they might be more readily appreciated by believers than by non-believers, it is most unlikely that Parry wrote them primarily with believers in mind; rather, he wrote them to give the Welsh nation suitable music to sing. Throughout his life, however, Parry was a devout member of the Congregationalist church. He had strong views on the place of music in worship and he wrote a significant body of music for use on religious occasions – church services and *cymanfaoedd canu*. These hymn tunes, anthems and chants were specifically intended for believers; not, to be sure, just Congregationalists but certainly all Nonconformists and, if he thought about it at all, Anglicans as well.

In his article in the *Cardiff Times and South Wales Weekly News* of 15 October 1887, number 19 in the series, Parry argues strongly for recognising and accepting the way in which music is used within the sanctuary in other countries, including England, and strongly rejects the idea that instrumental music should not be used for religious purposes. It may seem odd to us today that he should feel a need to make this argument. However, music in Welsh Nonconformist chapels was traditionally limited to the unaccompanied singing of hymns, in three parts, by the congregation under the leadership of the *codwr canu*. Four-part singing, the use of the harmonium and, later, the organ, anthems sung by a choir – or even by the congregation as a whole – and the chanting of psalms were all at times disapproved of by ministers and deacons.

Despite Parry's advocacy, neither the chanting of psalms nor the use of a choir was ever to become common in Welsh Nonconformist chapels. Nevertheless, the *Llyfr Emynau a Thonau y Methodistiaid Calfinaidd a Wesleaidd* ('Hymn and Tune Book of the Calvinistic and Wesleyan Methodists') published in 1929 contained forty-two anthems, including one by Parry, as well as settings of the canticles and over 100 chants.

Writing good hymn tunes requires special skills. Some composers have written excellent hymn tunes but nothing else worthy of mention, while some fine composers have tried, and failed.

Hymn tunes were important to Parry. The first of his

compositions that survives is the hymn tune with which he won first prize at the Fairhaven (Vermont) Christmas Eisteddfod in 1860, and he went on to write some 500 tunes – estimates vary. This was hymn tune writing on a heroic scale. Not even John Bacchus Dykes (1823–1876), the most prolific of nineteenth-century Anglican hymn-tune writers, managed more than 300, albeit in a life some nine years shorter. Inevitably, many of the tunes written by both are deservedly forgotten and one could wish that they had been more self-critical. Nevertheless, Parry, like Dykes, wrote a number of fine tunes that remained popular right through the twentieth century and are still widely sung today. *Caneuon Ffydd* ('Songs of Faith'), the book of hymns in Welsh published in 2001 and edited by a committee drawn from all the major Protestant denominations in Wales, includes eleven tunes by Parry – the only composer with more original tunes (as opposed to arrangements) in the book is J. Ambrose Lloyd, while there are ten of J. B. Dykes' tunes.

The unnamed tune with which he won first prize at the Fairhaven Eisteddfod (Example 1) is harmonically complex – the chromaticism is unusual and unexpected in a traditional hymn tune and suggests a bright, albeit inexperienced, student. It is clear that, if this tune won first prize, the competition was limited. However, given the extent of Parry's musical education and experience, it is not a bad piece of work. In particular, he succeeds in making all four vocal lines interesting.

In 1859, Ieuan Gwyllt published a collection of hymn tunes entitled *Llyfr Tonau Cynulleidfaol* ('A Book of Congregational Tunes'). Ieuan Gwyllt had a sophisticated if somewhat austere musical taste – at least until his last years when his religious enthusiasm, fired by the 1874 Sankey and Moody crusade, overcame his musical scruples and caused him to espouse Sankey's music. In *Llyfr Tonau Cynulleidfaol*, he sought to wean Welsh congregations away from the meretricious music that was then widely used in services, by making more suitable music readily available. The book was an instant success and some 30,000 copies were sold in the first three years after publication. An appendix was produced in 1870 and Parry was invited to contribute a tune. The result was *Llangristiolus*, the first of Parry's hymn tunes to be published in a major collection. According to Huw Williams,[13] it was written in a garden at Llangristiolus on 29 August 1869: that is, just before Parry started at the Royal Academy, and it shows how far his style had developed from the time of his success at the Fairhaven Eisteddfod. The melody, the part-writing and the harmony are satisfying without being memorable. What is remarkable about it is its competence, but apart from the use of the minor key – much less common in English hymn tunes than in Welsh ones – there is nothing here, good or bad, that could not have been written by J. B. Dykes or S. S. Wesley.

The most widely known of Parry's tunes is 'Aberystwyth'. In the English-speaking world Charles Wesley's fine hymn 'Jesu, lover of my soul' is now almost invariably sung to this tune, rather than to Dykes' tune 'Hollingside', which was once preferred. While Parry dated many of his hymn tunes, we do not have an accurate date for 'Aberystwyth' but it is clear that it was written during his time as Professor of Music in Aberystwyth. It was first published in 1879 in Stephen & Jones' collection *Ail Lyfr Tonau ac Emynau* ('Second Book of Tunes and Hymns'), where the words 'Beth sydd imi yn y byd?' (*What is there for me in the world?*), by Morgan Rhys (1716–79) are set to it. Percy Young, a distinguished and discriminating critic, wrote of it and of Parry 'As, however, the last named ['Aberystwyth'] is the noblest work of its kind composed by a British musician, Parry achieved more than many whose reputations were, and sometimes are, said to stand higher.'[14]

In the second half of the 1880s, Parry resolved to produce a book of his own hymn tunes. It was to be printed as a series of six parts, each containing some eighteen tunes, each with one or more possible sets of words, and one or two chants or congregational anthems. It was (and is) common practice for each denomination to produce each year a separate booklet (usually known as a *detholiad* or selection) of the hymns to be sung at all its *cymanfaoedd canu* in a district. Most, if not, all of the tunes in the booklet would be sung at each *cymanfa*. Each part of Parry's hymn book was just the right size to be used as such a detholiad and there is at least one recorded instance of this being done. Since the sections were sold at one shilling for versions in staff notation and sixpence for the sol-fa version (equivalent to £24 or £12 respectively in 2005), the profit to Parry, who sold them direct, was considerable.

The first part appeared under the title *Llyfr Tonau Genedlaethol* [*sic*] *Cymreig gan Dr. Parry* ('A Book of Welsh National Tunes by Dr. Parry'), and is shown as published by D. M. Parry (i.e. his son, Mendy), 23 Plymouth Road, Penarth. The title page of the second part describes it as *Llyfr Tonau Cynulleidfaol Cenedlaethol Cymru (fel cydymaith i lyfr emynau cenedlaethol Mr Gee) gan Dr. Joseph Parry, Coleg Cerddorol Cymru, Abertawe* ('A Book of National Congregational Tunes of Wales (as a companion to the book of national hymns by Mr Gee) by Dr Joseph Parry, Music College of Wales, Swansea'). It is stated that the booklet is available from all booksellers and from J. Parry and Son, Blodwen House, Swansea. Both parts are undated, although the date of composition of each tune is shown. It seems clear that Part 2 must have been published – or, at least, printed – before Part 1. Both parts, however, were presumably published around the time, in 1887, that Parry moved from Swansea to Cardiff and this is consistent with the dates on the tunes themselves. Most of the tunes in Part 1 dated from the first half of the 1880s but there are two from 1887; most of the tunes in Part 2 date from 1887 but a few are earlier, including one from 1873.

According to David Jenkins,[15] Parry wrote 'far too many' hymn tunes and at one stage in Swansea was writing a tune every Sunday. Given this, and his habitual lack of self-criticism, one would expect the tunes in these booklets to be little more than routine exercises. This is far from being the case. Two of the tunes, 'Dinbych' in Part 1 and 'Sirioldeb' in Part 2, are among Parry's finest.

'Dinbych' is dated 22 May 1881. John Wesley's fine translation of Paul Gerhardt's 1656 hymn 'Befiehl du, deine Wege' (*Commit thou all thy griefs*), one of the great hymns of Lutheranism, was set to a modified version of this tune in *Songs of Praise*, a collection of hymns and canticles intended for the use of schools, particularly public schools; the book was strongly Anglican in tone and set high musical standards. The same modified version was also selected for inclusion in *The Methodist Hymn-Book* of 1933, where Charles Wesley's hymn of death and judgement, 'Thou judge of quick and dead' is set to it. 'Dinbych' is perhaps the closest that Parry (or any other British composer) came to matching Bach's settings of German chorales. Another tune by Parry that has gained popularity in the Anglican church is the tune known, perversely, as 'Merthyr Tydfil' in England and 'Dies Irae' in Wales. 'Dinbych' and 'Merthyr Tydfil' are, like 'Aberystwyth', in minor keys, and have served to reinforce the stereotype of Welsh hymn tunes as being sombre tunes in the minor.

While the success of 'Dinbych' is attested by its popularity in the musically sophisticated, if somewhat austere, world of the Anglican church and English public school, the success of 'Sirioldeb' is largely confined to Wales, because its rhythms do not make it suitable for singing English words. The words usually sung to it, although not the ones in Parry's book, are by Eifion Wyn (Eliseus Williams, 1867–1926); the first verse runs as follows are:

> Un fendith dyro im,
> Ni cheisiaf ddim ond hynny,
> Cael gras i'th garu di tra fwy',
> Cael mwy o ras i'th garu.

> *One blessing bring to me.*
> *I look for nothing more than this;*
> *The grace to love thee while I live,*
> *And still more grace to love thee.*

The tune reflects the unstressed syllables at the end of the second and fourth lines of the Welsh by giving a full bar melisma to the stressed, penultimate syllable.

'Sirioldeb' is in A flat and the tunes in the hymn book contradict the general impression that all Parry's hymn tunes are in the minor; a good third of the tunes, including some of the best, are in the major. Number 22, 'Moliant' [Praise], for example, is a good tune in G major in the tradition of such fine eighteenth-century English tunes as 'St Stephen'.

A number of the tunes in the hymn book are derivative. Number 33, 'Llanelly', for example, bears a close resemblance to the tune 'Easter Morn' widely sung to the hymn 'Christ the Lord is risen today'; what is more, one of the two sets of words set to it is a translation into Welsh of the first verse of that hymn. This is not to suggest plagiarism

– the notes are different even if the rhythm is almost the same. A particularly amusing example of Parry unwittingly imitating himself is the tune 'Mynwy' (Monmouth), number 14. Although it is in the major, it bears a close resemblance to 'Aberystwyth', and a Welsh translation of 'Jesu, lover of my soul' is set to it.

To sum up, Parry was influenced by a variety of composers and his music suffers because of its eclecticism and lack of originality, which results from his lack of self-criticism. There are a few individual musical touches but 'His best compositions are not those that are most popular' as 'Asaph' wrote shortly after his death.[16] Parry had a longer composing career than Mendelssohn, Schumann and Sterndale Bennett – the three composers who most influenced his music – and Parry's technique improved as he got older but his style retained elements of inconsistency and too often harked back to his immature work. Nevertheless, he stands out as the most skilful and professional among the numerous Welsh composers of the period, who were less gifted and unsure in their musical technique, and as a writer of hymn tunes he can stand comparison with the best.

Today, the finest of Parry's music is no longer performed and so one cannot draw a complete and fair picture of the development of his musical style. It is only through the study and assessment of his work as a body that it is possible to evaluate his contribution to the music of Wales and of the world.

Notes Chapter 10

[1] *Y Faner,* 12 September 1901, p. 7.

[2] *A History of Music in England,* p. 260.

[3] Sunday Schools in Wales catered as much for adults as for children. They were an important means of sustaining the Welsh language and of spreading adult literacy.

[4] Cyril Jenkins in *The Sackbut,* November 1921, p. 21.

[5] *Y Cerddor,* November 1913, p. 118.

[6] NLW 19821E.

[7] NLW 19822E.

[8] That is, the music is different for each verse of the text. In contrast, in *strophic* songs the music is the same for each verse, as with a hymn.

[9] Joseph Parry, p. 24.

[10] *Y Cerddor,* 2 March 1903, p. 28.

[11] *Y Cerddor Cymreig,* 1 November 1871, pp. 82–84.

[12] *Y Cerddor,* 2 March 1903, p. 28.

[13] *Tonau a'u Hawduron* (Llyfrfa'r M.C., Caernarfon, 1967).

[14] *A History of British Music,* p. 492.

[15] *Y Cerddor,* February, 1914, p. 11.

[16] *Y Faner,* 25 February 1903, p. 11.

11

Epilogue

The latter half of the nineteenth century, and particularly its last thirty years, saw an astonishing growth in musical activity in Wales. With the benefit of over a century of hindsight, we can see that Joseph Parry was a key figure in this development. On the one hand, through his compositions, his teaching and journalism, his conducting and his adjudication, he contributed to, and stimulated, the musical life of Wales and influenced the direction in which it developed. On the other hand, the increasing number of people who were seriously interested in music created a demand for his services and a market for his compositions. The articles that he wrote for the *Cardiff Times and South Wales Weekly News* and later for the *Western Mail* would never have been published if the editors had not known that a significant proportion of their readership would want to read about the topics discussed, but they gave him the opportunity to put forward ideas in which he believed passionately.

It was for economic and demographic reasons that Cardiff became the centre of musical activity in Wales. As its commercial importance grew, so did its population – from 26,630 in 1851 to 172,629 in 1901 – an astonishing increase. Cardiff's growing role as an administrative and commercial centre meant a burgeoning of the professional classes, the people who traditionally had a taste for music and the arts, as well as the leisure and money to indulge that taste.

While much of the increase in musical activity was in the field of choral singing – where it was boosted by the competitive element – there was an increasing interest in instrumental music, something that Parry had long advocated. From the late 1880s onwards, the concerts of the Cardiff Orchestral Society, the inauguration of the Cardiff Triennial Festival, the regular concerts of chamber music and the visits of English opera companies brought a new variety to Welsh musical life. Furthermore, much of the music was either new or little known. The first Cardiff Festival in 1892 included performances of Berlioz' *Faust*, Dvořák's *Stabat Mater* (composed in 1876) and Hubert Parry's *Blest Pair of Sirens* (composed in 1887). In the following year, Joseph Parry was writing in the *Western Mail* about a forthcoming visit of the Rousbey Opera Company, which would be performing among other works *Cavalleria Rusticana* (premiered in 1890) and *I Pagliacci* (premiered in 1892). He wrote a lengthy review of a chamber concert given by Joachim and a piano recital given by Paderewski, which included Schumann's *Etudes Symphoniques* and Beethoven's Sonata in F minor, op 2 no 3.

Allsobrook has argued[1] that the musical activity in Cardiff was not a reliable indicator of changes in the general musical life and taste of Wales, but that it simply reflected the civic ambition of the 'hard-headed coal plutocrats' of Cardiff. Leaving aside this highly debatable description of such men as the third Marquess of Bute, the argument misses the point. One might just as well say that the musical activity in present-day London is not a reliable indicator of the general musical life and taste of England. The sophisticated music-making of the metropolis is supported by the existence of a mass of music-lovers throughout the country and, at the same time, filters down to broaden the tastes of the country as a whole. Particular evidence of this is provided by the success of the Welsh National Opera Company's tour in 1890, which visited many of the smaller towns of south and mid-Wales, and was called on to revisit many of them because of the success of the first visit. *Blodwen* and *Arianwen* may not have been at the leading edge of international operatic development but, for audiences used only to oratorio and hymn tunes, they represented a significant broadening of taste, which helped create an audience for '*Cav* and *Pag*'.

It would be difficult to measure precisely how much of the growth in musical activity was due to Parry's influence. We do know, however, that it was consistent with what he had been advocating in public lectures and in his journalism since the late 1870s. He was involved in the planning of the first Cardiff Festival and of the chamber music concerts, and he used his journalism to promote them. He was a successful conductor of the Cardiff Orchestral Society until his grief over Willie's death led him to resign. And as the composer of *Blodwen* and *Arianwen*, he sparked the interest in opera.

As a composer, Parry gave the people of Wales music that they could sing and enjoy and which was much superior to what was being written by other composers in Wales. At his best – in *Joseph, Nebuchadnezzar, Cytgan y Pererinion, Iesu o Nazareth*, for example – he wrote music comparable to the best of what was being written in England at the time. He also had a gift for composing substantial and playable music for children, as, for example, the collection of simple piano pieces and attractive songs entitled 'Y Llyfr Canu' ('*The Song Book*') of 1894. Too often, however, he wrote in haste and, as has so often been pointed out, he did not attempt to review or revise his work. As his former pupil, David Jenkins, wrote shortly after his death:

he believed strongly that he could compose, and he has proved that he was right, and, if he had been taught to be strict and critical about his own compositions, there would be no composer in England today, except for Elgar, who would excel him.[2]

(To have picked out Elgar at this date shows that Jenkins had an up-to-date knowledge of what was going on in the English musical world, as well as having sound judgement.)

It was probably inevitable that Parry's music would decline in popularity after his death, but the most vitriolic condemnation of his music was to come from the Swansea-born musician Cyril Jenkins (1889–1978). Jenkins wrote an article for *The Sackbut* attacking Parry;[3] surprisingly, he was invited to contribute a chapter to *Cofiant Joseph Parry*. The following excerpt is a fair example of the tone of his criticism:

When I was asked to give my considered opinion on the music of Dr Joseph Parry and the influence that it, and the personality of its creator, had on the artistic life of Wales, I felt reluctant to do it. Indeed, I still feel reluctant because I know that what I have to say will hurt the feelings of many who respect his memory and who will consider my judgement of his music to be intentional sacrilege. Still, I feel that someone should say what needs to be said, as clearly and as publicly as possible ...

Let me say at once that Parry's music is, at its best, no more than second rate, and, at its worst, is beneath contempt. I don't know of a single page that shows any sign of creativity.[4]

Jenkins had the advantage of having studied under Stanford and Ravel and thought of himself as a serious composer. His music has, however, lasted even less well than Parry's. He is now remembered only in the world of brass band music, where a couple of his pieces are still used as set pieces in competitions.

It is doubtful whether Jenkins' criticism had much effect on Parry's reputation, in Wales or elsewhere, although it certainly damaged Jenkins' own standing in Wales. The irony is that, in the years after Parry's death, Jenkins did much to advance the cause of instrumental music in Wales, along the lines repeatedly advocated by Parry. He even succeeded in bringing the London Symphony Orchestra to Cardiff to give several series of orchestral concerts, including ones in which Elgar and Vaughan Williams conducted their own works.

David Morgans, writing in 1922, defended Parry the composer on social grounds:

> To judge a musician of a working-class family, born in 1841 ... with the standard of today, is an unworthy and unfair act, and inclines us to believe that the object of such criticism is to wound the Welsh National feeling.[5]

It is easy for modern readers, accustomed to the opportunities offered by widespread public education, to dismiss this as special pleading, but it should be borne in mind that none of the composers contemporary with Parry were from anything less than a literate *petit bourgeois* background (and, in most cases, came from musical families). Even Verdi, who is often said to have been born in humble circumstances, was the son of an innkeeper and grocer in one of the most prosperous and food-loving parts of the Italian peninsula – a far cry from being the son of an illiterate iron worker in Merthyr Tudful. Dvořak's father was a butcher, an inn-keeper – and a professional zither-player. Even in the twentieth century it is difficult to find an example of a composer born into such poor circumstances as Parry. Nevertheless, we may admire a composer's efforts and sympathise with his struggles without necessarily having a high opinion of his music – and we cannot judge his music unless we have the opportunity to hear it.

It is unusual to hear any music by Parry on radio or television or in concert, except for 'Aberystwyth' or 'Myfanwy', although one or two numbers from *Blodwen* are occasionally to be heard in local concerts and eisteddfodau. In this respect, Parry has suffered in the same way as many English composers whose works fell out of favour after the First World War because of changes in taste. Stainer, Hubert Parry, Granville Bantock, York Bowen, Walford Davies (a later holder of the Aberystwyth chair), and Stanford are all examples that come to mind. The majority of their work was forgotten, with only a few pieces, not generally their best, remaining in the repertoire. It is a cause for concern that the male voice choirs in Wales today seem to prefer easier and lighter music at the expense of challenging works such as 'Cytgan y Pererinion' or 'Iesu o Nazareth'. This situation has been slowly changing since the beginning of the 1990s; thanks largely to the efforts of small recording companies eager to find new repertoire, the major works of these composers are now readily available on CD. The Welsh record company Sain bought the rights to a recording of the 1978 BBC broadcast of *Blodwen* and this is now available as a two-CD set. Sain has also produced a CD recording of a number of Parry's works for male voices, including 'Cytgan y Pererinion', 'Cytgan y Morwyr' and 'Iesu o Nazareth', performed by the Pendyrus Male Voice Choir.

Parry's reputation probably reached its low point in the 1950s and 1960s. Since then, interest in his life and work has increased slowly but steadily. We have already mentioned the centenary performance of *Blodwen* and the subsequent release of a recording. The University of Wales, Aberystwyth (now Aberystwyth University) named a hall, used for chamber music concerts, after him, and a performance of his string quartet was given there. Civic recognition arrived in 1979, when, thanks to the efforts of Mansel Richards of Cyfarthfa School, Merthyr Tudful Borough Council decided to restore Chapel Row and establish a Joseph Parry museum in number 4. It has been successful in attracting thousands of visitors from all over the world. The television adaptation of *Off to Philadelphia in the Morning* stimulated further interest. On 27 October 1985, the National Welsh American Foundation unveiled a memorial plaque on Joseph Parry's old house at 18 Chamber Street, Danville, and there are exhibitions relating to his life in America in the town library and museum. The Aberystwyth Civic Society has placed plaques on the house in Aberystwyth in which Parry and his family lived and on the chapel (now converted into a doctors' practice) where the tune 'Aberystwyth' is said to have been sung for the first time. From 2009, the National Welsh American Foundation has given an annual bursary to the four music departments in higher education institutes in Wales, to be known as Gwobr Gerdd Joseph Parry Music Awards, to sponsor musical links between Wales and America. Popular interest in Parry, 'Myfanwy' and 'Aberystwyth' and *Off to Philadelphia in the Morning* continues: there are many references to him on the worldwide web, many of which, including some on the BBC web site, perpetuate myths and inaccuracies. Nevertheless, neither a museum nor an exhibition nor any number of tributes, in speech or writing, can solve the fundamental problem that his best music lies largely unperformed.

Joseph Parry was undoubtedly the leading Welsh musician in the second half of the nineteenth century. As a composer he was a key figure in the story of the development of Welsh music, and his music deserves to be heard and fairly judged by today's audiences. But he had an enormous influence on the music and musicians of his nation, through his vision as well as his musical output. Many of the things that he unsuccessfully campaigned for were to come about after his death. The report of the Haldane Commission's investigation into the condition of the University of Wales, published in 1917, took music very seriously and its main recommendation in this area was for the appointment of a Musical Director for the University, who would chair a Council of Music for Wales. Henry Walford Davies took up this post in 1919, along with the Chair of Music in Aberystwyth. With the moral and financial support of the Davies sisters of Gregynog, he did much to further the developments that Parry had urged. He appointed a piano trio to the Aberystwyth staff, and they gave lecture concerts throughout Wales, an initiative taken up shortly afterwards by Bangor and Cardiff; he organised and conducted performances by united choirs that involved no competitive element; a Welsh Symphony Orchestra was formed; and annual musical festivals were started in Aberystwyth, Newtown (*Drenewydd*) and Harlech. The period immediately after the Second World War saw the establishment of the Cardiff College of Music, which was to become the Royal Welsh College of Music and Drama, the National Youth Orchestra of Wales (the first national youth orchestra in the world), and the Welsh National Opera Company. Fifty years after Joseph Parry's death, more or less everything that he had campaigned for had come about.

Notes Chapter 11

[1] *Music for Wales*, p. 33.
[2] *Y Cerddor*, 2 March 1903, p. 28.
[3] November 1921, pp. 19–22.
[4] Joseph Parry, p. 239.
[5] *Music and Musicians of Merthyr and District*, p. 186.

Appendix A

Catalogue of the Works of Joseph Parry

[R] = Catalogue number in Dulais Rhys' catalogue
[T] = Title. Where the original is in Welsh, an English translation is given in brackets.
[O] = Opus number, etc ('1.1' = Opus 1 no 1, etc). Note that there is duplication reflecting different publishers.
[A] = Author of the text
[D] = Date composed

1. Opera

[R]	[T]	[O]	[A]	[D]
1.168a	Blodwen	31	Mynyddog	1876–7
1.216	Virginia	–	E. R. Jones	1883
1.247a	Bronwen[1]	–	?	[1880s?]
1.247b	Arianwen[2]	–	Dewi Môn	c. 1888
1.285	Sylvia	–	D. M. Parry	1891–5
1.315	Cap and Gown[3]	–	Ivor B. John	1897
1.336	King Arthur	–	Elfed	1896–9
1.350	His Worship the Mayor	–	Arthur Mee	1899–1900
1.353	Y Ferch o'r Scer (*The Maid of Sker*)	–	?	1900–1
1.356	The Maid of Cefn Ydfa	–	Joseph Bennett	1900–2

2. Oratorio

[R]	[T]	[O]	[A]	[D]
2.178b	Emmanuel[4]	36	G. Hiraethog	1869–78
2.178d	Jehovah[5]	–	G. Hiraethog	c. 1881
2.273	Saul of Tarsus	–	scriptural	1891
2.361	Jesus of Nazareth[6]	–	scriptural	1902

3. Cantatas

[R]	[T]	[A]	[D]
3.004	Psalm 57	scriptural	1862
3.046	Y Mab Afradlon (*The Prodigal Son*)	Eos Bradwen	1866
3.106	Cantata y Plant (*Children's Cantata*)	Thomas Levi	1871
3.178a	Jerusalem	G. Hiraethog	1878
3.199	Joseph	Thomas Levi	1880
3.203	Nebuchadnezzar	scriptural	1881
3.286	Moses Bach (*Baby Moses*)[7]	Dewi Medi	1895
3.287	Bethlehem[7]	Dewi Medi	1895
3.311	Cambria	O. M. Edwards	c. 1896
3.327	Iesu o Nazareth [2] (*Jesus of Nazareth*)[7]	Ebenezer Rees	1898
3.343	Ceridwen[8]	Dyfed	1899
3.345	Caradog (*Caractacus*)	D. Adams	1900

Uncertain: The Pioneers

4. Sacred Choral

[R]	[T]	[O]	[D]
4.001	O, Give Thanks unto the Lord	1.2	c. 1860
4.002	A Temperance Vocal March	–	c. 1860
4.018	Gostwng, O Arglwydd dy Glust (Incline, O Lord, thine Ear)[9]	3.2	c. 1863
4.019	Te Deum [1]	–	1863
4.020	Achub fi, O Dduw! (Save me, O God)	4.1	c. 1864
4.021	Clyw, O Dduw fy Llefain (Henr, O God, my Cry)	4.2	c. 1864
4.022	Nid i ni (Not to us)[10]	–	c. 1864
4.038	Mor Hawddgar yw dy Bebyll (How Beautiful are thy Dwellings)	9.1	1865
4.054	Jubilate Deo	–	1867
4.055	Te Deum [2]	7.1	1867
4.065	Duw bydd Drugarog wrthym ni (God be Merciful unto us)	9.3	1868
4.091	Gweddi yr Arglwydd (The Lord's Prayer)	9.2	1869
4.092	Yr Arglwydd yw fy Mugail (The Lord's my Shepherd)	9.4	1869
4.095	Anthem Angladdol (Funeral Anthem)	9.5	1870
4.101	Hosanna i Fab Dafydd (Hosanna to the Son of David)	9.6	1870
4.123	Cân y Dŵr (Song of the Water)	–	c. 1873
4.158	Moliant i'r Iesu (Praise to Jesus)	–	[1870s]
4.159	Pebyll yr Arglwydd (The Pavilions of the Lord)	18.6	c. 1875
4.160	Bydd Drugarog wrthym ni (Be Merciful unto us)	29.3	[1870s]
4.161	Bless the Lord	–	[1870s]
4.162	Arglwydd, Cofia fi (Lord, Remember me)	–	[1870s]
4.169	Mi a Godaf ac a Af at fy Nhad (I will Arise and Go to my Father)	30.3	1877
4.170	Ysbryd yw Duw (God is Spirit)	30.4	1877

4.171	Molwch yr Arglwydd (Praise the Lord)	—	[1877]
4.172	Requiem Gynulleidfaol (Congregational Requiem)[11]	—	[1877]
4.173	Wele rwyf yn Sefyll wrth y Drws ac yn Curo (Behold me Standing at the Door and Knocking)	30.2	1877
4.174	Behold the Lamb	—	1877
4.180	Yr Utgorn a Gân (The Trumpet shall Sound)	30.5	c. 1878
4.181	Y Salm Gyntaf (The First Psalm)	—	c. 1878
4.182	Deuwch ataf fi (Come unto me)	—	1878
4.183	Teilwng yw'r Oen (Worthy is the Lamb)	—	1879
4.184	Mola Dduw O fy Enaid (Praise God, O my Soul)	29	c. 1879
4.198	Ar Lan Iorddonen Ddofn (On the Bank of the Jordan Deep)	30.1	c. 1880
4.204	Gwyn fyd Preswylwyr dy Dŷ (Blessed are they that Dwell in Thy House)	—	c. 1881
4.223	Toriad Dydd ar Gymru (Daybreak over Wales)	—	[1885]
4.250	Cofia yn awr dy Greawdwr (Remember now thy Creator)	—	1888
4.252	Te Deum [3]	—	1888
4.256	Sanctaidd! Sanctaidd! (Holy! Holy!)	—	1889
4.257	Am fod fy Iesu'n Fyw (Because my Jesus Lives)	—	1889
4.265	Bur Wreichionen (Vital Spark)	—	1891
4.312	In Memoriam	—	1896

Uncertain:

Elegie
Glory to God
Molwch (Praise Ye)
O! Come let us Sing
O! Give Thanks [2]
O! Lord God of Hosts

Oh, Mighty Father
Praise to the Lord
Praise Waiteth for Thee
The Rescue
Teyrnasa (He Reigns)
We will Rejoice

5. Secular Choral

[R]	[T]	[O]	[A]	[D]
5.005	Goodnight	1.1	?	c. 1862
5.014a	Gwŷr Harlech (*Men of Harlech*)[12]	12.2	?	1863
5.015	Ffarwel i ti, Gymru Fad (*Farewell to thee, Fair Wales*)	20	Ceiriog	c. 1863
5.023	Rhuo mae'r Môr (*The sea is Roaring*)	–	?	1864
5.024a	Heddwch (*Peace*)[13]	–	?	1864
5.025	Y Chwaon Iach (*Wholesome Breezes*) [1]	–	?	c. 1864
5.033	Patrons of Apollo's Lyre	–	?	1865
5.034	Merrily Chants the Soaring Lark	–	?	c. 1865
5.035	Ar Don o flaen Gwyntoedd (*On a Wave in the face of the Winds*) [1]	4.2	T. Levi	c. 1865
5.036	Ar Don o flaen Gwyntoedd (*On a Wave in the face of the Winds*) [2]	4.1	?	c. 1865
5.037	Y Cychod ar yr Afon (*The Boats on the River*)	–	?	c. 1865
5.052	Richmond	–	J. Harris	1866
5.056	Rhosyn yr Haf (*Rose of Summer*)	5.1	Ceiriog[14]	1867
5.084	Gweddi Gwraig y Meddwyn (*The Prayer of the Drunkard's Wife*)	8.2	T. Levi	1869
5.125	Sleep my Darling	–	?	1873
5.126	Sleighing Glee	20.6	Cynonfardd	c. 1873
5.163	Cytgan y Bradwyr (*Traitors' Chorus*)	20	Llew Llwyfo	c. 1875
5.164	Yr Ystorm (*The Storm*)	23.2	Hwfa Môn	c. 1875
5.175	Hiraethgan (*Song of Longing*)[15]	30.6	Hiraethog	[1877]

5.190	Rhyfelgan Gorawl (Choral War Song)	–	Granville-fab	[1879]
5.191	Molawd i'r Haul (Praise to the Sun)	–	Glan Padarn	[1879]
5.208	Â Chalon Lon (With Cheerful Heart)	–	T. Rees	[1881]
5.209	Hoff Dywysog Cymru Gu (Dear Prince of our Fair Wales)	–	T. Rees	[1881]
5.213	Hen Glychau'r Llan (The Old Church Bells)[16]	–	T. Rees	c. 1882
5.220	The Shepherds and the Fairies	–	J. Parry	1883
5.235	Yr Afon Fach (The Little River)	–	M. Emlyn	1886
5.255	Carmen Seculare	–	?	1889
5.266	A Dream	–	?	1891
5.283	A Monologue[17]	–	?	1894
5.330	Cytgan yr Orsedd a'r Cadeirio (Chorus of the Gorsedd and the Chairing)	–	Dyfed[18]	c. 1898
5.348	Degree Odes	–	Various[19]	1900
5.358	Life	–	?	1902

Uncertain:

Afloat on the Ocean	Greeting
Bessie's Grave	Haste we
Cartref y Cedyrn (Home of the Strong)	How Beautiful is the Night
Choral Fantasia	I will Call
Dismission	Pumlumon (Plynlymon)
Few and Precious	Through the Storm

6. Male Voice Choir

[R]	[T]	[O]	[A]	[D]
6.006	Cupid's Darts	–	?	[1862]
6.016	Man as a Flower	–	?	c. 1863
6.017	Rhowch i mi fy Nghleddyf (*Give me my Sword*)	–	?	c. 1863
6.129	Cytgan y Morwyr (*Sailors' Chorus*)	20	Mynyddog	c. 1874
6.149	Myfanwy [1]	4.3	Mynyddog	c. 1875
6.150	Rhyfelgan y Myncod (*War Song of the Monks*) [20]	24	Llew Llwyfo	c. 1875
6.189	Nosgan (*Serenade*)	32.1	Gutyn Arfon	c. 1879
6.206	The Village Blacksmith [3]	–	Longfellow	c. 1881
6.207	Yr un Hen Stori (*The same Old Story*)	–	I. Glan Dwyryd	1881
6.214	Cwch-Gân (*Boat Song*)	–	?	c. 1883
6.232	Cytgan y Pererinion (*Pilgrims' Chorus*)	–	D. Adams	c. 1886
6.233	Dwynwen	–	Gwynionydd	1886
6.238	Arianwen [2]	–	R. Williams	1886
6.243	Y Derwyddon (*The Druids*)	–	Alavon	1887
6.262	I Arise from Dreams of thee	–	Shelley	1890
6.264	The Village Sexton	–	?	1891
6.267	My Love, Good Morrow	–	Heywood	1891
6.274	Cymru Fydd (*Wales of the Future*) [2]	–	Dewi Môn	c. 1893
6.288	Suo-gân (*Lullaby*) [2]	–	?	[1890s]
6.289	Gwen	–	?	[1890s]
6.320	Iesu o Nazareth (*Jesus of Nazareth*) [1]	–	Elfed	1898
6.321	Belshazzar	–	?	1898

6.322	Annabel Lee	–	–	Edgar A. Poe	c. 1898
6.346	A Fantasia of Welsh Airs	–	–	Watcyn Wyn	c. 1900
6.347	Fel Gwannaidd Blentyn (*Like a Sickly Child*)	–	–	?	1900

Uncertain: Home Love
Life as a Flower   My Lassie

7. Vocal Quartet

[R] . [T]	[O]	[A]	[D]
7.024b	Peace Troubled Soul[21]	7.2	?	[1860s]
7.047	Be Merciful unto me	–	scriptural	1866
7.108	O na bawn eto'n Blentyn Rhydd (*O that I were a Carefree Child Again*)	12.1	Ceiriog	c. 1871
7.121	Oh! Lord Abide with me	16.1	H. F. Lyte	c. 1873
7.127	The Bells	–	J. Whyte	1874
7.128	Evan Benwan (*Silly Evan*)	20.4	Ceiriog	[1870s]
7.130	Ti Wyddost beth Ddywed fy Nghalon (*Thou Knowest what my Heart is Saying*)	–	Ceiriog	[1870s]
7.131	O Aros gyda mi (*O Stay with me*)	–	?	[1870s]
7.148	Mi Welaf mewn Atgof (*I See in Memory*)	20.3	Ceiriog	c. 1875
7.168b	O had I, my Saviour, the Wings of a Dove[22]	–	?	[1870s]
7.339	Come unto me	–	W. C. Dix	1899
7.340	Lead, Kindly Light	–	J. Newman	1899
7.341	Yn y Llwch, Waredwr Hael (*In the Dust, O Gentle Saviour*)	–	[hymn?]	1899

8. Vocal Trio

[R]	[T]	[O]	[A]	[D]
8.026	Sleep, Lady, Sleep	8.3	J. M. Price[23]	1864
8.057	O na bawn yn Seren (*Would that I were a Star*)	–	Ceiriog	c. 1867
8.079	Come Fairies Tribute	–	?	c. 1869
8.132	Fy Angel Bach (*My Little Angel*)	–	Glan Alun	c. 1874
8.133	Y Tri Aderyn Mwyn (*The Three Gentle Birds*)	–	?	[1870s]
8.197	The Village Blacksmith [2]	–	Longfellow	1880
8.275	Heddiw (*Today*)	–	J. M. Jones	1893
8.276	Y Llong King William (*The Ship King William*)	–	Eben Fardd	1893
8.277	Hoff Wlad (*Dear Country*)	–	J. M. Jones	1893
8.290	The Three Singers	–	?	[1890s]
8.337	Sleep Little Baby	–	?	1899
8.354	Faith, Hope and Charity	–	?	1902

Uncertain:	Hear our Prayer	The Music Lesson
	Home	Political Catch

9. Vocal Duet

[R]	[T]	[O]	[A]	[D]
9.039	O! Mor Hardd (*Oh! How Beautiful*)	18	Mynyddog	1865
9.134	Y Ddau Forwr (*The Two Sailors*)	21.1	Cynonfardd	c. 1874
9.176	Yr Heulwen Glir (*The Bright Sunshine*)	33.2	T. E. Griffith	1877
9.177	Yr Hen Deimladau Cynnes (*The Old Warm Feelings*)	–	?	c. 1876
9.236	Y Ddau Wladgarwr (*The Two Patriots*)	–	T. Lodwick	c. 1886
9.244	Cambria's Lament[34]	–	Elias Hughes	1887
9.291	Hen Wlad y Gân yw Cymru (*The Old Land of Song is Wales*)	–	Glan Prysor	[1890s?]
9.292	Dysg i mi dy Ffyrdd, O! Arglwydd (*Teach me thy Ways, O Lord*)	–	scriptural	[1890s?]
9.293	Rhwyfwn ein dau (*We Row Together*)	–	Elias Morgan	c. 1895
9.314	Mae Cymru'n Mynd i fyny (*Wales is Arising*)	–	J. M. Morgan	c. 1897
9.331	Y Bardd (*The Bard*)	–	?	1898
9.355	Plant y Cedyrn (*Children of the Strong*)	–	Eifion Wyn	c. 1902

Uncertain: Atat Ti (*To Thee*)   Gwenllian
Bow down   The Two Angels
Cambrian Minstrels

10. Solo Voice

[R]	[T]	[O]	[A]	[D]
10.003	Y Plentyn yn Marw (*The Dying Child*)	2.2	Alaw Llynfell	1861
10.007a	The American Star	–	?	1862
10.007b	Baner ein Gwlad (*Our Country's Flag*)[25]	28.1	Mynyddog	1862
10.008	Gwnewch i mi Feddrod (*Make me a Grave*)	28.7	Gwenffrwd	1862
10.029	Y Gwallgofddyn (*The Madman*)	–	?	1865
10.030	O Give me Back my Childhood Dreams (*Breuddwydion Ieuenctid*)	2.1	Joseph Parry	c. 1865
10.031	Yr Eneth Ddall (*The Blind Girl*)	5.2	Ceiriog	c. 1865
10.032	Prudd-Gân (*Serious Song*)	–	Telynog	[1860s?]
10.040	A Love Song	–	G. F. Powell	1866
10.041	Jefferson Davis	–	?	c. 1866
10.042	Lincoln's Grave	–	?	c. 1866
10.043	Cân Ymadawol (*Song of Parting*)	–	?	1866
10.044	Yr Ystorm ar Fôr Tiberias (*The Storm on the Sea of Tiberias*)	–	I. Gwynedd	1866
10.045	Dangos dy fod yn Gymro (*Show you're a Welshman*)	–	?	1866
10.048	Arglwydd na Cherydda fi (*Lord, Rebuke me not*)	–	scriptural	1866
10.049	Y Fenyw Fach a'r Beibl Mawr (*The Little Lady and the Big Bible*)	28.3	Ceiriog	1866
10.050	Y Trên (*The Train*)	11.6	Ceiriog	1866
10.051	The House on Fire	–	?	1866
10.053	Mari o Fedwig (*Mary of Medwig*)	–	Cuhelyn	1867
10.058	Cân Genedlaethol (*National Song*)[26]	–	?	1867
10.059	Gwraig y Meddwyn (*The Drunkard's Wife*)	8.1	Ceiriog	c. 1867

10.060	Friend of my Youth	—	?	c. 1867
10.061	Y Tŷ ar Dân (The House on Fire)[27]	—	Cuhelyn	c. 1867
10.062	The Playing Infant	—	Schiller[28]	1867
10.063	Home of the Soul	—	Bishop Heber	1868
10.064	He that doeth the Will of my Father	—	scriptural	1868
10.066	Excelsior [1]	—	Longfellow	1868
10.067	The Sad Farewell	—	?	[1868]
10.068	The Home of my Childhood	—	Joseph Parry	1868
10.074	Hoff Wlad fy Ngenedigaeth (Dear Land of my Birth)	—	Hwfa Môn	c. 1868
10.075	Adieu, Dear Home	14.1	?	1868
10.080	Fe'm Ganwyd innau'ng Nghymru (I was Born in Wales)	—	T. Levi	c. 1869
10.081	Yr Hen Ywen Werdd (The Old Green Yew)	11.4	Rhisiart Ddu	1869
10.085	Hen Gestyll Cymru (The Old Castles of Wales)	—	?	c. 1869
10.086	Y Milwr (The Soldier)	—	J. S. James	1869
10.087	Gwnewch Bobpeth yn Gymraeg (Do Everything in Welsh)	10.4	Mynyddog	c. 1869
10.088	The Village Blacksmith [1]	—	Longfellow	c. 1869
10.089	Y Melinydd (The Miller)	—	Dewi Môn	c. 1869
10.093	Mae'r Tywysog yn Dyfod (The Prince is Coming)	—	Taliesin o Eifion	1869
10.094	The Two Locks of Hair	—	Longfellow	1870
10.097	Judge not a Man by the Cost of his Clothing	—	?	1870
10.098	Gwraig y Morwr (The Sailor's Wife)	11.2	Mynyddog	1870
10.099	Gogoniant i Gymru (Praise to Wales)	10.1	Talhaiarn	c. 1870
10.100	Yr Ehedydd (The Lark)	11.1	Tydfylyn	1870
10.102	Y Danchwa (The Explosion)	—	J. S. James	1870

ID	Title	Author		Date
10.103	Y Carwr Siomedig (*The Disappointed Lover*)	D. Morgannwg	—	1870
10.104	The Old Cottage Clock	Charles Swain	10.3	c. 1870
10.107	Pleserfad y Niagara (*The Niagara Pleasureboat*)	T. Levi	11.5	1871
10.109	Song and Chorus Cenedlaethol	Rhisiart Ddu	—	1871
10.110	Yr Auctioneer (*The Auctioneer*)	Mynyddog	—	1871
10.111	Y Dyn sy'n Mynd â hi (*The Winner*)	Mynyddog	10.2	c. 1871
10.112	The Depot	Cynonfardd	—	1872
10.113	Cheer up!	?	—	1872
10.114	Ni Ddown yn Gewri yn y Man (*Heroes shall we be*)	?	—	1872
10.115	Y Gardotes Fach (*The Little Beggarwoman*)	I. Glan Aled	28.1	c. 1872
10.116	Cymry Glân Americ (*The fine Welsh People of America*)	I. Gwynedd	10.5	1872
10.117	All Hail to thee Columbia	?	—	c. 1872
10.118	Y Bachgen Dewr (*The Valiant Boy*)	Mynyddog	19.1	c. 1872
10.119	Slumber, Lie Soft	?	2.3	c. 1872
10.120	The Voice of Conscience	Knight Summers	12.4	c. 1872
10.122	King Death	Barry Cornwall	—	1873
10.124	Lady Mine!	Jennie Whyte	—	c. 1873
10.135	Atgofion (*Memories*)	Tydfylyn	28.5	[1870s?]
10.136	Glyndwr	Mynyddog	28.8	1874
10.137	Of thee, my Bleak House	?	—	1875
10.138	The Pauper's Drive	?	—	[1870s?]

No.	Title		Poet	Date
10.139	Atgofion Mebyd (*Memories of Youth*)	28.2	Hwfa Môn	c. 1875
10.140	I fyny fo'r Nod (*High be the Aim*) [1]	–	Mynyddog	[1870s]
10.141	Yr Hen Gerddor (*The Old Musician*)	–	Myfyr Emlyn	[1870s?]
10.142	Yr Eos (*The Nightingale*)	37.1	T. E. Griffith	[1870s?]
10.143	Paham mae Dei mor Hir yn Dod? (*Why is Dei so Long in Coming?*)	26.6	Ceiriog	1875
10.144	I fyny fo'r Nod (*High be the Aim*) [2][29]	28.12	Mynyddog	c. 1875
10.145	The Charge of the Light Brigade	–	Tennyson	c. 1875
10.146	Y Telynor Bach (*The Little Harper*)	19.2	Ceiriog	c. 1875
10.147	Ysgytwad y Llaw (*The Handshake*)	12.3	Mynyddog	1875
10.165	Myfanwy [2]	28.10	Mynyddog	1876
10.166	Morfudd	28.11	Mynyddog	1876
10.167	Excelsior [2][29]	–	Longfellow	1877
10.179	Ti nid wyt (*Thou art not*)	–	?	c. 1878
10.185	Cloch y Llan (*The Tolling Bell*)	37.3	I. Glan Aled	1879
10.186	Hen Gloch y Llan (*The Old Tolling Bell*)[30]	–	?	c. 1879
10.187	Cradle Song	–	?	1879
10.188	Y Milwr Dewr (*The Valiant Soldier*)	37.2	Granville-fab	c. 1879
10.192	Dinistr Derwyddon Môn (*Destruction of the Anglesey Druids*)	–	?	c. 1880
10.193	The Golden Grain	–	E. Brine	c. 1880
10.194	Come, Holy Spirit	–	?	[1880s?]
10.195	Malcombe's Serenade	–	Evan R. Jones	c. 1880
10.196	Sleep, my Love, Sleep	–	?	1880
10.200	Old Swansea Bells	–	?	c. 1881
10.201	The Telegraph Boy	–	Evan R. Jones	c. 1881
10.202	The Highland Brigade	–	Evan R. Jones	c. 1881?
10.205	O Happy Home of my Childhood	–	Dewi Môn	1881

10.210a	The Gates of Old Carlisle	–	Weatherby	1881
10.210b	Dyweddi'r Milwr (The Soldier's Fiancée)[31]	–	R. Bryan	c. 1902
10.211	The Old Pot-Pourri Jar	–	H. M. Burnside	1882
10.212	The Newspaper Boy	–	Evan R. Jones	1882
10.215	Gogoniant i Brydain (Praise to Britain)	–	?	1883
10.217	Cân y Morwr (The Sailor's Song)	–	Dewi Môn	1883
10.218	Y Chwaon Iach (The Wholesome Breezes) [2]	–	?	1883
10.219	The Days that are no more	–	Tennyson	1883
10.221	Lle y Cwrddasom (The Place where we Met)	–	Dewi Môn	1884
10.224	The Tangled Skein	–	?	c. 1885
10.225	O! Tyred yma Ngeneth Deg (O! Come here my Pretty Maiden)	–	?	[1880s?]
10.226	The Water Mill	–	?[28]	[1880s?]
10.227	As the Stream Flows	–	May C. West	[1880s?]
10.228	Y Fam a'i Phlentyn (The Mother and her Child)	–	Edeirnfab	1885
10.229	Dieu de Paix et Amour	–	?	1886
10.230	Doux Souvenir	–	Madame Evans	1886
10.231	Gwyndaf Sant (Saint Gwyndaf)	–	Dewi Môn	1886
10.234	Y Marchog (The Knight)	–	John Lodwick	c. 1886
10.237	Make New Friends but keep the Old (Y Cyfaill Pur)	–	Joseph Parry	1886
10.239	Ymweliad y Bardd (The Bard's Visit)	–	Ioan Tegid	1886
10.240	Fy Mam (My Mother)	–	Tudno Jones	1886?[32]
10.241	Yr Hen Delynor (The Old Harper)	–	?	c. 1887
10.242	Yr Hen Delynor Dall (The Old Blind Harper)	–	Tudno Jones	1887
10.245	The Tramp	–	?	1887

10.246	Cymru Fydd (*Wales of the Future*) [1]	–	Watcyn Wyn	*c.* 1887
10.248	My Captain	–	?	1888
10.249	Yr Eneth Glaf (*The Sick Girl*)	–	?	1888
10.251	Dreams of Childhood	–	?	1888
10.253	Birthday Feelings[33]	–	?	1888
10.254	Ein Tadau, pa le maent hwy? (*Our Fathers, where are they?*)	–	Dyfed	1888
10.258	Gone for ever	–	Edith Stone	1889
10.259	Cymru, Cymro a Chymraeg (*The Cambrian Triplet*)	–	Dewi Môn	1889
10.261	Hen Gymry oedd fy Nhadau (*The Welsh of Old were my Fathers*)	–	?	*c.* 1890
10.278	Eiluned	–	Dewi Môn	*c.*1893
10.279	Dymuniad y Cerddor (*The Minstrel's Desire*)	–	Dewi Môn	*c.*1893
10.280	Dewi Sant (*Saint David*)	–	Dewi Môn	*c.* 1893
10.281	Suo-gân (*Lullaby*) [1]	–	Dewi Môn	1893
10.282	Y Dyddiau Gynt (*The Days of Old*)	–	H. Davies	*c.* 1894
10.284	To Music	–	Herrick	1895
10.294	The two Christmas Eves	–	Dewi Môn	*c.* 1895
10.295	Come back to me	–	I. A. Fraser	*c.* 1895
10.296	Easter Hymn	–	Effie Sharpe	*c.* 1895
10.297	My Heart's Love	–	Effie Sharpe	*c.* 1895
10.298	Thy Life and mine	–	Effie Sharpe	*c.* 1895
10.299	Those Dear Eyes of thine	–	Heine[28]	*c.* 1895
10.300	She Knows	–	Heine[28]	*c.* 1895
10.301	Cymru Newydd (*New Wales*)	–	C. T. Thomas	1895
10.302	Oes y Byd i'r Iaith Gymraeg (*Long Life to the Welsh Language*)	–	Alafon	1895
10.303	Yr ydwyt fel Blodeuyn (*Thou art like a Flower*)	–	Heine[34]	1895
10.304	Mae gennyf Emau a Pherlau (*I have Gems and Pearls*)	–	?[29]	1895

10.305	Ti Ferch y Morwr Tyred (*Come, O Sailor's Daughter*)	—	Heine[35]	1895
10.306	The Moon is Fully Risen	—	Heine[36]	1895
10.307	Thine Eyes	—	Heine[37]	1895
10.308	Thy Cheek	—	Heine[38]	1895
10.309	Till Death	—	?	1896
10.310	Llais o'r Lli (*A Voice from the Sea*)	—	Alafon	c. 1896
10.313	Llywelyn, ein Llyw Olaf (*Llywelyn, our Last Leader*)	—	Anthropos	1896
10.316	Thraldom	—	Clifton Bingham	1897
10.317	The King's Bride	—	Clifton Bingham	1897
10.318	Llewelyn[39]	—	Ebenezer Rees	1897
10.319	Iesu Arwain fi (*Jesus, Lead me*)	—	Ebenezer Rees	1898
10.323	Childhood[6]	—	?	c. 1898
10.324	Y Lili Wen (*The White Lily*)	—	J. W. Thomas	c. 1898
10.325	Lord Roberts	—	?	1898
10.326	Cerdd Rhyddid Cymru (*Ode to Welsh Freedom*)	—	G. Jenkins	1898
10.328	Spring	—	Annie Howell	1898
10.329	Summer	—	Annie Howell	1898
10.332	Y Gloch (*The Bell*)	—	?	1898
10.333	Merch y Cadben (*The Captain's Daughter*)	—	Glan Padarn	c. 1898
10.334	Autumn	—	Annie Howell	1898
10.335	Winter	—	Annie Howell	1898
10.338	Hen Walia eto i fyny (*Old Wales Rises again*)	—	I. Williams	1899
10.342	Sorrow and the Angel Charity	—	?	1899
10.344	Sympathy	—	Annie Howell	1900

10.349	Sons of Britain[40]	—	?	1900
10.351	The Snuff Song[40]	—	?	1901
10.352	Come Home	—	?	1901
10.357	Mi Glywais Lais yr Iesu'n Dweud (I Heard the Voice of Jesus Say)	—	?	1902
10.359	Y Crythor Dall (The Blind Violinist)	—	John M. Jones	1902
10.360	Fy Mhriod (My Wife)	—	Joseph Parry	1902

Uncertain:

Am Gymru (Of Wales)
Beddgelert
Be Kind to the Loved Ones
The Children's Garden
Christmas Story
Columbia
Y Cymro Pur (The True Welshman)
Cymru (Wales)
The Day is Cold
The Day is Dark and Weary
The Day is Done
Degree Song
Deio Bach (Little Deio)
Devona's Vale
The Druid
Y Gadlys (The Courtyard)
International Celtic Song
Lead, Kindly Light
Life is a Dream
Life's Dreams

Mae'n Gymro byth (He's still a Welshman)
Merch Cadben y Loliwen (The Daughter of the Loliwen's Captain)
The Milkmaid's Song
The Minstrel
My Friends of Old
My Heart is Weary
My Love is Fair
Nothing but Leaves
Pa le mae Milwyr Arthur? (Where are Arthur's Soldiers?)
The Shepherdess
Song without Words
Ti Wyddost (Thou Knowest)
To my Friend
Wanton Gales
The Widow's Lullaby
When other Hands are Clasped in thine
Where are the Friends?
Where shall my Soul?
Yn Iach i Walia mwy (Farewell to Wales)

11. Works for Orchestra (including Brass Band)

[R]	[T]	[D]
11.082	Symphony [1]	1869
11.083	Symphony [2][6]	c. 1869
11.090	Overture	1869
11.178d	Tydfyl[41]	[1878?]
11.263	Suite: Three Tone Statuettes	1890–1
11.268	Cambrian Rhapsody	c. 1891
11.269	Peredur[18]	1891
11.270	Sleep[18]	1891
11.272	The Dying Minstrel	1892
Uncertain:	A Dead March	

12. Chamber works

[R]	[T]	[D]
12.076	String Quartet	1869
12.077	Fantasy for Violin and Piano	1860–70s?
12.078	Violin Solo	1860–70s?
12.260	A Short Fantasy on Welsh Tunes	1890
12.271	Ave Maria	1891
Uncertain:	Glyndwr March	Welsh Dance [1]
	Welsh Air Sonata	Welsh Dance [2]

13. Piano

[R]	[T]	[O]	[D]
13.069	Adagio Cantabile[42]	–	1868
13.070	Sonata no 1 in C minor	–	1868
13.071	Sonata no 2 in G major	–	[1868]
13.072	Rondo	–	1868
13.073	Galop	–	c. 1868?
13.096	Sonata no 3 in E minor	–	1870
13.105	Recollections of Spring	13.3	c. 1871
13.151	Maesgarmon [1][43]	24	c. 1875
13.152	A Seaside Reverie	27	[1870s?]
13.153	Recollections of Childhood	13.1	[1870s?]
13.154	Recollections of Courtship	13.2	[1870s?]
13.155	Little Willie's Waltz	–	c. 1872?
13.156	Little Eddie's Mazurka	–	c. 1873?
13.157	The Druids' March	25	c. 1875
13.168c	Overture to *Blodwen*	–	[1878?]
13.178c	Overture to *Emmanuel*	–	[1878?]
13.222	To *Dilys*[44]	–	c. 1884?

Uncertain: Cambrian Rustic Dance

14. Organ

[R]	[T]	[D]
14.009	Fugue in D minor	1862
14.010	David's Prayer[5]	[1862]
14.011	Piece for Organ	1862
14.012	Preludio	1862
14.013	Preludium and Fugue	1863
14.027	Six Melodies[6]	1864
14.028	Solo for Organ	1864

15. Hymns Tunes and Psalm Chants

At least 450 hymn tunes in some 100 different measures, and over 100 psalm chants.

Llyfr Tonau Genedlaethol [sic] Cymreig – Rhan 1 (*A Book of Welsh National Tunes – Part 1*), 1887–8.
Llyfr Tonau Cynulleidfaol Cenedlaethol Cymru – Rhan 2 (*A Book of Welsh National Congregational Tunes – Part 2*), 1887–8.

16. Collections

[R]	[T]	[D]
16.1	A Set of Six Songs	1872
16.2	Chwech o Anthemau (*Six Anthems*)	1871
16.3	Anthemau Cymulleidfaol (*Congregational Anthems*)	c. 1872
16.4	Pump o Anthemau (*Five Anthems*)	[1870s?]
16.5	Tair o Anthemau i Blant (*Three Anthems for Children*)	[1870s?]
16.6	Chwe' Quartett (*Six Quartets*)	c. 1879?
16.7	Deuddeg o Ganeuon (*Twelve Songs*)	c. 1879?
16.8	Book of Duets	1882
16.9	Book of Songs	1885
16.10a	Cambrian Minstrelsie	1893–5
16.10b	British Minstrelsie	c. 1899
16.11	Y Llyfr Canu – Rhan 1 (*Song Book – Part 1*)	1894

17. Books, Journalism, etc.

Elfennau Cerddorineth (The Elements of Music), by Joseph Parry, was published by Duncan and Sons, Cardiff, as the first of the 'Cambrian Series', described as a series of educational books on Music.

Between 11 June 1887 and 5 May 1888 Parry wrote thirty-five articles for the *Cardiff Times and South Wales Weekly News*. Between 1890 and 1895 he wrote frequently but irregularly for the *Western Mail*.

Notes for Appendix A

1 Incomplete, later [?] incorporated in *Arianwen*.
2 See note 1.
3 One act operetta with dialogue.
4 Includes the cantata *Jerusalem*.
5 Excerpts from *Emmanuel*.
6 Unfinished.
7 'A Musical Service' for Sunday schools.
8 Cantata or one act opera.
9 Motet for SSATB.
10 Three part canon.
11 Also published in an arrangement for TTBB.
12 Arrangement of the folk song for SATB, which was also used for *Maesgarmon* [2], that is, the second part of *Maesgarmon* [1].
13 Perhaps the same piece as the quartet 'Peace, troubled soul'.
14 Not by the Rev. D. C. Evans, as shown in some copies.
15 Secular words, although they were used for an anthem in *Congregational Anthems* [16.3].
16 Also included in the opera *The Maid of Scer*.
17 Also included in the opera *King Arthur*.
18 Co-authored by Dr W. Edwards, Principal of the Cardiff Baptist College,
19 Choruses I and V by Dr W. Edwards, II by E. N. Jones, III by Dewi Môn, and IV by Elfed.
20 Also included in the opera *Blodwen* as *The Soldiers' Chorus*.
21 See note 15.
22 Included in the opera *Blodwen* with the words "Rwy'n gwybod dy hanes' (*I know your story*).
23 Probably John M Price, Parry's teacher in Danville.
24 Included, with different words, in the opera Arianwen.
25 10.007a and 10.007b are the same piece of music, with different words.
26 Possibly the same song as *All hail to thee Columbia* (10.117).
27 Not the same song as 10.051.
28 Translated from the German.
29 Another setting of the same words.
30 In all probability a different song from 10.185.
31 The same music as 10.210a but different words
32 The composer's mother died on 11 June 1886.
33 Perhaps a piano solo. There is no voice part on the manuscript [19822E].
34 Translated into English from the German ("Du bist wie eine Blume") by Kate Freiligrath-Kroeker.
35 Translated into English from the German ("Du schönes Fischermädchen") by James Thomson.

[36] Translated into English from the German ("Der Mond ist ausgegangen") by James Thomson.

[37] Probably a translation of Heine's "Deine blauen Augen".

[38] Translated into English from the German ("Lehn deine Wang'") by F. Johnson.

[39] For baritone, male voice choir and piano.

[40] For baritone, chorus and orchestra.

[41] Arrangement for brass band of the overture to *Emmanuel*.

[42] Included as the second movement in 13.070.

[43] See note 12.

[44] ?A successor to *Little Willie's waltz* and *Little Eddie's mazurka*.

[45] This title, along with others, is deleted on the manuscript [9297E].

[46] Includes 11 of the arrangements in 16.10a.

Bibliography

Related Reading

David Ian Allsobrook, *Music for Wales: Walford Davies and the National Council of Music, 1918–1941* (University of Wales Press, Cardiff, 1992).

While this book is primarily concerned with later developments, it contains an extensive and insightful discussion of the Welsh musical world of the 19th century.

Owain T. Edwards, *Joseph Parry 1841–1903* (University of Wales, Press, Cardiff, 1970).

This is a very brief bilingual biography of Parry.

Alan Luff, *Welsh Hymns and their tunes: their background and place in Welsh history and culture* (Stainer and Bell, London, 1990).

The title of this enjoyable book describes its contents accurately. Almost all of the Welsh composers mentioned in the present volume are discussed in more detail there and examples of their work are given.

Dillwyn Miles, *The Royal National Eisteddfod of Wales* (C. Davies, Swansea, 1978).

The National Eisteddfod played an important role in Parry's career as a competitor, adjudicator, conductor, speaker and composer. Its history during Parry's lifetime was tortuous and complicated and is well described in this book.

Joseph Parry, edited by Dulais Rhys, *The Little Hero* (National Library of Wales, Aberystwyth, 2004).

This is Parry's fragmentary autobiography, edited and annotated by Dulais Rhys.

Gareth Williams, *Valleys of Song: Music and Society in Wales 1840–1914* (University of Wales Press, Cardiff, 1998).

A well-researched book that takes a sociological rather than a musical approach. It contains much fascinating background material as well as a very fair assessment of Parry's work.

Newspapers and Periodicals

Y Cerddor Cymreig (The Welsh Musician) was founded by Ieuan Gwyllt, who founded and edited a number of Welsh musical journals. *Y Cerddor Cymreig* lasted from 1861 to 1873.

Baner ac Amserau Cymru (The Banner and Times of Wales), commonly known as *Y Faner*. An influential radical Welsh weekly newspaper founded in 1859 by the merger of *Baner Cymru* and *Yr Amserau*. In 1971, it was relaunched as *Y Faner* but closed in 1992 due to falling circulation.

Cardiff Times and South Wales Weekly News

Y Drych (The Mirror). A Welsh-American newspaper that has been in continuous publication since it was founded in 1851 in New York City by John Morgan Jones, born in Llanidloes. It was originally a weekly and published entirely in Welsh. In the 1930s Welsh was gradually replaced by English and it became a monthly in the 1940s. In 2003, it was bought by another Welsh-American newspaper, *Ninnau* (We Ourselves) and the two are now published together under the title *Ninnau incorporating Y Drych*.

Y Gerddorfa (The Orchestra). A monthly magazine published from 1872 to 1881.

Yr Herald Cymraeg (The Welsh Herald). A Welsh language newspaper published in Caernarfon. The first issue appeared on 19 May 1855. It continued to appear as a separate publication until 2001 but it now survives only as a weekly Welsh language supplement to the *Daily Post*.

Y Cerddor ('The Musician'). A monthly magazine, published by Hughes and Son, Wrexham between 1889 and 1921, to promote the development of Welsh music. It contained articles in both English and Welsh, and was edited by David Jenkins, who became Professor of Music at the University College of Wales, Aberystwyth in 1910, and D. Emlyn Evans.

Cambrian News. An English language newspaper based in Aberystwyth. It had become very influential through the efforts of its young, crusading editor, John Gibson. While Gibson was an enthusiastic supporter of the Aberystwyth College in principle, he was a severe critic of its management.

Pall Mall Gazette. A London evening newspaper founded in 1865. It took its name from the fictional newspaper in Thackeray's novel *The History of Pendennis*. Its many distinguished contributors included Engels, Trollope, Robert Louis Stevenson and Oscar Wilde. It ceased publication in 1923.

The Sackbut. A musical periodical founded by Philip Heseltine (Peter Warlock) in 1920. It survived until 1934.

Other Sources

Alumni Cantabrigensis, Volume 5 1752–1900 (Cambridge University Press, 1952).

Elwyn T. Ashton, *The Welsh in the United States* (Caldra House Ltd, Hove, 1984).

Ifor ap Gwilym, *Y Traddodiad Cerddorol yng Nghymru* (Gwasg Christopher Davies, Swansea, 1978).

Thomas Bassett, *Braslun o Hanes Hughes a'i Fab* (Oswestry, 1946).

D. H. B. Brower, *Danville – Past and Present* (Lane S. Hart, Harrisburg, Pennsylvania, 1881).

Sir John Edward Lloyd and R. T. Jenkins (eds) *Y Bywgraffiadur Cymreig hyd 1940* (Honourable Society of Cymmrodorion, London, 1953).

Cambridge University Calendar 1872 (Cambridge University Press, 1872).

Gilbert Chase, *America's Music* (McGraw-Hill, New York, 1955).

C. E. Claghorn, *Biographical Dictionary of American Music* (Parker Publishing Co., W. Nyack, New York, 1973).

T. Wood Clarke, *Utica for a Century and a Half* (Widtman Press, Utica, New York, 1952).

Emrys Cleaver, *Gwŷr y Gân* (Llyfrau'r Dryw, Llandybie, 1962).

Cofnodion a Chyfansoddiadau Buddugol Eisteddfod Genedlaethol Llandudno 1896 (I. Foulkes, Liverpool, 1898).

Frederick Corder, *A History of the Royal Academy of Music 1822–1922* (F. Corder, London 1922).

Rhys T. Davies, *The Story of Henry Richard* (Hughes and Son, Wrexham, 1925).

Eleanor Deutsch, *Off to Philadelphia in the Morning* [Abridged version of the novel of the same name by Jack Jones] (No publisher given, 1977).

F. W. Diehl, *History of Montour County 1769–1969* (Keyside Publishing Co., Berwick, Pennsylvania, 1969).

Hywel Teifi Edwards, *Gwŷl Gwalia: Yr Eisteddfod Genedlaethol yn Oes Aur Victoria 1858–1868* (Gwasg Gomer, Llandysul, 1980).

William Edmunds, *Hanes Plwyf Merthyr* (Josiah T. Jones, Aberdare, 1864).

Owen M. Edwards, *Gwaith Mynyddog* (Hughes and Son, Wrexham, 1914).

Alfred Einstein, *Music in the Romantic Era* (J. M. Dent, London, 1947).

E. L. Ellis, *The University College of Wales, Aberystwyth 1872–1972* (University of Wales, Press, Cardiff, 1972).

T. I. Ellis (ed.), Thomas Charles Edwards' Letters (Cylchgrawn Llyfrgell Genedlaethol Cymru, Aberystwyth, 1952–1953)

E. Keri Evans *et al.*, *Cofiant Joseph Parry* [Memories of Joseph Parry] (The Educational Publishing Company Ltd, Cardiff and London, 1921).
A collection of essays, mostly about Parry rather than his music, written by people who had known him. It seems to have been written largely from memory and contains many inaccuracies. The one chapter that does concern itself with Parry's music is the chapter by Cyril Jenkins. There is no English translation of the book.

Arthur T. Foulke, *My Danville* (The Christopher Publishing House, N. Quincy, Mass., [1968?]).

John Graham, *A Century of Welsh Music* (Kegan Paul, Trench, Trübner & Co., London, 1923).

Frederick Griffith, *Notable Welsh Musicians* (Francis Goodwen, London, 1896).

Richard Griffith, *Y Gohebydd* (Gee and Son, Denbigh, 1905)

R. D. Griffith, *Hanes Canu Cynulleidfaol Cymru* (University of Wales Press, Cardiff, 1948).

Rhidian Griffiths, 'Swansea's "Mr. Music": the career of D. J. Snell, music publisher', *Y Llyfr yng Nghymru: Welsh Book Studies 1* (1998), pp. 59–90 National Library of Wales. Available on the website of the National Library.

Rhidian Griffiths, 'Isaac Jones: music printer and publisher'. *Y Llyfr yng Nghymru: Welsh Book Studies No 5* (2003). National Library of Wales. Available on the website of the National Library of Wales.

Sir George Grove, edited by John Alexander Fuller Maitland, *A Dictionary of Music and Musicians* (Macmillan and Co., London 1910).

Trevor Herbert (ed.), *The British Brass Band: A Musical and Social History* (Oxford University Press, Oxford, 2000).

W. H. S. Johnston, *History of the First Cardiff Festival 1892* (Novello, Ewer & Co., London, 1892[?]).

Jack Jones, *Off to Philadelphia in the Morning* (Hamish Hamilton, London, 1947).
The novel based on the life of Joseph Parry, on which the television series of the same name was based. The most recent edition was published by Pan Books in 1978.

Jacob Jones, *Hanes Eglwys Gynulleidfaol Bethesda, Merthyr Tudful* (Swyddfa'r Tyst, Merthyr Tydfil, 1909).

M. O. Jones, *Bywgraffiaeth Cerddorion Cymreig* (Cymdeithas yr Eisteddfod Genedlaethol, Duncan and Sons, Cardiff, 1890).

Jones, Philip Henry and Rees, Eiluned (eds), *A Nation and its Books* (National Library of Wales, Aberystwyth, 1998).
Contains a chapter by Rhidian Griffiths on music publishing in Wales, as well as more general material, including a chapter on Hughes a'i Fab and Gee a'i Fab.

Thomas Levi, *Caneuon Cymru* (Lewis Evans, Swansea, 1896).

Idris Lewis, translated into Welsh by Enid Parry, *Cerddoriaeth yng Nghymru* (Gwasg y Brython, Liverpool, 1945).
It appears that, although this work was originally written in English, it was written with the intention that it should be translated into Welsh and it was never published in English.

W. J. Lewis, *Born on a Perilous Rock* (Cambrian News, Aberystwyth, 1980).

Ken Llewellyn, *Disaster at Tynewydd* (Ap Dafydd, Cardiff, 1975).

Alfred Lowenburg, *Annals of Opera* (Roman & Littlefield, Totowa, New Jersey, 1978).

Mahoning County Register 1865 (Youngstown, Ohio, 1865).

David Morgans, *Music and Musicians of Merthyr and District* (H. W. Southey and Sons, Merthy Tydfil, 1922)

Louis C. Nelson, *The History of American Music* (Macmillan Co., New York, 1925).

W. R. Owen, *Transactions of the National Eisteddfod of Wales Liverpool 1884* (I. Foulkes, Liverpool, 1885).

Henry Raynor, *Music in England* (Robert Hales, London, 1980)

A. J. Heward Rees, *Symffoni Môr* (Bangor Normal College, Bangor, 1982)

Dulais Rhys, *Joseph Parry: Bachgen Bach o Ferthyr* (University of Wales Press, Cardiff, 1998)
The basis for the present book. In Welsh.

Glyn Richards, *Braslun o Hanes Ebenezer, Abertawe* (Gwasg John Penry, Llanelli, 1954).

Eleazar Roberts, *Bywyd a Gwaith Henry Richard* (Hughes and Son, Wrexham, 1902).

T. R. Roberts, *Mynyddog: Ei Fywyd a'i Waith* (Gee and Son, Denbigh, 1909)

Stanley Sadie (ed.), *The New Grove Dictionary of Music and Musicians* (Grove, London, 1980).

Percy A. Scholes, *The Oxford Companion to Music* (Oxford University Press, London, 1970)

E. W. Smith, *Passenger Ships of the World* (George H. Dean, Boston, Massachusetts, 1963).

J. Rees, *Report on the National Eisteddfod of Wales* (Caernarfon, 1866)

J Sutcliffe Smith, *Impressions of Music in Wales* (The Venture Press, Penmaenmawr, 1948).

Nicholas Temperley, *Music of the English Parish Church, Vols 1 and 2* (Cambridge University Press, 1979).

Nicholas Temperley (ed), *The Romantic Age 1880–1914* (The Athlone History of Music in Britain V), (The Athlone Press, London, 1981).

John Thomas, *Cofiant Thomas Rees* (William Hughes, Dolgellau, 1888).

R D Thomas, *Hanes Cymry America* (1872). Translated by Martha A Davies and Phillips G Davies. Second edition. (Great Plains Welsh Heritage Project, Wymore, Nebraska, 2008).

Roy Thorne, *Penarth – A History* (Starling Press, Risca, 1975)

University College of Wales Reports 1872–1881 (Aberystwyth, 1872–1881)

Ernest Walker, *A History of Music in England* (Oxford, Clarendon Press, 1907)

Huw Williams, *Canu'r Bobol* (Gwasg Gee, Denbigh, 1978)

Huw Williams, *Tonau a'u Awduron* (Llyfrfa'r M.C., Caernarfon, 1967).

Percy M. Young, *Choral Music of the World* (Abelard-Schuman, London, 1969).

Percy M. Young, *The Choral Tradition* (Hutchinson, London, 1962).

Percy M. Young, *A History of British Music* (Ernest Benn Ltd, London, 1967).

Index

Entries for key words that occur only in the bibliography and the catalogue of Parry's works are not included in the index.

'Cyfryngdod Emmanuel' (Gwilym
  Hiraethog), 117
Cymmrodorion, Honourable Society of,
  143,210,214
Cymmrodorion, National Society of, 165
Cymro, Y, 223
Cymru Fydd, 178, 185
'Cymru Fydd', 214, 235
Cymru Fydd Glee Society, 185
Cynonfardd, *see Edwards, Rev. Thomas*
'Cytgan y Briodas', 234
'Cytgan y Milwyr', 110
'Cytgan y Morwyr', 233,237,252
'Cytgan y Pererinion', 165,173,175,183,
  196,214,235-6,238,249,252

Daily Telegraph, 85,195
'Dangos dy fod yn Gymro', 71,220
Danville, 12,24,26-8,30-2,34-5,38,40-2,
  46,48,50-1,55,65-9,71,74,76,89-98,
  100,103,124,127,172-3,184,186,
  197-8,200,202,226,228-33,253
  Choral Society, 67
  Musical Institute, 92,95,124
  Welsh Chorus, 55,93
David, T. W., 222
Davies, Ben, 135, 146, 148,
Davies, *Rev.* D. Charles, 182
Davies, Madam Clara Novello, 148,185,
  214
Davies, *Dr* Evan, 22,42,46,68,134
Davies, Hattie, 111
Davies, Mary, 96, 146
Davies, Richard (Mynyddog), 71,87,95,
  108-9,115-6,124,133
Davies, William (Mynorydd), 29,69,111
Davis, David, 100,126-7,131
'Dead March' (Handel), 91,159
Denbigh, 41,81,121,123,136,165,210
Denver (Colorado), 174
'Derwyddon, Y', 214
Deutsch, Eleanor, 40
Dewi Môn, *see Rowlands, Rev. David*
Dickens, Charles, 18
'Dinbych', 171,243
Dr Joseph Parry Memorial Fund, 187,208
Dr Joseph Parry National Scholarship
  Trust, 188
Dolgellau, 78,204
Dowlais, 18,75,78-9,87,130

'Dream, A', 173
Dresden, 97
Drych, Y, 40-1,70,97,222
'Drylliwyd y Delyn' (David Jenkins), 185
'Dundee', 182
Durham University, 99
'Duw bydd Drugarog', 83
Dvořák, Antonín, 178,225,227,248,252

Ebbw Vale, 78
Ebenezer Chapel (Cardiff), 151,201
Ebenezer Chapel (Swansea), 132,135,
  142,147,151,162,167,202
Edinburgh, 191,221
  University 99,191
  Prince Alfred, Duke of, 215,223
Edison Bell, 173
Edmunds, William, 18
Edwards, E. J., 64
Edwards, H. M., 167
Edwards, Joseph, 85
Edwards, O. M., 169
Edwards, Owain T., 123
Edwards, *Rev.* Thomas Charles, 93,99,103
Edwards, *Rev.* Thomas (Cynonfardd),
  167,181
Edwardsville (Pennsylvania), 167,181
'Ehedydd, Yr', 85
Eifion Wyn, *see Williams, Eliseus*
Eifionydd, *see Lloyd, J. Ambrose*
Eisteddfod, 9,21,25-7,31,35,37,40,43-4,
  46-8,70,74,79,93-4,108,130-1,134,
  145,160,167,169,180,183,185,188,
  193,195,202-3,208,210,211,213-4,
  216-7,226,252
  Aberdare, 35
  Aberystwyth, 41-2,44-5,47,65
  Bala, 152,218
  Ballarat, 180
  Bangor, 96,98,130
  Barry Island, 187
  Blaenau Ffestiniog, 103,164
  Brecon, 152
  Caerwys, 144
  Cardiff, 165,175,237
  Carmarthen, 176
  Chester, 66
  Chicago, 165,238
  Coedpoeth, 152
  Danville, 30,32,197,202